STORYWORLDS OF ROBIN HOOD

STORYWORLDS *of* ROBIN HOOD

THE ORIGINS of a MEDIEVAL OUTLAW

LESLEY COOTE

REAKTION BOOKS

Published by Reaktion Books Ltd
Unit 32, Waterside
44–48 Wharf Road
London N1 7UX, UK
www.reaktionbooks.co.uk

First published 2020

Printed and bound in India
by Replika Press Pvt. Ltd

A catalogue record for this book is available from the British Library

ISBN 978 1 78914 232 7

Contents

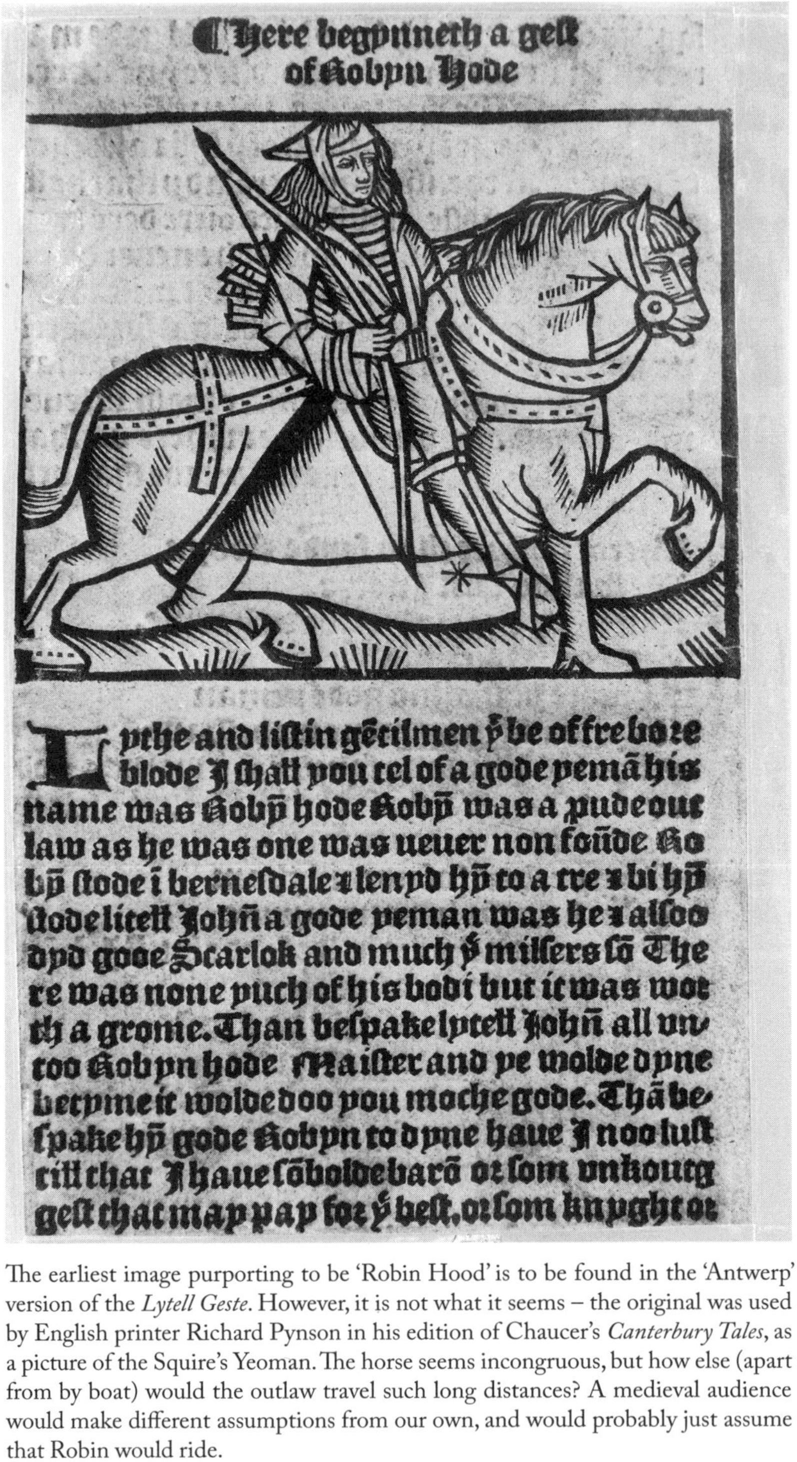

Here begynneth a gest of Robyn Hode

Lythe and listin getilmen yᵗ be of fre bore blode I shall you tel of a gode yemā his name was Robyn hode Robyn was a prude out law as he was one was neuer non foūde Robyn stode i bernesdale & lenyd hym to a tre & bi hym stode litell Johñ a gode yeman was he & alsoo dyd gode Scarlok and much yᵉ millers sō There was none ynch of his bodi but it was worth a grome. Than bespake lytell Johñ all vntoo Robyn hode Maister and ye wolde dyne betyme it wolde doo you moche gode. Thā bespake hym gode Robyn to dyne haue I noo lust till that I haue sō bolde barō or som unkouth gest that may pay for yᵉ best, or som knyght or

The earliest image purporting to be 'Robin Hood' is to be found in the 'Antwerp' version of the *Lytell Geste*. However, it is not what it seems – the original was used by English printer Richard Pynson in his edition of Chaucer's *Canterbury Tales*, as a picture of the Squire's Yeoman. The horse seems incongruous, but how else (apart from by boat) would the outlaw travel such long distances? A medieval audience would make different assumptions from our own, and would probably just assume that Robin would ride.

Introduction: Who Was Robin Hood?

It is the purpose of this book to re-examine the character and the idea of Robin Hood, both at the point of his emergence in the culture of medieval England and in the early, pre-Reformation years of his development. It is rooted in an attempt to understand the culture that surrounded the early Robin Hood stories, in the light of some of the other storyworlds that complemented and competed with Robin's. The idea of the storyworld has entered scholarly criticism quite recently, but approximates closely to what Maurice Keen (writing in 1961) wanted to call 'the Matter of the Greenwood'.[1] Simply put, a storyworld consists of the stories, locations, events, characters, objects and ideas that have accumulated around a particular character or event.[2] Everyone who enters a storyworld interacts with it, selecting different elements to create something new, whether that is a work of literature, art or some other cultural product, a piece of scholarship or simply a viewpoint particular to themselves. The storyworld of Robin Hood is now (at least) eight hundred years old, and throughout that time has seen many additions, of all kinds and all chronological periods. These may differ in their content, their quality and their intent and purpose, but they all use elements derived from within that same storyworld.[3] The process is well described by William Shakespeare in *As You Like It*. The old duke has been displaced by his younger brother Frederick, and has taken up residence in the Forest of Arden with a few of his loyal courtiers. When Oliver, the young nobleman, asks the old duke's whereabouts, the wrestler Charles tells him: 'They say that he is already in the Forest of Arden, and many merry men with him;

and there they live like the old Robin Hood of England; they say many young gentlemen flock to him every day, and fleet the time carelessly as they did in the golden world' (Act I, Scene I).

To be attractive, a storyworld needs to offer two main benefits: escape and relevance. At the end of Shakespeare's play, the melancholy courtier Jacques chooses to escape to permanent marginality, while the old duke, restored to his position, chooses to return to the 'real world', and the rest of his followers with him. Having escaped to the greenwood, and stayed for a while in its 'play space', absorbing the lessons it has to offer them, they return, restored, revitalized and re-empowered, to the world from which they came. Jacques, like Robin Hood in the end, turns from the court and returns to the greenwood, back to a past which, however golden, is gone. Visiting storyworlds of the past is beneficial, Shakespeare is saying, but we must take what they have to give us and move on into the future.

Shakespeare was writing in the late 1590s, so his 'past' was the world of the later Middle Ages and of Henry VIII (r. 1509–47), before the reformation of religion and the dissolution of the monasteries and chantries swept away the bases of cultural patronage that had existed before them. This movement was completed in the 1560s and 1570s by the demolition of much of the festive culture, based originally on the liturgy of the pre-Reformation Church, which preceded it.[4] How did the people of this 'past' understand Robin Hood, and how did that differ from the way he was understood in the aftermath of these cataclysmic events? How did it differ from the way in which he is understood today?

There are four major elements in the way that people have understood and represented Robin Hood in the twentieth and twenty-first centuries. These are social function, appearance, chronology and place. A quick glance at these, compared with the way in which they were understood and presented in the Middle Ages, reveals that there may be problems in projecting our own view on to audiences of the early, pre-Elizabethan (that is, before the 1560s) stories. 'He robbed the rich to give to the poor' is probably the most common response of people today when asked what they know about Robin Hood. Nowhere in the surviving medieval/early Tudor stories does Robin do this. He and his merry men are thieves, of that there is no doubt, and they keep a stash of stolen luxuries in the greenwood, but they dole out their treasure only to those needy people they meet by chance on the highway and whose stories merit it. The only person who benefits from Robin's generosity in the surviving early stories is an impoverished knight, not someone who would strike a modern reader as qualifying for membership of 'the poor'. Nor is there any issue of taxation involved, although unjust taxation has become a staple of Robin Hood films and television retellings. In relatively recent times, Robin Hood has been depicted as a superhero, a rebel, a war-weary NCO, an outsider with 'issues' and a hoodie-wearing 'lad'.[5] These roles are all seen by their creators to have some relevance for the modern world, but some or none of these things may have had relevance for earlier audiences. In consequence, Robin may have been some or none of these things in his former 'lives'.

The earliest image of Robin Hood still surviving is that of a Flemish edition of around 1495 (probably by the Antwerp printer Gerhaert Leeu, a friend and collaborator of William Caxton, the first English printer) of *A Lytell Geste of Robyn Hode*.[6] This shows an adult male on a moving horse. He is wearing a plain short riding tunic, hose and riding boots. He also has a hat with a deep brim, pointed at the back (a style referred to as a 'bycocket' hat), held on to his head by a band tied under his chin. He carries a bow slung across his shoulder (he grips it with his hand), and arrows in a quiver behind his back. It looks authentic for the great archer, but this was not the first use of that particular image. It appeared originally in an edition of Geoffrey Chaucer's *Canterbury Tales* by the English printer Richard Pynson, where it is used in the 'General Prologue' to depict the Squire's Yeoman:

> . . . he was clad in cote and hood of grene.
> A sheef of pecok arwes, bright and kene,
> Under his belt he bar ful thriftily
> Wel koude he drese his takel yemanly;
> His arwes drouped noght with fetheres lowe,
> And in his hand he baar a myghte bowe.

> He wore a coat and hood of green.
> A sheaf of peacock [feathered] arrows, bright and sharp,
> He wore very neatly tucked under his belt
> He knew how to take care of his yeoman's tools;

His arrows' feathers didn't droop,
And in his hand he carried a mighty bow.[7]

He was, says Chaucer, a forester by trade. Pynson published an edition of the *Lytell Geste* in 1492, but only fragments survive. It could be that he reused the picture for Robin Hood, because of the bow and arrows and the suitability of the forester's appearance. Leeu's workshop would then have copied it – although concrete evidence is lacking. Early printers used existing images, for reasons of economy, wherever they were considered suitable. The costume of the Pynson/Leeu picture is very similar to that worn by foresters in the illustrations created for the *Livre de chasse* (Book of Hunting) commissioned by Gaston Phébus, comte de Foix.[8] All that can be said about this early image is that, allowing for economic and availability issues, an image with this profile was considered suitable for use as 'Robin Hood'. It may have been the bow and arrows, or the forester's outfit, which appealed most, or all of these in equal measure. The tiny, rather ineffectual figure of Robin in Wynkyn de Worde's printed version of the *Lytell Geste* (see the beginning of Chapter Three) of circa 1506 is evidence of the rather inconvenient truth that, given the need for an image, an early printer would use whatever was available as a default, no matter how it fitted the subject matter (or not).[9]

The forester, hunter and hunt employee figures in the *Livre de chasse* usually wear green, especially when they are hunting in wooded countryside. More recent film-makers have made a point of avoiding green clothing (as worn by Errol Flynn in *The Adventures of Robin Hood* in 1938, by countless film and television Robins from the 1940s to the 1980s, and by Disney's fox Robin) on grounds of 'medieval authenticity' (and medieval doublet and hose, too, possibly because of modern homophobic reactions to men in little skirts). In Otto Bathurst's 2018 film version, Robin's clothing is mostly dark grey/brown. He wears grey trousers tucked into leather riding boots (as in the Antwerp image), but his neckwear is bright blue. As the film is set in a largely urban, built environment the need for green clothing evaporates, and Robin's clothing reflects this.[10] The *Lytell Geste* tells us, however, that Robin and his men wear green clothing, and the cloth he keeps in the forest is green and scarlet, like that of the *Livre de chasse* hunters:

'Ye must gyue the knight a lyueray
To helpe his body therin;
For ye haue scarlet and grene, mayster
And many a riche aray.
Ther is no marchunt in mery Englond
So ryche I dare well say.'
'Take hym thre yerdes of euery colour
And loke well mete that it be.'

'You must give the knight a suit of clothes
To look after his body inside [it];
Because you have scarlet and green [cloth], Master
And a lot of rich cloth[ing].
There is no merchant in merry England
That is so rich, I dare well say.'
'Bring him three yards of each colour
And see that it's good quality.'[11]

In this case, then, modern 'authenticity' is medievally inauthentic. It conforms to our idea of what the medieval world was like (and to our own social and ideological imperatives), not to the medieval world itself, nor to the early storyworld of Robin Hood. In the early stories, Robin's hood is only ever mentioned in the little Paston play script, where he uses it to carry the sheriff's head. It seems to have no relevance to the name, which may instead refer to a place (such as Hodde in Denmark) or to a trade (as is the case with pseudonyms such as Wat Tyler and Jack Straw, two leaders of the Peasants' Revolt in 1381). It might just refer back to the hat characteristically worn by the Old Norse god Odin on his journeys through Midgard – Hood replaced Odin/Grim, or the Devil, in the nomenclature of some ancient heritage sites from the sixteenth century onwards. The hood, in modern retellings, has become a more significant artefact, seen as being in need of explanation. It has also become more sinister, as a means of concealment related to the cultural trope of the 'hoodie'. It may simply have been, for reasons outlined in Chapter Three, a dialectical pronunciation of the word 'wood'.

Modern retellings of Robin Hood stories are usually set in the late twelfth century, during King Richard I of England's absence on the Third Crusade (1189–92). Richard Lester (*Robin and Marian*,

1976) and Ridley Scott set their films slightly later, during Richard's final campaign in France (1199), featuring his death by means of a chance arrow fired from the walls of Chaluz, and the early years of his unpopular but also much-maligned successor, his younger brother John (r. 1199–1216).[12] In many films the huge ransom demanded for Richard's release is used as the basis for Robin's link to crippling taxation; this was the case in Allan and Minghella's television *Robin Hood*.[13] The Third Crusade was used as a background by Sir Walter Scott in his highly influential novel *Ivanhoe*, and became a feature on stage and in film during the nineteenth and early twentieth centuries.[14] A similar historical setting had already been selected by Anthony Munday in the late 1590s for his twin plays *The Downfall of Robert, Earl of Huntingdon* and *The Death of Robert, Earl of Huntingdon*, while the roughly contemporary *George à Greene*, set in the reign of Edward I, simply regards the story as 'old' by then. The early Robin Hood stories do not adopt this chronology, however; its earliest known appearance is in the chronicle (*c.* 1520) of the Scottish scholar John Major, or Mair, who states: 'About this time it was, as I conceive, that there flourished those most famous robbers Robert Hood, an Englishman, and Little John.'[15] Another Scottish chronicler, Walter Bower, writing around 1440 (eighty years before Mair), places Robin Hood and Little John among those punished for their part in the rebellion of Simon de Montfort against Henry III (1263–5):

> At this time there arose from among the disinherited and outlaws and raised his head that most famous armed robber Robert Hood, along with Little John and their accomplices. The foolish common folk eagerly celebrate the deeds of these men with gawping enthusiasm in comedies and tragedies, and take pleasure in hearing jesters and bards singing [of them] more than in other romances.

As a nationalist Scot writing in the face of English claims to the kingdom of Scotland, Bower prefers to see Robin and Little John as noble rebels in a common national cause against the corrupt rule of a recognizably Plantagenet (rather than Angevin – although they were the same family, really) English king, although he is also at pains to note that they are criminals, and not worthy of the rapt attention they are getting from 'common folk' in Scotland:

> In that year [1266] also the disinherited English barons and those loyal to the king clashed fiercely; amongst them Roger de Mortimer occupied the Welsh Marches and John d'Eyville occupied the Isle of Ely; Robert Hood was an outlaw amongst the woodland briars and thorns. Between them they inflicted a vast amount of slaughter on the common and ordinary folk, cities and merchants.[16]

It was these 'common and ordinary', and particularly urban, people who, in Bower's own day, celebrated Robin Hood and Little John the most.

The king who appears in the *Lytell Geste* is called Edward in surviving versions:

> Full curteysly Robyn gan say,
> 'Syr haue this for your spending;
> We shall mete another day.'
> 'Gramercy,' than sayd our kyng,
> 'But well the greteth Edwarde our kynge
> And sent to the his seale . . .'

> Very courteously Robin then said,
> 'Sir, have this for spending [money]
> We shall meet another day.'
> 'Many thanks,' then said our king,
> 'But Edward our king greets you well,
> and sends you his seal . . .'[17]

By the time the text was published, at the end of the fifteenth century, there had been five kings of that name. They were Edward I (r. 1272–1307), 'Hammer of the Scots' and conqueror of Wales; Edward II (r. 1307–27), a weak king in thrall to his favourites, murdered on the orders of his wife and her lover; Edward III (r. 1327–77), victor of Crécy, Sluys and Poitiers, conqueror of Calais and regarded in the fifteenth century as a mirror of kingly rule; Edward IV (r. 1461–83), first ruler of the House of York and regarded as a strong and stable king; and Edward V (r. 1483), the elder of the 'princes in the tower', who was proclaimed but neither crowned nor anointed. Much debate has surrounded who the *Lytell Geste*'s Edward actually is, but none of it has produced any definitive answers. In 1492 the name could have been included as homage to Elizabeth of York, queen of Henry VII (r. 1485–1509), who died in 1503, and was sister to Edward V and daughter to Edward IV. It could equally well refer to Edward III, owing to his long reign and his great reputation, or to Edward II because of his fondness for 'common pursuits' and the company of 'lesser' men, or even to Edward I, owing to the years of his reign (as Prince of Wales Edward had opposed and finally defeated Simon de Montfort, making him contemporary with Bower's belief about Hood's chronology), and to his reputation as a strong and wise ruler. All of these are possible, and none can be fully ruled out. As there are no earlier versions of the *Lytell Geste* stories, any further conclusions are, at best, informed guesswork. The king in the Robin Hood story appears to be mature, strong, noble and wise, a fact which rules out two of the candidates. It could, however, be any of the other three.[18]

Only two mentions of Robin Hood are earlier than Walter Bower's chronicle. Writing twenty years before Bower (that is, about 1420), Andrew Wyntoun (yet another Scottish chronicler) says:

> Litil John and Robert Hude Waythmen war commendit gud
> In Ingilwood and Bernnysdale
> Thai ossit al this tyme thar travale
>
> Little John and Robert Hude, outlaws, were well praised
> In Inglewood and Barnsdale
> They carried out their work all this time[19]

Wyntoun thus places Robin Hood in the northwest of England, on the Cheshire–Lancashire border, rather than in Sherwood Forest (which ran from just north of Mansfield to the southern border of Yorkshire in the Middle Ages). Robin is nowadays associated with Nottingham and with Sherwood, but various locations are given for him in the earlier records. The earliest mention of Robin is in *The Vision of Piers Plowman*, written by William Langland (probably a pseudonym) in the 1370s. His characterization of Sloth (idleness) says:

> I can nought perfitly my pater-noster as the prest it syngeth, but I can rymes of Robyn Hood and Randolf earle of Chestre,

> Ac neither of owre Lord ne of owre Lady the leste that euere was made.

> I do not know by heart my 'Our Father' as the priest sings it, but
> I know rhymes of Robin Hood and Randolf earl of Chester,
> Also neither of Our Lord or of Our Lady, the least that was ever written/created.[20]

Langland was a man of the West Midlands; his narrator and alter ego Will begins his dream vision by falling asleep on the Malvern Hills, in Worcestershire, and he appears to be suggesting that the stories he mentions are known in the western and northwestern Midlands at least. During the course of the story, Will journeys to London to work, implying that the 'rymes' were known there, too. In the early stories, Robin Hood travels between Nottingham and the home of Sir Richard atte Lee, near Plumpton Park in northern Lancashire, and he is murdered at Kirklees, in the Pennine foothills of northwestern Yorkshire. This is a wide geographical spread, suggesting that Robin's original geography was much less specific than it is now; it may have differed according to the area in which the stories were being told.[21] By the end of the fifteenth century, and probably before, Robin Hood was appearing in performance in many geographical locations all over England and Scotland.

Enough questions are raised by comparing medieval to modern in these four important areas to indicate that Robin Hood may have appeared to his early audiences very differently from the way he does now. It is not enough simply to make that observation, however, without trying to understand how he *was* received and understood. There has been enough work done on the meagre survivals from the period 1400–1600 to suggest that the more immediate lines of enquiry have been all but exhausted. There are, however, some more points to be made, particularly in relation to the culture of which the Robin Hood stories formed a part.

British culture at the end of the thirteenth century was multilingual, and it remained so through the fourteenth and for much of the fifteenth centuries. In addition to the vernaculars of different parts of the islands – Welsh, Irish, Manx, Cornish – English itself was made up of many different dialects, any of which might be incomprehensible to another. Middle Scots was a variant of the language spoken south of the border, and the people of Scotland's marginal regions spoke different languages (including Gallic and the Scandinavian-based tongues of the north). There were two common vernacular languages, which people understood (or not) with different levels of facility. Latin was the language of education, of the Bible and of church services. It was a living language, written and spoken by those educated to the level of the grammar school and above. French, particularly in its Anglo-French dialect variant, was the language of the upper-class laity: the nobility and the gentry. This meant that it was the language of courts and of courtly entertainments. It was also the language of law. The writers and performers had to be bilingual, but others lower down the social scale were not necessarily excluded from an understanding, of sorts, of material in French and Latin. They were used to hearing Latin in church, to hearing its meaning explained by the priests, and thus, if they were not able to translate, they were able to develop a knowledge of what words, phrases and paragraphs of Latin were 'meant' to mean. This cognitive process would have extended to material in French. The servants who worked in households might have had to use some French in pursuit of their occupations; not only families and guests, but tenants and servants, would be present in noble and gentry halls during festivals when minstrels and actors performed.[22] They would all learn, at their own level, to understand and to appreciate any French songs and stories they heard or saw performed there.

In the thirteenth and early fourteenth centuries, the cultural links between England and France were very strong. The royal families of both countries were particularly close. Henry III of England (r. 1216–72) was married to Eleanor of Provence, and his son Edward I married as his second wife Margaret of France in 1299. In 1308 Edward's second son, Edward II, married Isabelle, the daughter of King Philippe IV of France; her three brothers, Louis X, Philippe V and Charles IV, became kings of France in turn. It was expected that queens would not only bring with them from their own country a household retinue of knights and ladies (with minstrels and other performers in tow), but patronize composers, artists and performers from their new countries. Composers and performers travelled in both directions. In 1297 Adenet 'le Roy' visited Edward I's court from the court of the count of Flanders, and one John de Cressin (from Cresy or Crécy in northern France) entertained Queen Margaret of England in 1307. Cressin may have come from France with the queen as part of her household, just as Edward's lute player Janin (Little John/Iago), who was Spanish, may have come to England in the retinue of the king's first wife, Eleanor of Castile.[23] In 1335 Edward's grandson, Edward III, paid for two of his bagpipers to visit an international minstrels' gathering (rather like a trade conference today) in order to improve their skills by networking with practitioners from the rest of Europe.[24]

France was the centre of courtly culture, and French influence on English royal courts percolated down through noble and regional courts and halls, whose owners were Francophone if not always Francophile.[25] The thirteenth and early fourteenth centuries were a golden age for the vernacular literature of northern France. Writers and performers such as Jean Erart, Jean Bodel, Adenet le Roy, Raoul de Houdenc, Hélinand de Froidmont, Rutebeuf, Gautier de Coinci and Adam de la Halle all flourished at different times throughout these years when the court cultures of England and of France were very closely connected. Courtly material in French exerted influence on works that were written and performed in English – in churchyards, in taverns and on the streets. Given that cultural movement was largely downwards, from the elites at the top to the workers at the bottom, it is very possible that early Robin Hood stories were written and performed in the 'French of England', although it is only in Middle English that they have survived. Moreover, much material that has been lost from medieval English culture has survived in French from a similar time.[26] Because of this, this book uses not only English, but French examples in order to illustrate the type of works that would have been known to the audiences of early Robin Hood tales, and would have influenced the way in which they understood them. Beginning with an overview of the early material remains and the early stories, this book will pursue an understanding, through a largely bilingual medieval context, of what subsequent generations – including our own – understand, and did/do not understand, about Robin Hood.

ONE
Robin Hood and the Written Word

The earliest surviving stories of Robin Hood date from the 1460s, although Langland's testimony that they were known to his audiences in the 1370s indicates that they were in existence even earlier than that, perhaps as early as the beginning of the fourteenth century or the late thirteenth (as Walter Bower believed). Such a date for works written in English, perhaps developed from French examples, is very feasible. By the early fourteenth century Edward I of England was already at war with the Welsh and the Scots, but he had also begun hostilities with King Philippe IV of France that would later develop into the Hundred Years War. Although he was Francophone himself and married a French princess as his second wife, Edward promoted the English language as part of his anti-French war propaganda.[1] The court of his son Edward II was essentially French in its culture, but the writer of *Adam Davy's Dreams about Edward II* thought it appropriate and acceptable to address advice to the new king (in the form of prophetic visions) in English instead of the usual Latin.[2] Edward was rumoured to enjoy spending his time conversing in 'low' English language to craftsmen, labourers and other peasants, although – like his equally much-maligned great-grandson Richard II – he seems to have been a very cultured and talented individual. The atmosphere his court provided was highly congenial to the production, or translation, of work in English, using widely available French models.[3] Such a process, in such an environment, could very well have produced the first English Robin Hood stories.

The earliest of these (almost) complete stories is usually called *Robin Hood and the Monk*, although this is something of a misnomer as Robin Hood in person is absent for much of the tale; the main actor in the story is Robin's second-in-command, Little John. John is not always on stage either, and neither is the monk, although he is pivotal to the story. The story unfolds as follows (it has been told and retold many times before, so this is simply my version) . . .

Robin Hood confesses to Little John a desire, and a need, to go to Mass, so he intends to go to church in 'notyngham' (Nottingham):

> 'Hit is a fourtnet & more,' sayd he,
> Syn I my sauyour see.'
>
> 'It is a fortnight and more,' said he,
> 'Since I saw my Saviour.'[4]

John agrees to accompany Robin, but he refuses to be Robin's bow-bearer ('Thou shall bere [carry] thin own seid litull Jon'), putting Robin's nose out of joint in front of the other outlaws. On the way through the forest, Little John suggests to Robin that they pass the time by competitive shooting – with a money stake.

> '. . . we well shet e a peny,' seid litull Jon,
> 'Undur the grene wode lyne . . .'
> '. . . euer for on as thou shetis,' seid Robyn,
> In feith I holde the thre.'
>
> '. . . we will shoot for a penny [stake],' said Little John,
> 'under the green wood canopy . . .'
> '. . . for every one [that is, penny] that you shoot,' said Robin,
> 'In faith, I will wager you three.'[5]

With the stakes raised, John proves to be the better shot, but when he asks for his payment, Robin refuses to pay up and even strikes him. John departs in high dudgeon at being unjustly called a liar. We then leave Little John for a while, and follow Robin into town to St Mary's Church (a popular designation at the time, but obviously St Mary's, Nottingham, in this version). As he enters the town, Robin prays to the Virgin Mary (whose church he is visiting and who therefore rules the space) to help him in this hostile environment. Here Robin is recognized by a monk who had been robbed by the outlaws on a previous occasion. The monk rouses the sheriff, who makes for the church with his men, having also called out the watch (the city's defence force) and alerted the townsfolk. There is fighting in the streets, and ultimately in the sacred space of the church itself. Eventually, Robin's sword breaks and he is captured, then imprisoned in the sheriff's castle to await execution. He is an outlaw who has already been condemned, and may be killed by anyone on sight, so the sheriff does not have to go through this due process at all: he is making a point while enjoying the satisfaction of seeing Robin Hood hang.

There follows a tantalizing gap in the story; a section is missing due to manuscript damage. There may have been something about the sheriff's appointment of the monk and his page as messengers to the king, and a link to the forest, which is where we catch up with the story as the disconsolate outlaws mourn the loss of their leader. In this leaderless state, Little John takes charge, calling on the Virgin Mary to help him in the rescue of Robin Hood.

He has seruyd Oure Lady many a day
And yet wil securely.
Therfor I trust in hir specialy
No wyckud deth shal he dye . . .
. . . let this mourning be
And I shal be the munkis gyde
With the might of mylde Mary.

He has served Our Lady many a day
And surely will continue to do so.
Therefore I trust in Her especially
No wicked death will he die . . .
. . . let this mourning be;
And I shall be the Monk's guide
With the might of mild Mary.[6]

Disguised as a traveller, with Much the miller's son dressed as his page, John watches for the monk from the house of Much's uncle. John and Much ride out to meet the monk, and John ingratiates himself by pretending that he, too, has been a victim of Robin Hood's gang. On a lonely stretch of road John reveals his identity,

In *Robin Hood and the Monk*, Robin is held in the 'deepest dungeon' of Nottingham Castle. The deepest of the castle's dungeons were in the caves (some still accessible) tunnelled into the rocky outcrop on which the castle is built.

pulls the monk from his horse and decapitates him. Much does the same to the page in order to eliminate any incriminating witnesses. After burying these two in shallow graves by the roadside, Little John and Much take on the identity of the sheriff's messengers. They go into the king's presence (we are not told where the king is; he is likely to be in London, or at least at some distance, as news has not travelled to him yet) and deliver the news of Robin Hood's capture. The king is delighted but suspicious – where is the monk? Thinking quickly, John says that the sheriff was so glad of the monk's help that he was given a rich abbey, and John was sent in his stead. The king accepts this, gives John and Much twenty pounds, declares them 'yemen [servants] of the crown' and sends them back to the sheriff with the king's seal and his thanks. John and Much return to the sheriff, who is also delighted but suspicious. Where is the monk? Thinking quickly again, John tells him that the king was so pleased with the news that he made the monk 'Abot of Westmynster [Abbot of Westminster] / a lorde of that abbay'. The sheriff accepts this, thinking the pair to be royal messengers, and gives them the usual hospitality – bread and board – that such men would expect when on missions. The story does note, however, that the sheriff gives Little John 'wyne [wine] of the best', which is an unexpected honour for an employee, even a royal one: the sheriff is really pleased with himself at this point. In the middle of the night John and Much make their way to the gaol, where John kills the porter, takes his keys and frees Robin. The sheriff does not dare tell the king in person, 'For sothe [in truth] he wil me heng [hang].'

The story ends not with this happy outcome to the action, but with a confidential conversation and a royal outburst. In the first, between Robin Hood and Little John, John leaves Robin in no doubt about the moral lesson of what has happened:

> I haue done the a gode turne for an euyll,
> Quyte the whan thou may
>
> I have done you a good turn for an evil [one]
> Pay me back when you can.[7]

In an unforeseen and impulsive act, Robin offers to resign his position as leader to John, but John refuses, saying he would rather be a follower than a leader.

> 'I make the maister,' seid Robyn Hode,
> Off alle my men and me.'
> 'Nay by my trough,' seid litull John,
> 'So shalle hit never be.
> But lat me be afelow . . .'
>
> 'I make you master,' said Robin Hood,
> 'Of all my men and me.'
> 'No, by my troth,' said Little John,
> 'So shall it never be.
> But let me be one of the men . . .'[8]

So John accepts the divinely appointed social order, although his ruler (Robin) may be a morally lesser man in need of his subject's advice and example.[9] In an outburst to nobody in particular, but which is 'overheard' by the composer and the audience (and ourselves, as readers), the frustrated – and not a little embarrassed – king expresses his anger that everyone, including the king himself, has been well and truly duped by Little John.

'Litill John has begyled the Schereff
in faith so hase he me:
Litul John has begyled vs bothe
And that full wel I se –
Or ellis the Schereff of Notyngham
Hye hongut shuld he be.
I made hem yemen of the crowne
And gaf hem fee with my hond!
I gaf hem grith,' seid oure kyng,
'thorow out all mery Inglond!'

'Little John has beguiled the sheriff
In faith, so he has me;
Little John has beguiled us both
And that I can full well see –
Or else the sheriff of Nottingham
Hanged high, should he be.
I made them yeomen of the Crown
And gave them fee with my hand!
I gave them a pardon,' said our king,
'Throughout all merry England.'[10]

In a perhaps even more unforeseen socio-political shift, the king notes that Little John loves Robin Hood more than his own servants and subjects love *him*. On reflection, best keep it quiet, he says, '[s]peke no more of this mater.' The writer ends with a familiar 'book-ending' appeal to the audience, which is also a cue for applause:

Thus endys the talking of the Munke
And Robyn Hode, I wysse.
God that is euer a crowned kyng
Bryng us all to his blisse . . . Amen.

Thus ends the talking of the Monk
And Robin Hood, indeed.
God, who is always a crowned king
Bring us all to his bliss![11]

The volume itself is quite small in size, at 8½ × 5⅞ inches and 135 paper folios. It is not small enough to be carried in a sleeve or purse, but is portable enough to be carried in a pilgrim's or a messenger's bag, or in a *male* (a travel bag, box or case) – roughly the size of a modern A5 notebook. It is also large enough to fit comfortably on a bookshelf. The book has become disorganized, and some pages are missing. They are not in the order intended by the original scribe, who appears to be the sole compiler.[12] On folio 43r the scribe names himself in an inscription two lines high, with three-line capitals, the first with elaborate penwork decoration, contained in an elaborate cartouche.[13] The inscription reads: 'Explicit Passio D[o]mini nostri ih[es]u xpi [Christi] Q[uo]d D[omi]n[u]s Gilbert[us] Pylkyngton Amen' (Here ends the Passion of our Lord Jesus Christ by Master Gilbert Pilkington Amen).[14] The handwriting evidence implies that this was a personal rather than a family or institutional volume.

Gilbert Pilkington was a member of a well-known northern family whose main residence was at Rivington, in Lancashire. A minor branch of this family also resided at Kirklees near Brighouse in West Yorkshire – the place given in the late fifteenth- and early sixteenth-century printed books as the site of Robin Hood's death.[15] They belonged to a group of independent, self-sustaining local gentry who controlled most of the land in Lancashire, Cheshire and the northern Peak District, where royal and ecclesiastical control was limited to less than a quarter of the local area. Being a Lancashire family, the Pilkingtons were clients of the earls, later the dukes, of Lancaster; Robert Pilkington of Rivington served in the armies of John of Gaunt, Henry IV's father, in Spain. A certain Gilbert Pilkington is listed in the register of the Bishop of Coventry and Lichfield (whose diocese stretched from the West Midlands across the Cheshire border at this time) as having been ordained a subdeacon in 1463, a deacon in 1464, and a priest in 1465, although there is no record of his being ordained to a living. This Gilbert's dates coincide with the dating of *Robin Hood and the Monk*, and his likely place of origin matches the dialect in which the whole manuscript is written, that of the area running from the northern Peak District (Derbyshire and Staffordshire) to south Lancashire, in which Pilkington family homes were situated.[16] The assumption, therefore, is that this book was compiled by Gilbert Pilkington, priest, probably over a period of several years or perhaps longer, and was originally his property.[17]

Gilbert Pilkington must have had a personal interest in, and a personal use for, the contents of this book, in which he invested much effort over many years.[18] What Gilbert thought useful is a very interesting mix of materials. The first section of the book (as it is now) contains a variety of religious items (the *Passion of Christ*, John Mirk's *Instructions for Parish Priests*, *Christ's Wounds*, the *Signs of Death* and the *Seven Deadly Sins*, and addresses to the Virgin Mary), along with several items that we might find odd in this context. These are the satirical *Tournament of Totenham*, in which a group of 'churls' ape their betters by organizing their own alternative tournament, a moral ghost story with similarities to other northwest Midlands stories such as *The Awntyrs of Arthure at the Tarn Wathelyn*, and a comic tale of adulterers and fornicators being 'outed' by an enchanted chamber pot to which they become stuck fast (*The Adulterous Falmouth Squire* and the *Tale of the Basyn*). *King Edward and the Shepherd* is a 'king and commoner' story of how a king meets a peasant, who then tells him some home truths about the corruption of his officials and the practical effects of his rulership on the rural working-class population.[19] There is also an *Anonymous Short Metrical Chronicle of England*, along with popular religious miracle material based on the transformational theology of the Mass (*The Lady Who Buried the Host*). Finally, there is *Robin Hood and the Monk*, along with *Thomas of Erceldoune's Prophecy*. We might be tempted to call these folklore elements, but there is danger in this, as the idea of 'folk' developed later and therefore is not applicable to this manuscript. *Erceldoune* was, however, a text of the Anglo-Scottish and Anglo-Welsh borders, so it is entirely appropriate to find this text in the manuscript of a Pilkington. Thomas of Erceldoune, also known as Thomas the Rymer, was seen as a prophet both in the form of 'fore-telling' and of 'forth-telling', or speaking out words of divine wisdom. Robin Hood was also seen as a 'forth-teller', as Gilbert Pilkington would have been in his office as a preacher. Prophetic truth-telling is, more than anything, what binds the seemingly disparate contents of this collection together.

Gilbert Pilkington must surely have been a parish priest, responsible not only for preaching, confessing and instructing his flock, but for festive activities, perhaps overseeing them and/or writing the scripts.[20] If Pilkington was a parish priest, we do not know where. He does not seem to have been as favoured as his contemporary, one George Pilkington from the diocese of York (so possibly of the trans-Pennine Kirklees branch of the family), a graduate of the University of Cambridge, who was ordained in April 1457, at about the time Gilbert may have been beginning his book.[21] George was presented to a third part of the rectory (that is, the freehold living) of Clipston in Northamptonshire, in 1456, presumably as a support for his studies. The rectory was in the gift of Christ's College, Cambridge, in an area originally part of the earldom of Lincoln, which then became part of the duchy of Lancaster. In 1456/7 the duke of Lancaster was also the king, Henry VI, and the armed conflict now known as the Wars of the Roses had already begun (with the first battle of St Albans in 1455). These two Pilkingtons reveal the range of the house of Lancaster, whose tendrils of ownership and influence reached from the far northwest of England down to the University of Cambridge and the affluent Midlands, from which members of their affinity in apparently isolated places were able to derive considerable benefits. The road travelled by the young George Pilkington from Lancashire or Kirklees to Cambridge would have been the same road identified by James Holt as the 'Robin Hood road', surrounded by the Duke of Lancaster's lands.[22] This is less a line, as Holt suggests, and more like an ellipse, or a pair of giant pincers. Along these lines a link can be established (in the form of the Pilkington family) between the areas mentioned in the surviving Robin Hood stories: Lancashire/Cheshire, North Yorkshire, Sherwood Forest and Nottingham, also with the Peak District and the West Midlands where Langland may have heard them. Members of this same family took each of the two major north–south routes down the eastern and western sides of England in search of preferment and a living.

Robin Hood and the Potter is of similar date. This tale is close in length to *Robin Hood and the Monk*, and is also contained in a 'miscellany', a manuscript book made up of a variety of different items (now University Library, Cambridge, MS Ee.4.35).[23] The book as it stands has also been written in a single hand.[24] One very interesting thing about the contents is their similarity to those of Gilbert Pilkington's book. The sermons and other instructions for parish priests are missing, although it does contain (on folio 5r) instructions on how to calculate the date of Easter, something that all parish priests would require. *The Lady Who Buried the Host* is there, along with *The Adulterous Falmouth Squire* and *The Kynge* [*King*] *and the Barker*, another 'king and commoner' story similar in generic content to that of *King Edward and the Shepherd* in Pilkington's book. What is different is the presence of two conduct books (instructions for how to bring up children to be good and moral Christian members of society, and to practise good manners). These were very popular in the later fifteenth century with members of the aspirational merchant and professional classes; if they were to rise in the world, as their parents hoped that they would, it was important for middle-class children to have the courtly manners proper to the gentry and to share their tastes and interests. Courtesy books provided a form of courtly education that they could not otherwise acquire (generally – Geoffrey Chaucer is an exception to this), as their aristocratic peers could, from education and experience (*noriture* or nurture) in another aristocratic household.[25] Robin Hood and Little John, it should be noted, also display courtly manners – at least, most of the time!

One important thing that we can say is that the collection is moral, devotional and confessional. The 24 folios it contains today were not originally the major works in the book, but were written on the remaining blank leaves in a fourteenth-century copy of *The Prikke of Conscience*, a devotional, apocalyptic poem about the last fifteen days of the world.[26] The *Prikke* was extremely popular with faithful laypeople in the fifteenth century – a beautiful example can still be found in the late fourteenth-century windows of All Saints' Church, North Street, York, where it was sponsored by the donations of wealthy merchants of the parish. This is interesting, because the *Potter* manuscript appears to have had a similarly urban context and point of origin. On the back of folio 24 (its recto) there is a merchant's mark, a trade identifier or brand logo, and above it there is an autograph: 'iste liber constat ricardo calle' (this book belongs to Richard Calle). The Calle family were grocers in Framlingham, Suffolk (a seat of the dukes of Norfolk), but the name is best known because a family member, Richard Calle, was steward to the Paston family of south and east Norfolk in the fifteenth century. The Pastons are famous for their large collection of letters, spanning more than half a century, from which can be deduced the interests, aspirations and daily lives of an English gentry family during the period often known as the Wars of the Roses. When John Paston, the first member of the family to be officially a 'gentleman', died in 1466, his daughter Margery announced to her mother, Lady Margaret Paston, that she had secretly married Richard Calle, with whom she had fallen in love. The family's efforts failed to break the marriage, which was found to be legal in the eyes of both Church and State. Calle was forced to leave his employment; he moved to London with his wife, and was able to use his connections – professional and family – to make a good living as a member of the Grocers' Company in the City.[27] A note concerning the provision of victuals for the marriage of Edward IV's sister Margaret to Charles the Bold of Burgundy in Bruges – an event that Sir John Paston (the first John's eldest son) is known to have attended – on 3 July 1468 confirms both the mercantile associations and the date of the book.[28] The Calle household was well established in London by this time.

In *Robin Hood and the Potter*, Robin himself is much more of a star than he is in *Robin Hood and the Monk*. One day, Robin and his men are waiting for someone to ambush on the highway when a potter comes along in his cart. This potter is well known to Little John, who declares that he has fought with him on a previous occasion (at Wentbridge on the Great North Road – this story, unlike *Robin Hood and the Monk*, is located in Yorkshire), and he can still feel the bruises. Robin bets John and the other outlaws that he can get the better of the Potter, and the bet is laid. Robin blocks the way and challenges the Potter to pay *pavage*, a local tax used to maintain roads and bridges – which is most likely being used ironically here (this is actually theft or 'protection money': Robin's *personal* taxation). The Potter gets a big stick from the back of his cart, Robin readies himself with a sword and buckler (the curved sword and small round shield of an ordinary fighting man, as illustrated in the margins of the Luttrell Psalter and other illuminated books), and they fight, while John and the men enjoy the fun of it all.[29] Things turn more threatening when the Potter fells Robin 'with a caward [sly or crafty] stroke', and the outlaws reach for their bowstrings. Unlike the nastier and more quarrelsome Robin of *Robin Hood and the Monk*, this Robin quickly defuses the situation with good humour, announcing that Little John has won his ten-shilling bet:

'Yeff they were a C,' seyd Roben,
'Y feyth they ben all theyne.'

'If they were a hundred,' said Robin,
In faith, they are all thine.'[30]

As in later narratives, such as the later ballad stories of Robin's fights with Little John and Friar Tuck (beloved of illustrators from Howard Pyle onwards and of film-makers), Robin offers a place in his band to the victorious Potter, but the latter refuses. Robin then has a sudden idea – he asks the Potter to exchange clothes and to let him take his pots to Nottingham, to which the Potter agrees. This begins a second stage of the story.

Robin arrives in Nottingham with his pots, and sets up his stall outside the sheriff's (castle or maybe hall) door. There, he sells the pots at a deliberately low price, and attracts a lot of attention as a result:

> . . . all that say hem sell
> Seyde he had be no potter long . . .
> Preveley seyde man & weyffe,
> 'Yownder potter schall neuer the.'
>
> . . . all who saw him sell
> said he'd not been a potter long
> In private, men and women said,
> 'Yonder potter will never thrive.'[31]

Having almost sold out of pots, Robin sends his five remaining pots as a free gift to the sheriff's wife and she, in return, invites him to dine with her, the sheriff and his men. The sheriff is a genial host, happy to oblige his wife. During the meal, Robin 'the potter' overhears two of the men talking about a shooting contest, which he joins and, of course, wins the prize. The festive atmosphere changes when 'the potter' announces that in his cart he has a bow given to him by Robin Hood, with whom he has taken part in shooting games: 'Knowest thow Robyn hode?' seyde the screffe, 'Potter, y prey the tell thow me.' ('Do you know Robin Hood?' said the sheriff, 'Potter, I pray you to tell me.')[32] The 'potter' promises to take the sheriff to Robin the following day. Having thanked the sheriff's wife 'of all thyng' (for everything) and given her a gold ring, 'the potter' takes the unsuspecting sheriff into the greenwood, where he blows his horn, assembles his men and reveals his true identity. After a night sleeping rough in the forest, the sheriff is sent home on foot, accompanied by a white palfrey, which is Robin's gift to the sheriff's wife. When the good lady sees the shame and discomfiture of her returning spouse, she just laughs. Back in the greenwood, Robin asks the Potter what his pots were worth: 'they were worth ij nobellys [two nobles],' seyde he.' Robin gives him ten pounds, an improvement on his original investment, and invites him to visit the outlaws in the greenwood whenever he likes.

This story lacks the moral severity, the violence and (to us, at least) the general nastiness of *Robin Hood and the Monk*. It may be that this difference in emphasis reflects a more secular taste than that of Pilkington the priest. The Calles were a comfortably off merchant family in a major European city (London) which was also Britain's greatest port. Like many London merchants, they were incomers who had made good, established families and interests in the city, and stayed. They are very representative of the middling sort of all European towns and cities of their time, and this book demonstrates something of what such people were then collecting, reading and, in a practical sense, using. It complements Gilbert Pilkington's book in that it shows how many interests and points of view the gentry-bred priest and the City merchants actually shared. Priests like Pilkington were providing services to people like these, and to their clients,

The gatehouse of Nottingham Castle has medieval foundations, and the arches of its medieval entrance survive within the rebuilt (from the 17th century) shell. Is this the 'sheriff's door' where Robin sold pots in *Robin Hood and the Potter*?

customers and employees, as well as to the local gentry, their tenants, labourers and servants. It shows that they all had a basic solidarity of ideology, morality and belief in the second half of the fifteenth century. In Britain, Robin Hood belonged to that context.

The wealthy citizens of London (like those of other major European cities and towns) sponsored and enjoyed a cultural and social life that centred on city guilds and the social events and performances, such as plays, pageants and processions, which they organized and funded. Events staged by wealthy guilds and their associated social and religious organizations, or confraternities, in major English and Scottish towns and cities cannot have been any less impressive in their quality, spectacle or scale than those of their European counterparts. The governing class of these places saw themselves, and wanted to be seen, as *probi homines*, or 'worthy men'.[33] Worthy men had to demonstrate their moral credentials in ways that also demonstrated their wealth, because their right to social prominence was based solely on their economic power. In a society where the only truly dependable source of power and sustained wealth was still land ownership, these men aspired to marry their children into landed families, or to acquire landed estates, because a position based on capital alone was precarious. Their claim to power was also, therefore, problematic. It could not be based, as was the aristocracy's, on land, so they laid claim to a special moral worth that was both the reward for, and the basis of, financial fortune. This worth and its resulting status had to be continually displayed: before their peers, before their social betters, and before the people over whom they claimed authority. The saints owed their power and status to their own virtue and to the power of God. The blessings given to the saints made the City merchants' own debts to fortune – backed up, no doubt, by a few dealings of less than peerless morality – look more like divine favour. In this way, their claims to authority were backed up by heaven as much as, if not more than, the claims of those above them in the social hierarchy. It was with God's permission that they had been able to leapfrog over the usual status barriers. Richard Calle would have seen himself as such a worthy man; he was able to look the aristocratic young Pastons (whose family, in his eyes, might be seen as having wronged him and his wife) in the eye and to deal with them on equal terms. In the same way, Robin Hood and Little John, although they have impeccable manners, can think themselves equal, in God's eyes at least, to potters, sheriffs, monks and kings.

In the towns, Robin Hood was also seen as a worthy man, thus aligning him with members of the urban elite. This was the case in Rye, East Sussex, in 1511, when Robin is described as 'the worshipfull man'.[34] Names of individuals in some records show that it was often the churchwardens themselves, leading men in their communities, who played the outlaw's part in a variety of festive events.[35] The burgesses of Edinburgh were repulsed when they offered the part of 'Litiljohn' to the Earl of Arran in 1518, but the fact that they were prepared to make the offer to a high-ranking noble of royal blood shows the esteem in which they held this form of participation. In Scotland, Robin Hood was a feature of activities in Aberdeen, where in 1508 all able-bodied men were obliged to process with Robin Hood and Little John with bows and arrows (is this an oblique reference to an archery contest?), and also in Ayr, Cranston, Dalkeith, Dumfries, Dundee, Haddington, Peebles, Perth and St Andrews.[36] The first mention of a performance in Scotland is for Edinburgh in 1492, but we know from Wyntoun and Bower that they had been going on before this. The Robin Hood tradition in Scotland must have been separate to that of England in that Scots were highly unlikely to have been celebrating Robin Hood's Englishness. The Scottish manifestations of Robin, however, do belong to the same context as those from elsewhere, in that the worthy men of Scottish towns saw themselves competing with, and alongside, other urban elites throughout Europe. Like the merchant oligarchs of English (and continental) towns, they were engaged in impressing their own people, their sovereign, local aristocrats and (perhaps more important) other major towns and cities in their part of the European trading world. For the citizens of Aberdeen, the Baltic towns of the Hanse were as close, if not closer, than those of southern England. If Robin Hood formed part of celebrations in competing Scottish and English towns, they would feel the need to keep up with trends. As with other towns and cities, Scottish urban communities already had their own festive life, so Robin Hood could just be fitted in. This is probably why he is recorded as taking part mostly in processions in Scotland rather than plays, as in England. Each area had its own particular festive forms.

The 'Potter' book gives little evidence, apart from its dialect, about original ownership of the texts. Was it made for Calle, was it purchased, or was it a gift? If a gift, was it given by a member of his family, his employer or maybe even his first wife, Margery? Did he simply take it when he was dismissed? There is evidence that John Paston and his family sponsored festive performances in which Robin Hood played a part, in the form of a short text fragment, on a single paper sheet (now bound into Trinity College, Cambridge, MS R.2.64, a collection of papers that also originated with the Paston family). The fragment contains what can be described as a medieval 'working' script.[37] Actors at this time did not, on the whole, learn whole scripts from text in the way that most modern actors do. They used cue-lines for entries (and possibly exits) and delivered the rest from memory (aided by audio-visual techniques) and improvisation. A short working script like this would be entirely sufficient for an experienced performer such as Sir John Paston's 'man' William Woods to produce one of his Robin Hood or sheriff of Nottingham performances. The reference is a well-known one: in one of his letters, Paston complains that he has been deserted by his master of horse, William Woods, whom he has kept for three years 'to pleye Seynt Jorge and Robynhod and the shryff of Notyngham' (to play St George and Robin Hood and the sheriff of Nottingham), who has 'goon in-to Bernysdale' (gone into Barnsdale) and left him without a horse-keeper.[38] The full narrative of the little play has to be imaginatively reconstructed (as it originally was), but it runs like this . . .

Speaking to the sheriff (Nottingham is not mentioned), a character offers to kill Robin Hood 'for thy sake', while the sheriff offers him 'golde and fee' in return. Robin is then depicted having a shooting contest with an individual, who may very well be the same person, and winning. This is followed by 'casting the stone' and 'casting the exaltre' (axle tree, a heavy piece of wood). 'Syr knyght ye haue a falle' ('Sir Knight, you have fallen', or perhaps 'you have scored a fall') suggests that either the other person slips, or that a wrestling contest follows this. Robin blows his horn, and two fight 'at ottraunce' (*à l'outrance*, or to the death). Robin kills the knight, puts on his clothes, cuts off his head and puts it in his hood. Two people then meet, one asking the other for news. The other says that Robin Hood and his men have been taken by the sheriff. The two decide to 'sette on foote' (make their way on foot) and kill the sheriff: Friar Tuck 'dothe his bowe pluke' (plucks his bow [string]). Someone orders (possibly the same two characters) to yield to the sheriff, and they are bound and taken to prison with the others. In the final line, a character calls to the guards to open the gates, perhaps of a castle or of a city. The final scene may have been similar to *Robin Hood and the Monk*, where Robin is freed by means of an inside job, or to the later ballad of *Robin Hood and Guy of Gisborne*, where they are freed at the gallows.[39] It may have been entirely different, but obviously would have ended with the outlaws either freeing themselves or being 'sprung' in some way.

The text occurs on the recto side of a piece of paper, perhaps originally folded, but certainly ruled for some other purpose (the play lines are written over the ruled line). On the verso (back), there are three drawings: a cannon-like instrument firing stones, whose likeness also to an erect penis firing semen 'balls' cannot be ignored, was probably obvious to the artist and was therefore deliberate; a head-and-shoulders image of a woman, which may be connected and by the same hand, in broad, semi-faded pen strokes; and a dragon, which is almost heraldic, very precise and definitely added later, as it overlaps the bottom corner of the woman's wimple. Unfortunately these tell us nothing (although John Marshall thinks that they may be somehow connected to the St George's guild processions in Norwich), as they seem to have been carried out by different people at different times.[40] Along with the drawings, the back of the paper carries the record of a series of payments received by one John Sterndalle from Richard Wytway, a 'peynter', for the lease of a building, or room, called the 'wardarrop' (wardrobe?), and rents paid for a 'hosse' (house?) by the same Wytway, between May 1475 and August 1476. In the light of his researches, Marshall suggests that Wytway may have been working for the Paston family at Caister Castle (near Great Yarmouth in Norfolk) during this time. The period in question marked the negotiations leading to the final cession of Caister to the Pastons, who had laid claim to it since the death of its former owner and builder, Sir John Fastolf, in 1459. The claim had been subject to a long-running dispute with the dukes of Norfolk, but Caister had finally been restored to the Pastons in August 1476. The castle at Caister had a famous large 'Wardrobe' building, in which Fastolf had kept his considerable valuables, including rich fabrics and tapestries, at the time of his death. Marshall suggests that Wytway's tenancy would have represented a means of gaining some form of revenue while the Norfolks (who, unlike the Pastons, never lived at Caister) waited for the final resolution of the dispute.

Of course, all of this is possible but unproven. If the play-lines relate to a performance at all, it could have been given in Norfolk, Suffolk or London – or not given at all. There is no reason to link the dragon drawing with the dragon which took part in the St George's guild processions on 23 April in Norwich, although the guild's members were the most 'worthy' men in the city, and they included various members of the Paston family (who had a house on what is now Elm Hill in the city). Apart, that is, from John Paston II's assertion that William Woods, in addition to being a horse-keeper, had been retained to play St George, Robin Hood and the sheriff of Nottingham for him. The reference might just have been to the Norwich procession, but in that procession St George was usually accompanied by St Margaret (another dragon-slaying saint), not Robin Hood.[41] As the records are so ambiguous and incomplete, it is very hard to tell. Woods probably played these characters at different times and in different places. It may be that the cannonballs and the woman are more closely connected to the play-lines. The obscene joke would be fitting for a representation of Maid Marian's lusty part in the local, pastoral play-games. In these she was linked with Friar Tuck, who appears to take a prominent part in the play described on the other side of the paper.[42] If this is so, then the lines are a record of the type of performance which took place all over England (and Scotland) in the late fifteenth and early sixteenth centuries, and which contributed so much to the popularity of Robin Hood.[43]

The play may have been performed in the Pastons' own household, and/or that of a patron or kin, rather than in a public space. Courts, royal and aristocratic, provided regular employment for players and musicians throughout the medieval period, so it would have been very strange if the family had not sponsored performers of some kind. Other households besides Paston's, great and not quite so great, 'hosted' Robin Hood, and other plays and entertainments. The detailed accounts of Prior William More of Worcester show a regular and frequent stream of players and performers visiting his household at several of the great houses his priory owned. These included musicians and singers from the households of King Henry VIII and Cardinal Wolsey, as well as players of various kinds from neighbouring areas. At each of his residences, More hosted Robin Hood performances by local community groups in 1528, 1529–30, 1530–31 and (for the last time before the dissolution of the priory) 1534–5, when More paid *12d.* to the 'Robyn Whod & Litle John of Ombursley'.[44] More also kept his own household entertainers; one Roger Knight, for whom he provided a 'coote [coat] of moteley' in 1518–19, appears to have been a 'fool'.[45] Although both prior and king supplied and maintained their own entertainers, it was part of the reciprocal relationship between the great household and its surrounding communities that this patronage of local groups should happen. One of the major problems with locating and analysing Robin Hood in performance – and British minstrelsy and 'playing' in general – is the lack of detailed seigneurial household accounts for this period.[46]

Parish communities, towns and great households paid 'players' and 'minstrels' on a regular basis.[47] The records generally do not tell us what they played, and it is very dangerous to argue from a vacuum. It is highly likely that some of them 'played' a game of Robin Hood or told stories about him, but again there is no surviving record. Travelling performers such as these were the lifeblood of the medieval entertainment industry. At the time when Robin Hood's storyworld was being created, minstrels were *trouvères*, multi-talented individuals who composed, played and performed their own material, as well as that of others, and who often led and managed groups of performers. The patronage of minstrels by society's elite members had a very long history before Robin Hood was even thought of, and he simply entered the system at some point, probably in the mid- to late thirteenth century. Minstrels in the pay of great men (including the higher clergy) were well rewarded for their services, the more favoured ones being given grants of land that enabled them to found gentry families. Through the fifteenth into the early sixteenth century 'minstrel' came to mean 'musician' – the meaning generally associated with it today.[48] The term 'game', 'play' or 'player' might still include the ability to play music, sing and dance as well as act, however.

Licensed minstrels were those attached to a lord or the 'waits' attached to a town or city. By the fourteenth century, great households rarely retained their minstrels for more than the major feasts or the family's special occasions. At other times, a lord's minstrels might be used for other tasks, as above, or expected to go on the road. This was the case for most of them, but their journeys were not haphazard. They had planned itineraries, often taking a well-known route, visiting regular patrons, and the fees they were paid tended to be standardized, too. In his household ordinances of 1512–34, Lord Percy, Earl of Northumberland, offers 3*s*. 4*d*. to performers for annual visits, with 6*s*. 8*d*. for those who visited less regularly. However, if the minstrels belong to a member of his kin or a close friend, they get the whole fee anyway.[49] Minstrels, players or waits might travel long distances during the course of a year; the waits of Nottingham travelled widely; they were recorded in York in the fifteenth century and in Shrewsbury. Waits, usually in groups of three or four, constituted the watchmen of a town or city. They were tasked with not only keeping watch, but playing loud musical instruments such as trumpets and bagpipes at the setting of the watch, and to sound the alarm in case of attack or emergency. They played other instruments, and gradually their ceremonial and entertainment activities (providing music for civic meetings, official and unofficial gatherings, performances and processions) became more important than their guard duties. Waits toured just like the minstrels of the nobility, sometimes travelling long distances. The Nottingham waits were well travelled; they may have been under the jurisdiction of a Minstrels' Court in Tutbury, Staffordshire, and are recorded as far away as York in 1446–9. The waits of Coventry were so much in demand that the City Fathers limited their touring to within a 16-kilometre (10-mi.) radius of the city. Local performances seem to have been frequent and regular: in addition to their local duties, the Norwich waits are recorded in Thetford regularly between 1497 and 1513, and they were summoned by Edward IV to accompany him to France in 1475.[50]

The only other medieval manuscript version of a possible Robin Hood story is the text known as *Robyn and Gandeleyn*. It is written in a small book (British Library, London, MS Sloane 2593) that consists, in its present form, of almost nothing but poems, songs and carols, in English with some Latin, relating to named saints, religious festivals and the Virgin Mary. Some are secular drinking songs, some are satires (such as poems on the power of money) and some have moral subjects. One or two range from rude to rather obscene.[51] The nature of its contents led to scholarly speculation that this was a minstrel's miscellany.[52] *Robyn and Gandeleyn* is a short text; unusually for this manuscript, the text is written as prose, but it is very rhythmical and can also be written as poetry.[53] The text begins and ends with the repetition of a single line: 'Robyn lyth in grene wode bowndyn.' At the beginning of the story, we are given some interesting information about 'gode robyn & gandeleyn'; they were 'strong theuys' (tough – or possibly valiant – thieves) and 'bowmen gode & hende' (good and skilful archers). We are also told that they are 'childer' or young adults. They are not poachers; they go to the wood to get food, but find no deer. As evening draws on, they see a herd of a hundred fat fallow deer, and Robin swears to kill one. He does so and begins to flay the corpse, but as he does an arrow flies out of the west and kills him. Gandeleyn looks about for the perpetrator, swearing deadly revenge. He sees a 'lytil boy' who gives his name as Wrennok 'of donne': he carries a bow and twenty 'goode arwys' tied in a lace about his body. He and Gandeleyn agree to a deadly archery contest, and Wrennok fires the first shot. Mortally wounded, Gandeleyn fires an arrow straight to Wrennok's heart, which he 'clef on too'. Before he dies, Gandeleyn boasts over the boy's body that he will never be able to boast of killing 'goode robyn & gandelyn his knawe' (good Robin and Gandeleyn his page/servant/boy).[54]

Although small and largely unadorned, the Sloane book is carefully made and written, with rubrics (red letters) and bracketing, and a few little leaf-and-trefoil drawings in the lower margin of folio 15v. The hand is of a mid-fifteenth-century type, and the scribe has used the unmistakable 'chi' symbol – based on the Greek alphabet and looking like a saltire cross or a large letter X – for the 'sh' sound, which is typical of manuscripts made in the county of Norfolk at that time, and the use of 'qw' instead of 'wh' also indicates the dialect of north Norfolk. The manuscript also contains verses in honour of St Nicholas, patron of St Nicholas's Chapel in Lynn, now King's Lynn in northwest Norfolk.[55] Other verses praise St Edmund and St Thomas Becket, two saints who were particularly venerated in Norfolk. The coastal area immediately north of Lynn had a special association with the kingly martyr Edmund, who was believed to have landed there on his way back from exile to claim his throne of East Anglia.[56] Snettisham, just north of Lynn on the coast road leading to Wells and Cley, held a regular procession in honour of the saint, about which there are few recorded details, except that it was held annually and was a major local event.[57] A play of St Thomas

Becket, *Sancti Thome martiris* (St Thomas the Martyr), is noted in the Lynn records of 1384–5, although this is the only actual record of the subject at this location. Further records mention plays (*ludes*) but do not give any information on the subject matter.[58]

At first sight, the book does appear to be a personal collection. A note on folio 36v says that this book belonged to one Johannes Bardel or Bradol, who 'is of dwellyd in C' but it does not give the place name.[59] A note on fol. 35v refers to a payment of 25*s.* 4*d.* made 'ffor [th]e dy of Cley', which indicates a possible connection between the manuscript, its owner, and the north Norfolk coast. Cley next the Sea is now a sleepy village around 2 kilometres from the North Sea coast, but in the early fifteenth century it was still a thriving port town with a twin port, Blakeney, on the other side of the River Glaven's mouth. Along the nave of the church of St Margaret of Antioch at Cley, sculpted stone figures of minstrels perform in the spandrels of the arches, together with St George and a lion. There may have been processions here in the Middle Ages, as there were in other towns such as Snettisham and in the city of Norwich. Cley would also have been a point of disembarkation for pilgrims on their way to Walsingham, as the town lies a relatively short travelling distance from the famous shrine of Our Lady of Walsingham; the Sloane manuscript's owner may have travelled there, too. The imposing churches of Cley and Blakeney testify to the wealth of the communities they once served, as do the merchants' monuments in Cley church, and the remaining undercroft of a wealthy merchant's home in Blakeney.[60] The owner's name could be interpreted as Bardwell or Bradwell (it is given as 'Bradol' and 'Bardel'), or it could be Bradlee or Bradley. No fifteenth-century Bradley is recorded as a local vicar in the area, but there was a family of that name at Louth in Lincolnshire. In a record of 1462–3 relating to the Pentecostal performances at Lincoln, there is an entry stating that 3*s.* 4*d.* was paid to John Bradley 'pro labore suo habito circa le Orlege' (on account of his usual work on *le Orlege*).[61] *Orlege* here is not a clock, as in modern French, but clockwork, and the entry refers to the machinery that controlled the fake dove (possibly with accompanying firecrackers) which was lowered from the crossing ceiling into the cathedral during the Whit Sunday liturgy. This performance, which represented the descent of the Holy Spirit on the first Pentecost, was a regular feature of the cathedral's liturgy: in 1458–9 one William Muskham was paid 7*s.* 4*d.*

The church of St Margaret of Antioch, Cley next the Sea, North Norfolk. The ornate south porch bears the arms of the main donors, including those of Anne of Bohemia, first wife of King Richard II.

for work on 'columbam et vexillam in choro' (the dove and the banner in the choir).[62] From Lincoln or Louth to Lynn or Cley was only a short journey by sea. (The Vaux family, the post-Conquest lords of Cley, also had lands in Lincolnshire, around the port of Boston, and their successors by marriage, the Roos family, hailed from Helmsley in North Yorkshire.)

It is not inconceivable that the Sloane book's owner was not a monk, but a merchant, or maybe he could even have been a 'performer' of some kind himself, or a patron of performers travelling the road between Lynn, Snettisham, Cley and possibly Walsingham or Norwich. This road was well known to performance artists; the account books of the Lestranges at Hunstanton show that they were accustomed to paying visiting players.[63] Perhaps this book was compiled for use by groups of players, such as the Lynn waits, in a merchant's home visited by them, and others, on their travels through the year.[64] It may, on the other hand, have been a book of personal devotion. An alternative interpretation would be that the performance material was used locally in festive events, and by the middle of the fifteenth century it was being recorded, and kept by a confraternity member on behalf of the group.[65] Judging by the dirtied and worn state of the corners and page edges, it has seen much use.

There is a possible reference to the northwest, the land of the 'minstrel earl' Ranulf of Chester, whose 'rimes' were mentioned by Langland alongside those of Robin Hood in *Robyn and Gandeleyn*. Wrennok is a British name, and Don is an area in the Delamere Forest in Cheshire. In 1245 the king's house of Delamere was committed to one Wrennok son of Kenewrek as his dwelling. Wrennok was obviously a forester, living in a lodge.[66] The Dones were a local Cheshire family; in 1353 Richard Done claimed that his family had a hereditary right to the office of chief forester. The claim was successful, and the family kept the office until the seventeenth century, with an ancient hunting horn as the symbol of their title.[67] Royal patronage for members of their Chester affinity did extend to north Norfolk: for example, Sir Robert Knolles, a Cheshire gentleman and war captain under King Edward III and his son Edward, Prince of Wales, moved to Sculthorpe (between Walsingham and Lynn) in the later fourteenth century after a royal grant of land in the area, and died there in 1407. The *Monk* and *Potter* manuscripts also demonstrate a range of geographical and cultural movement. They were made on different sides of England, its western and eastern limens (boundary areas), yet both have stories set in and around Nottingham in the heart of the English Midlands. In each book the Robin Hood story is different, but in both it is associated with *Thomas of Erceldoune's Prophecy*, a borderland text of the north and west. *Erceldoune* was originally associated with Dunbar and Melrose on the Anglo-Scottish border, but moved south and west through interaction between noble and gentry families, and dominant border families such as the Percys who created loyalties through their patronage.[68] If *Erceldoune's Prophecy* moved south by this means, it is highly likely that Robin Hood (among other options) could have moved north in a similar way.[69] Both types of text turned up in contemporary Norfolk, and were then transported to London by internal migration. People got around in the Middle Ages, bringing their cultural inputs with them. At the very least, it gives us an insight into the means by which books and texts could move around in later medieval Britain and Europe, and into how the cultural references they contained were shared.

TWO

Robin Hood and the Printed Word

In the late fifteenth and early sixteenth centuries, printed books were part of a 'blended' culture that included images and performed, printed and handwritten (that is, manuscript) work. For example, Henry VIII is known to have taken part in Robin Hood events during the first decade of his reign. The first was in 1510, when Henry and some of his most intimate friends entered the queen's chamber dressed as Robin Hood and his merry men as part of the New Year's festivities. The best known of Henry's Robin Hood events was that at Shooter's Hill in 1515, where the king and Queen Katherine were 'ambushed' by Robin Hood and his outlaws (two hundred royal guardsmen dressed in green costume), then led off to a feast in the woods with Robin, in an arbour decorated with herbs and flowers. Such an event would have made a significant impact on those who witnessed or took part in it.[1] Five years earlier, in 1510, Henry (then resident with his new wife Katherine of Aragon in the palace at Richmond-on-Thames) had received the villagers of Kingston-upon-Thames, who were taking their Robin Hood 'game' around the neighbouring Thames Valley in order to raise funds. The parishioners of the area surrounding Kingston would have had connections with the palace anyway, in terms of trade and provisioning and the supply of servants. They probably had family insiders working there, and lines of communication would have already been open for them. The players were well received, and doubtless also well rewarded, for their performance. At the time of this Robin Hood performance, Henry VIII had been king for less than a year, so the visit from the Kingston Robin Hood takes on a particular significance, in that the local elites and their neighbours were presenting themselves to the young, newly married king and queen through the storyworld of Robin Hood. In such a context, they would appear as loyal, humble subjects, morally responsible and 'good', honest, prosperous, united, friendly and aspirational, and pious, too, for Robin also carried associations with faithfulness in religious belief and practice. In the light of their shared culture, Henry would have understood the references.

The period of Robin Hood's greatest recorded popularity as a performance character coincides with this period in the first half of the sixteenth century, when stories of his exploits were circulating in print for the first time. That the stories were available in print may also have helped their distribution and their popularity. If there were hundreds, or perhaps a couple of thousand, of copies in circulation, then any boom in Robin Hood performance events between about 1500 and 1530, including that of the Kingston players, may also be early evidence for the power of the printing press. Members of the local elites would have constituted many of the new readers of printed works, and therefore a market for the early printers and booksellers. It may have been their reading that prompted them to take up this character for their festive celebrations, in the same way that favourite film and television characters are presented at local carnivals and fundraisers today. Having been created by members of educated elites, they are taken up as media creations and repurposed. When Henry received the Kingston Robin Hood players and their sponsors, therefore, an extremely literate and well-educated young man was also acknowledging his subjects' literacy. (This should not, however, hide the fact that Robin Hood was only one of a myriad of options available for the purposes of festive celebration in the 'long' fifteenth century. Sometimes he was selected, sometimes not. Plays about the lives, and particularly the gory deaths, of saints were more popular and far more widespread.)

Five editions of a single Robin Hood text and its variants were printed within about 25 years in the 1490s and early 1500s, four in England and one in the Low Countries for export to England. We cannot know whether all of these copies were sold, but given that the usual number in a print run was four hundred, this means that more than 2,000 books of Robin Hood stories (at least) would have been in existence around that time.[2] Early printers had to be canny entrepreneurs who published for a market, so this large number indicates that there was a wide audience for the stories. The Robin Hood narrative presented in these books quickly became the favoured, in fact the only, version on offer, eclipsing the short written narratives in the existing manuscript versions – although it seems from the content of later ballad versions that oral stories continued to circulate, and to be passed on down the generations. This longer, printed version was generally known as *A Lytell Geste of Robyn Hode*, and was made up of at least three shorter stories (probably of a similar length to *Robin Hood and the Monk* and *Robin Hood and the Potter*), with at least one more alluded to.

The first story tells how Robin Hood's men, led by Little John, see a knight coming along the road, and take him for the usual meal with Robin Hood. The knight, who explains that his name is Sir Richard atte Lee, is poorly dressed and unattended. When questioned (somewhat cheekily) by Robin Hood, he reveals that, although of an old family, he has been forced to mortgage his lands to the abbot of St Mary's. He needs the money in order to ransom his son, who has accidentally killed 'a knight of Lancaster' in a tournament. In order to test the knight's worth, Robin imposes a 'truth test'. He asks the knight how much money he is carrying:

> 'I haue no mor but x.s.,' sayd the knyght.
> 'So gode haue parte of me.'
> 'Yf thou haue no more,' sayde Robyn,
> 'I wyll not one peny,
> And yf thou haue need of ony more
> More shall I lend the.'
>
> 'I have no more than ten shillings,' said the knight,
> 'As God is my witness.'
> 'If you have no more,' said Robin,
> I don't want one penny,
> And if you have need of any more
> More shall I lend you.'[3]

Robin requires a pledge for repayment, and the knight offers God as his guarantor, but this is rejected by Robin:

'Do waye thy Iapes,' sayd Robyn,
'Therof wyll I right none.
Wenest thou I wyll haue god to borowe,
Peter Poule or Johan . . .?'
'I haue none other,' sayd the knyght,
'The sothe for to say,
But yf it be our dere lady;
She fayled me neuer or this day.'

'Stop joking with me,' said Robin,
'I won't have any of that.
Do you believe I'll have God as a guarantor,
[Saints] Peter, Paul or John . . .?'
'I have no other,' said the knight,
'I'm telling the truth,
Unless it be Our dear Lady;
She never failed me up to this day.'[4]

Now that he knows the knight is worthy (because he values the Virgin Mary), Robin's generosity flows. He gives Sir Richard a loan of four hundred pounds, along with a considerable amount of rich fabric, a horse, boots, gilded spurs and Little John, who offers to go with the knight as his body servant. The knight then goes to meet his 'day' with the abbot. Sir Richard has dressed in his dowdy old clothes, and even the abbot's porter is dismissive and rude. The abbot and the king's justice sit in judgement in the abbot's hall, refusing to accept any further extension of the loan period. To the amazement of all, the knight dramatically throws the money on the table, and leaves.

He sterte hym to a borde a none
Tyll a table rounde,
And there he sholde out tha bagge
Euen foure hundred pounde.
'Haue here thy golde, syr abbot,' sayd the knyght . . .

He went immediately up to a cupboard
up to a round table,
and there he shook out of the bag

a full four hundred pounds.
'Here, have your gold, Sir Abbot,' said the knight . . .[5]

It takes Sir Richard a year to raise the repayment money, but raise it he does. On the way back to Robin Hood to deliver it, he is delayed by a wrestling match, in which he intervenes to save a yeoman who is in danger of being killed.

The knyght presed into the place
An hundred followed hym fere
With bowes bent and arowes sharpe
For to shende that company . . .
He toke the yeman by the honde
And gaue hym all the playe;
He gaue hym fyue marke for his wyne . . .
And bad it sholde be sett a broche
Drynke who so wolde . . .

The knight pushed on into the place
A hundred fit [men] followed him
With bows bent and arrows sharp
To destroy that company . . .
He took the yeoman by the hand
And declared him the winner;
He gave him five marks for his wine...
And ordered it to be opened
So that any who wanted might drink . . .[6]

While the knight is 'paying it forward' in this way, Robin's men ambush a couple of rich monks from St Mary's Abbey. After eating, the monks fail the same truth test passed by Sir Richard, lying about how much money they are carrying. Robin gives them enough for their needs and takes the rest. This amounts to four hundred pounds, the amount owed by Sir Richard. When the knight turns up, he is told that the Virgin has paid his debt, so *he* does not need to. The story ends at this point, although Sir Richard later plays a small part in advancing the plot, when he shelters the outlaws during their flight from the sheriff.

The 'Knight and Abbot' plot is dissected by a diversion on Little John and the sheriff, which may be related to the stories of Gamelyn and the 'king and commoner' tradition (discussed in a later chapter). Seeing Little John shooting with the other young men, and 'alway he sleste the wande' (he always slit the marker), the sheriff asks Sir Richard if he may have Little John as a servant, and John (with the knight's permission) agrees, calling himself Reynold Greenleaf:

Say me Reynaud grenelefe
Wolte thou dwell with me,
And euery yere I wyll the gyue
Twenty marke to thy fee.

Tell me, Reynold Greenleaf,
If you want to live with me [be part of my household],
And then every year I will give you
Twenty marks for your fee.[7]

One day, while the sheriff is out hunting, John gets up really late. He goes to the kitchens, where he demands his food, eating and drinking a prodigious amount. The sheriff's cook is angry and attacks 'Reynold' with his big ladle. They fight and John, unable to overcome the bellicose cook, reveals his identity and offers his adversary a place with Robin Hood's men. The cook agrees, and together they steal the sheriff's valuables, including his plate, before heading off into the woods. When he catches up with the sheriff, John offers to show him the way to find a 'grete green harte'. The sheriff is delighted, but John leads him to Robin Hood, who makes the sheriff and his men spend the night in the forest in their underwear. They cannot wait to give up their valuables and their fine clothing, to get back to 'civilization'.

This is followed by another episode featuring the motif of the shooting contest (now much favoured by film directors). The sheriff 'dyde crye a full fayre play / that all the best archers of the north / sholde come vpon a day' for the prize of a silver arrow.[8] Robin Hood, Little John, Will Scathelock, Much, 'Reynold' and Gilbert of the White Hand defeat all comers, but Robin Hood is 'euer more the best'.[9] Horns blow, and the sheriff's men close in on Robin and the outlaws. They, however, shoot so well that they manage to escape, although Little John is sorely wounded in the knee. John begs Robin to leave him to his fate, but Robin picks John up and carries him on his back to safety in Sir Richard atte Lee's castle. The sheriff sends word to the king, who supports his officer and promises to come himself to Nottingham to aid the sheriff. Sir Richard goes hawking by the river (not necessarily the most advisable thing to do, given the situation – but Sir Richard is a knight and must live a knight's life) and is captured. He is taken to Nottingham 'Bounde both fote and hande' to await his execution for treason.[10] Sir Richard's wife escapes the castle and finds the outlaws in the forest. With 'mo than seuen score' bowmen, Robin lays an ambush, frees Sir Richard and kills the sheriff, cutting off his head with his 'bryght bronde'.[11] He takes the knight to the greenwood to await the arrival of the king. This appears to have been a separate story. A new story now begins.

The king arrives in Nottingham to find his sheriff dead and the knight escaped. Acting according to the laws of attainder, the king takes the traitor's possessions into his own hands. He is, however, fascinated by the thought of the outlaw and his men. Following the advice of 'a fayre olde knyght' (a common romance trope, used in the romance of *Richard Coer de Lyon* and other stories), the king takes a few men and dresses as an abbot with his company of monks. They are, of course, ambushed and invited to dinner by the outlaws, who submit them to the 'truth test' about how much money they have. The honest 'abbot' gets his spending money back. After a shooting contest, which Robin wins, he and the 'abbot' agree to a game of pluck buffet (every time the arrow fails to hit the mark, the shooter has to stand and take a punch from his adversary, and *vice versa*), in which Robin is matched blow for blow. Ultimately, Robin recognizes (we are not told how – have they met before, is it the king's bearing, or does he resemble his likeness on the coinage, perhaps?) the king in the abbot's guise. The king (called 'Edward' in this tale) takes on Robin's livery, along with his men. Robin and the outlaws accompany the king back to Nottingham, where the king (in the manner of the 'king and commoner' stories) gives them a feast in return. Sir Richard, along with Robin and his men, are pardoned, and the king offers Robin Hood a place in his own household. Robin accepts, goes off to live with the king, and another story ends.

That is the end of the overall narrative, except that there is a codicil, taken from another narrative about Robin Hood. Displaying the excessive generosity and conspicuous consumption expected of knights (although he isn't one), Robin spends his way through the fee he gets from the king. He becomes listless, missing his old life in the greenwood. Telling the king that he wants to make a brief visit to a chapel he has founded, Robin returns to the greenwood. He kills a deer and blows his horn, at the sound of which a group of young outlaws appears. Robin never returns to the king. Eventually, Robin goes to be bled at Kirklees, where a female relative of his is the abbess. Unknown to him, she has agreed with her lover, Roger of Doncaster – an enemy of Robin's – to murder him:

Syr Roger of donkestere
By the pryoresse he lay
And there they be trayed good Robyn hode
Through theyr false playe
Cryst haue mercy on his soule . . .

Sir Roger of Doncaster
By the Prioress he lay
And there they betrayed good Robin Hood
Through their false intercourse
Christ have mercy on his soul . . .[12]

It looks as if these stories existed already as independent, shorter manuscript narratives, and were blended together to form a 'historified' account. The printed 'compendium' edition is the only evidence we now have for the prior existence of these stories. The late fifteenth- and early sixteenth-century printed editions largely copy one another, and there has been controversy about which of them was the earliest, although this honour has now been settled on the edition of Richard Pynson, printed in London about 1495, followed by Wynkyn de Worde's edition some ten years later, also printed in London. In between these there exists an edition of the same text – often known as the 'Lettersnijder' edition from the type of lettering used – printed in Antwerp towards the end of the 1400s; this copied both Pynson's text and his frontispiece illustration. The printer is unknown, but was most likely Gerhaert Leeu, a friend and associate of William Caxton in the 1470s and '80s.[13] The early printers of the *Geste* were all closely associated with one another. After the death of Caxton, Britain's first printer, in 1492, Pynson and Wynkyn de Worde (who had been Caxton's assistant and inherited his printing house, materials and stock) were the two major competitors in the country, although de Worde was bigger – for the purposes of taxation, he was listed as worth £201 11*s*. 1*d*., while Pynson was worth only £60.[14] Early printers had to be entrepreneurial, and they were sellers and advertisers of their own books, while also acting as factors, importing and selling copies from abroad; chiefly Germany and France, but also Italy and the Low Countries. This is interesting in terms of the Lettersnijder edition of the *Geste*. Direct copying of other people's work was common among the early printers. If he needed a book to compete with de Worde and could not produce it quickly, Pynson might even have sold copies of the Continental edition. Given the nature of arrangements between competing book-makers and -sellers at home and on the Continent, and the fact that most of the people involved in the book business in England (and Scotland) at the time were aliens, that is, non-natives – or 'economic migrants' to use the current term – nothing can be taken for granted.

Hugo Goes, a Flemish migrant, whose edition was produced in York in 1506–9, had been an associate of de Worde (also Flemish in origin) and had bought some of de Worde's type (that is, wooden letter-blocks used in the printing press). He may have produced Robin Hood in York because the story had some local associations, or he may have been simply trying to set up his business in England's northern capital to supply a demand for books that were more immediately available and did not have the added costs of transporting them from London.[15] This is suggested by his later move to Beverley, midway between York and the port of Hull, the home of the lucrative shrine of St John and also a local centre of education and book production. Julian Notary (originally from Normandy) set up in Pynson's old workshop in Westminster after Pynson followed de Worde to Fleet Street, where printers and book traders were beginning to congregate at this time.[16] He appears to have specialized in reprinting or copying works previously printed by others, so his edition of the *Geste* was likely drawn from one of the pre-existing texts.

No manuscript version exists, and we do not know when, or why, the stories were joined together. There may, however, be a clue in the Reynard stories, as printed by William Caxton in 1481, as *The Historye of Reynart the Foxe*. The stories of Reynard the Fox were largely canonical by the end of the fourteenth century, having been developed from classical beast fables from the twelfth century onwards. They were very well known across continental Europe, and probably in England as well. They existed as shorter, stand-alone narratives and as longer versions, in which several stories were juxtaposed and (quite simply) linked as a loosely chronological narrative. Although many of these were French, Caxton used a Dutch/Flemish manuscript for his edition.[17] This was *Die Historie van Reynaert de Vos* (The Story of Reynard the Fox), composed in the late fourteenth or early fifteenth century from a combination of Reynard's trial (Branch Va – 1160–80), Reynard's duel (Branch VI – 1190–1205) and Reynard's pilgrimage (Branch VIII – also 1190–1205), with the addition of a story of Reynard and the She-ape, which may also have existed in a shorter form (the fox is often depicted with apes in fifteenth-century English church carvings).[18] The *Historie*, in prose, was adapted from an earlier, thirteenth-century verse source, *Van Den Vos Reynaerde* (About Reynard the Fox). The version used by Caxton was that printed in Antwerp by Leeu, in 1479. The text of the *Historie*, as printed by Caxton (and reprinted several times), is a blend of about three or four major stories, with elements of one or two other (in this case, known) stories also blended in, just as they are in the *Geste*. They have been arranged to form a continuous 'historical' narrative, which reads very much like a romance narrative, unlike the shorter tales in the manuscript version. The finalized text of *The Historye of Reynart the Foxe* is of a similar size to that of the *Geste*, although it is arranged in prose, not verse. (It should be noted that the printer of the Lettersnijder edition did not see any problem in printing part of the *Geste* as prose, though.) Both books were of a good economic size for a printed edition, and both were compendium versions of very popular stories: this was an all-round winning formula. It may be that the success of the *Historye* formula was influential in the decision to use the *Geste*, if this was available in manuscript form. Early printers generally used texts they knew were already popular, even if they needed to translate them themselves. Caxton translated, but did not originate his own works. In the process, he *did* alter the composition of the works he translated. It would be very unlikely that Wynkyn de Worde, in Caxton's workshop, was not involved in some of these projects.

Thomas H. Ohlgren suggests that de Worde's 1506 edition of the *Geste* may have been printed in collaboration with, or even by,

Robert Copland, de Worde's assistant from around 1506, who became Britain's second native-born printer when he set up at the sign of the Rose on Fleet Street in 1515. Robert Copland was a typesetter, compositor and (I think) text editor for de Worde, and (again, this is my own preference) he may be responsible for the differences between de Worde's edition of the *Geste* and that of Richard Pynson. Copland was not a writer, but he was a rewriter and an accomplished one: he was most likely the writer, or adapter, of the two plays published alongside the *Lytell Geste* by his close relative and successor, William Copland, around 1560.[19]

Interestingly, there seem to have been no more editions of Robin Hood stories immediately after this initial flurry of interest. The next publication was that of William Copland at the end of the 1550s. *The Historye of Reynart*, and the stories of the German trickster *Till Eulenspiegel* (translated into English as *Howleglas* or *Owlmirror*), also ceased being published in 1515 and 1530, respectively. It may be that the market was saturated with Robin Hood, with more than 2,000 copies of the *Geste* alone already in circulation. Printing of *The Historye of Reynart* resumed in 1550, around the same time as Copland's *Robin Hood* publications, and *Till* (in the form of compilations and single stories) was later reprinted.[20] Robin's association with the 'Catholic' idea of the Virgin Mary may have led to self-censorship in what were very difficult times for printers. It is also possible that tastes simply changed, as the advent of printing quickly led to a change in what people wanted to read. New readers were more interested in fresh work and current events, and there was a developing taste (how could there not be?) for religious and political controversy.[21] It may be that Robin Hood, in his pre-Reformation form anyway, was simply too old-fashioned for the discerning Elizabethan reader. His later revival in broadsheet ballad form implies that he was seen as cheap, somewhat lower-class entertainment for those lacking a good education.

In the early print versions, there may have been a similarity of purpose and (perceived) audience reception between Reynard and Robin Hood (and possibly *Till*, too). Caxton's introduction to the *Historye of Reynart the Foxe* says:

> In this historye ben wreton the parables goode lerynge and dyuerse poyntes to be merkyd by whiche poyntes men maye

> lerne to come to the subtyl knoweleche of suche thynges as dayly ben vsed and had in the counseyllys of lordes and prelates gostly and worldly and also emonge marchantes and other comone peple. And this booke is maad for nede and prouffyte of alle god folke. As fer as they in redynge or heeryng of it shal mowe vnderstande and fele the forsayd subtyl deceytes that dayly ben vsed in the worlde not to thentente that men shold vse them but that euery man shold eschewe and kepe hym from the subtyl false shrewis that they be not deceyuyd.
>
> In this history are written stories of good instruction and diverse points to be noted by which points men may learn to come to cunning knowledge of such things as are daily rehearsed and form part of the counsels of lords and holy prelates, and also among merchants and common people. And this book is made for the needs and the profit of all good people, as far as they in reading or listening to it shall understand better and imagine the aforesaid subtle deceits that are used in the world, not with the intent that they should use them but that every man should avoid and keep himself from the cunning false villains, so that they are not deceived.[22]

It is highly likely that this was how readers viewed Robin Hood, as a way to 'eschewe and kepe' themselves from falling into sin and more practical trouble by means of avarice, dishonesty and poor conduct. Along with the availability of manuscripts and printed copy, the choices made by the printers were very much affected by the expectations and preferences of their potential readers. These were, in the main, clergy, teachers, students and the new readers. They were to be found among the mostly urban middle class, among 'children who formerly did not go to school, among women, and among the "economically less forward" classes'.[23] The aim was for dialect-neutral, simple, easy-to-read and above all useful material, which would be attractive to anyone (male or female) who could afford to buy it. Numerous were the primers (Books of Hours) and calendars, school textbooks and legal books, sermons, news and propaganda, devotional works and indulgences, along with midwifery/

housewifery and medical books, and other books of instruction relating to everyday life. Martin Luther, in the early 1500s, said that reading helped 'men to govern, and women to attend to house, children and servants'.[24] It is in that light, I think, that we should see not only the *Historye of Reynart the Foxe*, but the *Lytell Geste of Robyn Hode*. It was entertainment, but also a work of devotion and moral instruction.

As an extension to his reprinting of the *Lytell Geste* (which he retitled *A Mery Geste of Robyn Hoode*) of around 1560, London printer and publisher William Copland also published two play texts, one based on a story of Robin Hood and Friar Tuck, and the other based on a version of *Robin Hood and the Potter*, although this differs somewhat from that in the Calle manuscript (see Chapter One). Copland describes them in the introductory rubric as being 'verye proper to be played in Maye games'. Copland had just taken over the licences of Robert Copland, the former assistant of Wynkyn de Worde. It seems that William was Robert's son, or a similarly close relative, who had taken over the entire assets of his predecessor's business. He seems to have put out the Robin Hood material immediately, maybe to test the market or in the hope of making a quick profit from it. In the circumstances of the time, with the death of the Catholic Mary I and the succession of the Protestant Elizabeth, William might have had anxieties about the long-term appeal of this material. Government policy on religious observance and public performances of this kind had shifted constantly since the 1530s, creating a problem with which printers and booksellers simply had to deal. The plays must surely be Robert Copland's work (or why not finish them both?), and so reflect source material in circulation in the previous ten years, or maybe more.

Although there is surviving evidence for the existence of a 'Potter' tradition, the Friar play is different; there is no known source for this story, either published or handwritten, although there is a later ballad with similar content.[25] Friar Tuck does, however, appear in the little Paston play script, and he was also a known character in morris dances at the time, where he often appears with Maid Marion, as he may do here. The play centres around a conflict (a play fight between Robin Hood and the Friar), like the unfinished *Potter* play; this seems to have been a popular motif for Robin Hood stories. In addition, there are touches reminiscent of earlier *pastourelle* poems, in the presence of the friar's mastiffs and the girl given to the friar by Robin Hood at the end of the play, who may be a version of the shepherdess Marion or a reference to the Marion of the morris. The friar's final lines could also be an invitation to some form of coarse display:

> She is a trul of trust, to serve a frier at his lust
> A prycker a prauncer a terer of shetes
> A wagger of ballockes when other men slepes
> Go home ye knaves and lay crabbes in the fyre
> For my lady & I wil daunce in the myre for veri pure joye.

> She is a trull [a sexual innuendo implying 'loose woman'] of trust, to serve a friar at his pleasure
> A rider [sexual], a prancer, a tearer [or perhaps 'smearer'] of sheets
> A wagger of bollocks before men sleep.
> Go home, you knaves, and lay crabs [crab apples] on the fire
> For my lady and I will dance in the mud for true, absolute joy.[26]

A dance, possibly (but not necessarily) a morris dance, is indicated here. There may also be an oblique reference to what Ronald Hutton calls the 'man-woman', or the practice that developed of having a man play the part of Marion, which often involved some coarse display of the player's masculinity.[27] Copland's texts are very different in nature and in content from the Paston play, which is altogether more violent, and any humour involved would have been decidedly black. These differences cannot be entirely laid at the door of the Protestant Reformation of the 1530s, as a similar difference exists between earlier stories, such as *Robin Hood and the Potter* and *Robin Hood and the Monk*. Copland designates these two plays as 'very plesaunte and full of pastyme', and herein may be a difference between two types and uses of Robin Hood in performance. His descriptions of the content and potential uses of the texts may indicate that Copland was aware of a difference between two forms of Robin Hood play. In representing friars as 'degenerate', he may also have been attempting to please both sides in the religious controversy, within a year of Catholic queen Mary I's death, and her Protestant sister Elizabeth's accession.

In late May (mostly) – in story, dance and song, in courts, yards and the streets – Robin Hood was performed in urban and rural communities as spring turned to summer. Britain had a long established – so long established as to be almost organic – festive life, with May games and church ales, summer kings and queens, and lords of misrule. Shrewsbury and Stafford, like Scottish communities, had an abbot rather than – or as well as – a lord of misrule; he was generally known as the 'abbot of marram [Marham?]' in the West of England.[28] Summer or May kings and queens sometimes held their 'court' in bowers or 'houses', temporary structures specially built for the occasion, along with games or plays, music, singing and dancing.[29] The structure would then be broken up and the wood sold for profit. Robin Hood might also have a bower. At Stratton in Cornwall in 1543, the wood of Robin Hood's house was sold off, indicating that Robin had, at some time, replaced or joined with the 'king' custom.[30] In 1555 at Bridport in Dorset, 32 shillings were raised 'for the Bowth [booth] that was solde'.[31] As this record immediately follows the receipts for the Robin Hood ale, it would seem that the booth was part of that event (although it might not have been). The wardens of Woodbury in Devon purchased canvas 'for maken of Robert Hoodes House' in 1574–5.[32] At St Ives in Cornwall in the 1580s, there were May kings and queens as well as Robin Hood. Robin and Maid Marion were King and Queen of the May in Manchester in 1522, and the Robin Hood game seems to have alternated with the 'king game' at Kingston-on-Thames in Surrey, but there is little convincing evidence that Robin was generally a 'summer king' replacement.[33] The Kingston 'summer king' toured widely in the area, and there were also 'king games' at Reading in Berkshire and at Henley-on-Thames.[34]

Many towns and cities record the purchase of bows and arrows as part of May or midsummer celebrations, but do not link these to a Robin Hood. Archery figured in some festive events, for example in Chagford in Devon, where the prize for the archery contest was a silver arrow.[35] As a legendary archer, Robin would easily have been fitted in, or taken out, of local archery-based events without compromising the existing arrangements too much.[36] Custom was probably dictated by local requirements, availability of people, money and materials, and local traditions. It is impossible to tell whether or not celebrations marked simply as 'May games' or 'church ales', as many are in Norfolk and Suffolk for example, used Robin as a character.[37] They may well have done, but nobody thought to record the fact. What evidence remains supports the fact that Robin Hood as a performance character had a variety of different uses.[38] This is because he was mostly fitted into pre-existing festivals and formats. It seems that Robin Hood, as a performed character, was adapted to fit into whatever was already in place, and that this was the type of event, and audience, which Copland was targeting with his plays.

Robin Hood performances of varying kinds were particularly popular at parish level because he appears to have been a really good fundraiser. Fundraising became increasingly important for parish churches, as donated income ceased to provide enough funds to keep the buildings and their liturgical requirements going year on year. Medieval worship was particularly 'candle heavy', and sometimes the profits of revels or ales would help to maintain lights in churches and chapels. If rural and small-town parishes often struggled with upkeep – as today – when the church buildings needed repairs they could struggle even more. Donors alone could not provide sufficient funds for general maintenance, let alone extra expenses.[39] From the existing evidence, Robin Hood seems to have been something of a godsend for church maintenance, repairs, extensions and rebuilding. Plays or games (which may have been similar or the same thing) were good for raising funds, but the major way of employing the outlaw as fundraiser seems to have been the 'ale' or 'revel' (which, again, may have been similar or the same). The local church would provide materials and facilities such as ovens and brewing equipment, sometimes in their own church house (which could also be let out for a fee), and then the profits from sales would help with the running of the church for the year or half year. An account from Chudleigh in Devon for 1561 lists expenditure for such an event, including coats for Hood and the Vices, material for sixty (other?) coats, and expenses for a cook, a brewer and a clerk to write up the accounts. The profit is given as 44*s.* 7*d.*, a not inconsiderable amount.[40] In Braunton (Devon) in 1562 payments were made for coats, horses, wood and carriage, use of the church house, a cook, a brewer (one Johanna Crowne), food and drink 'when we brew', and a pastry cook to make 'bread and pies'.[41]

There are several instances of Robin Hood being used to raise money for building projects, especially well documented in the records for the West of England. In Somerset, Croscombe's Robin

The parish church of St John the Baptist, Glastonbury, Somerset, where 'Robin Hood' helped to raise funds for the addition of pews. These would have been a fashionable luxury at the time, as most people stood or knelt during services.

Hood events coincide with the building of the church house, the vestry and the St George Chapel, while other running expenses were met from elsewhere. Glastonbury and Tintinhull seem to have used the money raised by Robin to install pews in their churches. Stratton paid for a new rood loft, and at Bodmin in Cornwall the proceeds helped to build the church's 'Berry' tower.[42] Some places held an ongoing series of Robin Hood events, while others, such as the Glastonbury and Tintinhull events, seem to have held them only once for a special purpose.[43] It was not the fact that he was a thief *per se*; it was rather the work of the Virgin Mary in turning Robin Hood's theft into profitable labour that made him acceptable in the raising of funds for religious purposes. This also made it possible for respectable members of community elites to play the character. Like the Robin Hood stories, this performance of the outlaw character served to turn economic power into moral superiority. It may be that the power of Robin Hood as a fundraiser was based on a combination of religious association (who would *not* pay up to the messenger of the Virgin Mary?) and the fact that the player inside the green suit was recognizable as a figure of local power and authority.

It is tempting to see Copland's plays as representative of simple folk performance, but the evidence is that, like 'saint' plays and liturgical drama, they were major events locally. This meant that local communities were prepared to undertake the expense involved: all that quality green cloth did not come cheap. Indeed, cloth for coats and other items of clothing appears regularly as a major expense for Robin Hood performances. Quality was important for all medieval plays and other performances, and large amounts were spent on costumes. This was not a feature of English, or British, events alone; drama and festivity were considered worth investing in across Europe.[44] In European drama, the fool's costume was green or green and yellow (as was Robin's costume in Aberdeen in May 1508).[45] Sometimes Lucifer might also wear green, being considered a fool for defying God.[46] Costumes could be renewed, restored, loaned and hired. In 1552, the year before the accession of the Catholic Mary I reversed the government's Reformed religious policy, the wardens of Holy Trinity the Less in London disclosed that they still possessed fifteen Robin Hood coats.[47] This looks like the remains of a profitable costume hire business, but it also demonstrates something interesting about the relationship of Robin Hood events to the existing records. No such events are recorded for London, and yet – even if only a portion of these costumes were hired out at any one time – the coats are evidence that Robin Hood performance events must have been held on a relatively regular basis in the area.

At the end of *Robin Hood and the Monk*, the writer says, 'thus endys the talking of the Munke.' 'Talking' here is a translation into English of the French term *dit*, designating a relatively short poetic narrative that could not be classified in any other way or, simply put, a 'general poetry-story'.[48] The audience, or at least some of it, seems to have been expected to understand this designation. It may very well be that William Langland was referring to *dits* when he described stories of Robin Hood and Ranulf of Chester as 'rimes'.[49] *Dits*, it seems, could be used alone, in a context of worship, or as an intermediate form between narrative and dramatic script. The existing stories of Robin Hood, manuscript and print, show that the form in which they were written, the *dit*, was very flexible, with multiple potential uses and changes of form built in. They could be enjoyed in their own right, as enlightening moral tales or simply fun stories, or adapted as short pieces for performance in a secular or spiritual setting. They might be adapted to enlighten sermons in order to make their biblical messages more accessible (or simply more entertaining), and they could be turned into dialogue and used as the basis for performance scripts, whether as formal plays or less formal presentations in a more festive setting such as Copland's 'Maye games'. Robin Hood had, therefore, many possible faces and many possible applications inherent in the form in which his stories were told. This may be why he has proved so slippery and difficult to fathom in later centuries: we need to look to the form of the stories, as well as the content, to see it. This form fitted a cultural context that required and valued flexibility, which may be why Robin, among others, was so popular as a character in medieval Britain. It is highly likely that he was both written *and* performed from the very beginning of his cultural life.

THREE

Robin Hood and 'Maid' Marion

Robin and Marion first appear together in a genre of romance poems known as *pastourelles*. These were popular in courtly and clerical circles from the second half of the twelfth to the beginning of the fourteenth centuries, when their popularity declined rapidly. At their height, the influence of the *pastourelles* could be found all over Europe, from the Mediterranean to the Baltic, in the vernacular tongues of many lands.[1] *Pastourelles* in French would have been known and performed in English courts throughout the period. Their influence can be seen in surviving Middle English texts, though these are not 'word-for-word' Middle English translations from French *pastourelles*. The lack of Middle English versions may be due to the aristocratic nature of the form; as England's/Britain's upper classes were French-speaking in the thirteenth century anyway, there was no need to make translations.[2]

In *pastourelle* stories, Robin is the lover of a shepherdess called Marion. She may also herd goats or cattle, something that often depends on the region of the poem's origin. Robin and Marion are not the only names of these lovers: the tradition also includes other peasant names such as Perrin and Peronelle, Guiot and Emmelot. Marion may also be referred to by other (diminutive) versions of 'Mary', such as Mariette, Margot or Marot/e, often in the same poem. However, Robin, together with Marion, Marote or Mariette, is the most common name used in French versions of *pastourelles*. At first Robin is only present as an absent lover described by Marion:

The frontispiece of Wynkyn de Worde's *c.* 1506 edition of the *Lytell Geste*. Each 'factotum' image, respectively, appears elsewhere in publications with no connection to the Robin Hood stories. It is unclear whether the figure in the centre is Robin, although this would be the logical assumption. The figure to the right may be Little John (he is saying, 'My lord') or possibly Sir Richard atte Lee. The woman to the left is very interesting. She could be Lady Lee, but equally she may represent Marion. If that is the case, then Marion already had some recognizable association with Robin Hood by that time – despite her absence from the surviving early stories.

. . . je sui amie
au filz dame Marie,
Robinet le cortois
Qui me chauce et lie,
et si ne me let mie
sanz biau chapeau d'orfrois'

. . . I'm the love
of the son of Lady Mary,
Robinet the courtly
Who [gives] me shoes and a girdle
and who never leaves me
without a pretty gold-embroidered hat[3]

In this version Robin is both *courtois* and the son of a Lady called Mary, which calls to mind the relationship between Robin Hood and the Blessed Virgin in the early Robin Hood texts. That we may be glimpsing an early version of that relationship here is a possibility, but of course there is absolutely no direct evidence for it. The author of the poem is also unknown. In this anonymous thirteenth-century French *pastourelle*, Robin is also handsome and an ideal, true lover:

. . . ami ai,
plus biax que nus que je voie.
Mon fin cuer doné li ai;
Ja n'en partirai.
Sa très fine amourete
e fet a li penser.

. . . I have a lover,
More handsome than any that I see.
I have given him my noble heart;
I will never leave him.
His very true love
Makes me think of him.[4]

The refrain of this poem is an example of 'borrowing' common to these texts, which are often self-reflexive in nature:

Robin m'aime, Robin m'a,
Robin m'a demandee, si m'aura!

Robin loves me, Robin has me,
Robin has asked for me, so he will have me!

Robin is (almost) always a peasant in the *pastourelles*, and his actual physical presence is not required by the plot, which really concerns the narrator's attempt – successful or not – to seduce, or otherwise get sexual satisfaction from, the shepherdess. The girl herself is objectified, described to the audience by the narrator, who may be a knight, a clerk or a persona adopted by the composer/performer himself. When her age is given, the shepherdess is a young girl, usually about fourteen years of age. In medieval society this age marked the boundary between childhood and womanhood, fourteen being the earliest accepted age at which a young bride might have sexual relations with her husband.[5] The point of view is that of the would-be seducer, which focuses on the shepherdess's fetishized body parts, the sight of which inflames the passion of the speaker/writer:

N'avoit sourcot ne peliçon,
Ne guimplete ne chaperon,
Toute estoit desfublee.
Blanche ot la gorge et le menton
plus que noif sur gelee.

She had neither an overgarment nor a tunic,
Nor a little veil nor a hood,
She was entirely unprotected.
Her throat and her chin were whiter
than the snow on the frost.[6]

je sui sade et brunet
et joenne pucelete;
s'ai color vermeillete,
euz verz, bele bouchete;
si mi point la mamelete
que n'i puis durer

I am agreeable and dark,
and a young maiden;
I have a ruddy complexion,
sparkling eyes, a lovely little mouth;
my little breast pricks me
so that I cannot bear it[7]

In what is a very structured generic format, the girl rejects his advances, claiming her fidelity to Robin above anyone else. The seducer is not, however, put off. Falling back on their respective financial positions, he offers to pay her for sex – in the form of valuable clothing and/or jewels:

Touze, juaulz et bone robe entire
senture et gans aureis et amoniere,
se vos voleis
Les juaus li ai moustreis,
Dix, 'teneis!'
Lors se fist un pouc moins fiere
Se nes ait pais renfuseiz.

All, jewels and a whole good dress,
a belt and gold-embroidered gloves and an alms-purse,
as you want.
I showed her the jewels,
Said, 'Take them!'
Then she became a little less proud,
She did not refuse them.[8]

These are standard, generic items, repeated in many French and Occitan *pastourelles*. An interesting variation occurs in a poem by Ernoul de Gastinois, in which the knight offers the shepherdess a cloak:

Cote noire,
c'est la voire,
ne vos donrai mie;
d'escarlate,
iert vermeillete,
de vert mipartie.

An overgarment of black
It is evident,
I will not give you at all;
Of scarlet,
Bright red it will be,
Half of green.[9]

The colours scarlet and green here indicate the quality and value of the cloth being offered. They echo the colour of the hunters' clothing in the *Livre de chasse* illustrations, and also the green and scarlet cloth given by Robin to Sir Richard in the *Lytell Geste*. It suggests a possible *pastourelle* origin for their use in the Robin Hood stories. It is also possible the name 'Will Scarlet' indicates expensive dye (he might just as well have been called Dyer), rather than being derived from 'Scathelok' or 'safe-breaker'.[10]

In many *pastourelles*, the offer is enough and the shepherdess gives way. On occasion, she continues to refuse and may become distressed. In these cases, the 'lover' simply takes what he wants. The rape scenario seems to be most common in northern European *pastourelles*, including those most likely to have percolated into English culture from northern France:

Quant par ma prioere n'I poi avenir
Par les flans l'ai prinse, si la fis chair.
Levai la pelice,
La blanche chemise;
A molt bele guise
Mon jeu li apris.

Since by my plea I could not make it happen,
I took her by the sides and made her fall.
I lifted her tunic,
Her white shirt;
In a very lovely way
I taught her my game.[11]

Where is Robin? In most cases, he hardly lives up to Marion's description of him. When the audience meets him, he turns out to be coarse, slow and not very intelligent. He may not appear at all, and if he does turn up, he is usually too late to prevent coitus from happening:

Robins sens demorance
Vint o grant esmaiance;
Bien voit par sa semblance
kau jeu de pic-en-pance
on jué ambedui.
Lors dist, 'Conchiez sui,
si fail a covenance,
tu as fait autre ami.
Quant ma foi te plevi
Bien deceüs m'anfance.'

Robin without delay
Came in great alarm
He could see very well by her appearance
What game of poke/peck-in-the-belly
They had played between the two of them.
Then he said, 'I've been deceived/shat on,
The covenant is broken,
You have taken another lover,
When I plighted my troth to you
You well betrayed my youth.'[12]

The courtly narrator has nothing but contempt for Robin, the peasant: 'Lai Robin cel garçonel / Garder ses pors el boschel' (leave that little boy Robin / to watch over his pigs in the wood), and Robin's distress is presented as laughable.[13] In any event, Robin is likely to be castigated as neglectful by his unfaithful or violated lover:

s'il demore longement
del tout a a moi failli
Amis, vostre demoree
me fera faire autre ami

if he tarries long
he will have lost me entirely

Friend, your delay
will cause me to get another lover.[14]

There are variations in which greater power is accorded to the peasants. In one such scenario they turn up in time to drive the knight away:

Avai les prez regardai,
s'oï criant
deus pastors par mi un blé
qui venoient huiant
et leverent haut cri.
Assez fis plus que ne di.
Je la les si m'en foï
n'oi cure de tel gent.

I looked over the meadows,
I heard them whooping,
Two shepherds in a wheat field
Who came, yelling,
and raising a loud cry.
There was nothing else that I could do.
I left her and ran away
I don't want to [be involved with] such people.[15]

The knight may also be the victim of a carefully laid plot or ambush, in which Marion 'plays' him for financial gain. One would-be rapist is well paid in blows for his attack on a girl's virginity:

Et Robins li fils Fouchier
I ait fait grant asemblee
Ki d'un baston de pomier
M'ait l'achine mesuree.
Pués m'ait dit en reprover,
'Vasauls, retorneis airrier . . .'

And Robin the son of Fouchier
Had got a large crowd together there;
With a club of applewood

He took the measure of my spine.
Then he reproached me, saying,
'Vassal, go back where you came from . . .'[16]

It is a very serious, as well as comic, inversion for a peasant – who should doff his hat, lower his eyes and wait until spoken to in the presence of such a social superior – to call a knight 'vassal'. In the later Robin Hood stories, it is mirrored by the respectful insolence that Robin, Little John and their men display towards their social superiors. In a comic overturning of the expected denouement, one knight is attacked and 'raped' by an aggressive shepherdess:

Lors me prist a embracier
Et molt m'aloit estraignant
Qu'ele mi vouloit bezier,
Més je m'aloie eschivant.
Voirement
de moi fist tout son talent
Et me descouvri
et me foula et ledi
plus que je ne di

Then she began to embrace me
And to hug me tightly
Because she wanted to kiss me,
But I stepped back out of the way.
Truly,
she did all she wanted with me
and uncovered me
and crushed and abused me
more than I can say.[17]

In many cases, even after being raped, the girl finds that she enjoys this new game; she responds with praise and an invitation to come back for more:

Quant je vi ke por proier
Ne por prometre juel

Ne la poroie plaixier
K'en feïsse mon avel,
Jetai lai en mi l'erboie;
Ne cuit pais k'elle ait grant joie,
Ains sospire,
Ces poins tort, ces chavols tire
Et quiert son eschaipement;
Et pués la fix je bien rire
Tant l'acollai doucement.
A departir me dist, 'Sire,
Per si reveneis sovent;
Vostre jeus paid nen empire –
Muels valt k'el commencement!'

When I saw that by pleading
Or by offering jewels
I could not move her
And have my desire,
I threw her down in the grass;
I don't think she had great joy,
Rather she sighed,
Wrung her hands, tore at her hair
And tried to get away;
And then I made her laugh a lot,
So sweetly I embraced her.
As she left she said, 'Sir,
Come back this way often;
Your game doesn't get any worse –
It's better than at the beginning.'[18]

Peasant girls, being viewed by upper-class men as little better or more educated than the sheep they tended, were fair game for members of the knightly class. The shepherdess, appreciative or not, may (in social terms she *should*) be abandoned after the deed – even if devastation is the result:

Mult longuement
L'alai proiant
Que riens n'I conquis.

Estroitment
Tout en riant
Par les flans la pris.
Sur l'erbe la souvinai;
Mult en fu en grant esmai,
Si haut a crié,
'Bele douce mere Dé,
gardez moi ma chasteé!'
Tant i luitai
Que j'achevai
Trestout mon desir;
Je la trouvai
De bon essai
Et douce a sentir.
Adonc sime sui tornez,
Et quant je fui remenbrez
Si pris a chanter . . .

For a long time
I begged her
But got nothing.
Tightly
With a smile
I took her by the sides.
I laid her back on the grass;
She was in great distress
And cried loudly:
'Fair sweet Mother of God
Protect my chastity for me!'
I wrestled
Until I achieved
All my desire;
I found her
Good to try
And soft to touch.
Then I went away,
And when I remembered
I began to sing . . .[19]

Is this a more honest – if callous – account of a common seduction event, or is this distress the girl's just reward for holding out against nature?[20]

Pastourelles open with a similar scenario to those of the Robin Hood stories:

Quant noif remaint et glace funt,
Qe resclercisent cil ruissel,
Et cil oiseiel grant joie funt
Por la doçor del tens novel,
Et florissent cil arbrisel
Et tuit cil pré plain de fluer sunt,
Et fine amor ce mi semunt
Que je face un sonet novel,

When the snow stops and the ice melts,
And the little rivulets are clear again,
And the birds make very merry
For the sweetness of the new time
And the bushes are in flower
And all the meadows are full of flowers
And true love calls on me
To make a new little song,[21]

Robin Hood and the Monk begins thus:

In somer when the shawes be sheyn
And leves be large and long
Hit is full mery in feyre forest
To here þe foulys song
To se þe dere draw to þe dale
And leve þe hilles hee
And shadow hem in þe leves grene
Undur the grene wode tre . . .

In summer, when the woods are bright,
And leaves are broad and long,
It is a great joy in the fair forest
To hear the birds' song,

To see the deer go down to the valley
And leave the high hills,
And shade themselves in the green leaves
Under the greenwood tree . . .

And *Robin Hood and the Potter* begins in similar vein:

In schomer when the leves spryng
The bloschems on every bowe
So merey doyt the berdys syng
In wodys merey now . . .

In summer, when the leaves spring,
The blossoms [are] on every bough,
So merrily do the birds sing
In woods [that are] merry now . . .[22]

This is not the only similarity. The chance encounter between knight and shepherdess usually takes place beside a wood, or sometimes an orchard.

Lés le brueill
d'un vert fueill
truis pastore sanz orgueill
chantant et notant un son

Beside a wood
Of green foliage
I found a shepherdess without pride
Singing and playing a song[23]

In *our* Robin Hood stories, the action usually takes place on a road, with Robin or other outlaws coming out of the wood to ambush travellers, just as some of the more ill-fated knights are ambushed on the road. The dogs are missing, but the group is there and the violence is similar. The mastiffs are, however, encountered in William Copland's *Friar Tuck* play, and in the later ballad of *Robin Hood and the Curtal Friar*, indicating that this element of the *pastourelle* world may have survived in medieval texts (written and/or orally transmitted) now lost to us.[24] Robin, or the lover, also comes out of the wood in *pastourelles.* Not only is the lover associated with woodland, he is sometimes described as being 'of' it:

> *. . . autrui sui ami,*
> *si ai ma foi plevie*
> *a Robin del sauçoi.*
>
> I have another lover,
> I pledged my faith
> to Robin of the willow grove.[25]
>
> *J'ai amin, faites amie,*
> *jai ne serons d'un acort;*
> *a Robin dou boix m'acort,*
> *a cui je seux otroieie!*
>
> I have a lover, go get a mistress,
> we will not be of one accord!
> I am content with Robin of the wood,
> To who I am promised![26]

The storyworld of Robin Hood is the world of the *pastourelles*, something that would have been easily understood by his early audiences. In the beginning, they would have known and appreciated the older genre, although this direct association would have become weaker over the course of two centuries.

Class prejudice runs all the way through the *pastourelles*. The story of the young man's attempt to take (or to buy) the girl's virginity, the country setting, one girl's observation that she will be beaten if her family thinks she has given herself to a man: these all add realistic touches to what is essentially a courtly fantasy. The flashes of white skin which the young man finds so exciting were far more likely to be found on a noble girl than a peasant, and the idea of country girls sitting around under trees or in gardens, playing their panpipes instead of doing manual tasks around the house and farm, is equally fantastic. Inherent in the form, though, is also the potential for satirical observation and self-deprecation. When her lover appears with his well-armed friends, a shepherdess taunts the fleeing alter ego of the aristocratic Thibaut, king of Navarre:

Quant ele m'en vit aler
Si me dist par ramposner
'Chevalier sont trop hardi'

When she saw me making off
She said, jeeringly,
'Knights are very brave.'[27]

The settings, therefore, and some important elements of the *pastourelles* are recognizable also in Robin Hood stories, but the characters (apart from their names) are not. In particular, there is no 'Maid' Marion in the existing early Robin Hood stories. Where has she gone? An insight into this is provided by the celebrated late thirteenth- to early fourteenth-century *trouvère* Adam de la Halle, one of the greatest, if not *the* greatest, of the French *trouvères* of his day. He lived and worked in Arras, at a time when the city was a cultural centre of great reputation; he was an author, composer, performer, instrumentalist and actor, the full range of *trouvère* skills. At the time he wrote *Robin et Marion*, Adam de la Halle was living in Sicily at the Anglo-Norman court of his patron Charles of Anjou, king of Sicily. In the 1290s Charles's position was particularly unstable, so part of Adam's job would have been to bolster the morale of the court.[28] In addition to its significance as one of the earliest play scripts in northern Europe, Adam's treatment of the *pastourelle* story about a shepherdess, her peasant lover and a sexually marauding knight offers echoes of what would become the Robin Hood stories.[29]

Robin et Marion is based on two forms of narrative poetry popular in French courts at the time: the *pastourelle* and the *bergerie*. The former we have met, while the latter is related: a voyeuristic member of the social and educational elite spies on a group of peasants playing, feasting and dancing, and describes their antics for the audience. (*Pastor* in Latin is the equivalent of *berger* in French, or 'shepherd' in English.) The viewer is as contemptuous of peasants as the narrator of the *pastourelles*. One of the shepherds apes the *trouvère* himself:

. . . an piez saillit sus toz drois,
de chanteir savance,
car il fut de niviaz reis.
Ces hoziaz ot takeneiz
et par grant bobance
estiot d'un sac afubleis.

. . . he jumped to his feet immediately
he made as if to sing,
because he was the new 'king'.
His hose were newly repaired
And with great vanity
He was adorned with a bag.[30]

One of them acts farcically above his station:

Li quairs, qui ot non Gatiers,
Si ce fist trop cointes,
Por ces moufles sans pouchiers
C'ot de novel ointes.
Vait faisant lou roubardel,
Vestus fut d'un giperel,
Deguixiez sans pointe.

The fourth, whose name was Gautier,
He made himself very elegant,
With his mittens without thumbs
Which were freshly oiled.
He pranced around like a young gallant,
Wearing a rustic garment,
Unusual for [its] lack of stitching.[31]

Adam takes a *pastourelle* story, joins it to a *bergerie* in the middle, and removes the narrator, thus creating a story told by actors (that is, *par personnages*) rather than a narrated story. Removing the narrator has the effect of reapportioning some of his power to the peasants and the poet, and allowing the characters to speak for themselves. Adam's version of this familiar material puts Marion at the centre of the text, but not in the same way as in *pastourelle* texts. Her voice, singing of her love for Robin, is the first the audience hears, before that of the knight, who is no longer privileged by first-person narration. The story is no longer about him but about her, and the second – *bergerie* – half is no longer about a courtly voyeur's view of peasants arguing, showing off and doing clunky, drunken dances, but about how she negotiates, and in fact manipulates, their social intercourse (rather than just being reactive).

The knight (we later discover that his name is Aubert) is, as is usual in *pastourelles*, at leisure. He is on his way to do some hawking by the river. On a road beside a wood – the usual *pastourelle* landscape – he comes upon Marion singing of her love for Robin. Also in generic fashion, the knight begins his attempt at verbal foreplay, which is thwarted by Marion's sharp and witty replies, twisting and turning his words:

> LI CHEVALIES
> *Di moi, veïs-tu nul hairon?*
> MARIONS
> *Hairens, sire? Par me foi, non!*
> *Je n'en vi nes un puis quaresme*
> *Que j'en vi mengier chiés dame Eme*
> *Me taiien, cui sont ches brebis.*
>
> KNIGHT
> Tell me, have you seen any herons?
> MARION
> Herrings, sir? By my faith, no;
> I've seen not one since Lent,
> When I saw some eaten at the house of Dame Eme,
> My grandmother, who owns these sheep.[32]

Marion has mistaken herons (*hairons*) for herrings (*hairengs*). This is one of a series of transpositions that opposes the knight's elite experience and her peasant lifestyle. It is unclear from this whether Marion is being an ignorant peasant girl unable to conceive of a more elevated form of life, or if she is cleverly playing dumb. Such a verbal exchange, allowing the shepherdess an intellectual verbosity equal to the courtly lover's, is not outside the parameters of the *pastourelles*. In this part of *Robin et Marion*, Adam allows his heroine – unlike the usual *pastourelle* heroine – to save herself by her skill with words.[33] There is a coarse element to the exchange when Marion asks the knight what he has in his hand. He says it is his falcon, which then prompts Marion to ask if it eats bread. He says that it eats 'bon char' (good meat). The falcon has a leather hood on its head, the hood worn by game birds to prevent them being distracted or attempting to free themselves from their handler. In a comic double entendre, this could also refer to a medieval condom, made of leather. The comparison between the knight's horse and Robin's, which 'ne regiete me / quant je vois apres se karue' (doesn't hurt me when I follow after his plough), also has a potential double meaning, ploughing being a medieval euphemism for the sexual act.[34] The knight leaves, bested, and Robin appears (eventually) at Marion's call; they sing of their love for one another in the manner of *pastourelle* lovers.

In another potentially comic exchange, Marion offers Robin some of the cheese she has been keeping down the front of her dress. They also have bread and apples, the simple natural food Arcadian shepherds prefer to the prepared meats of the wealthy. Robin eats: 'Diex, que chis froumages est cras!' (God! This cheese is so rich!) Although carrying things in one's bodice or hat was common practice in the countryside, there is a hint of blasphemous fun, too.[35] The apples can refer both to the Garden of Eden and to the Song of Songs ('comfort me with apples, for I am sick for love'), and the cheese to the Virgin's breast milk, which was a valued relic.[36] In an inversion of the knight's offers, Robin says that he, not the courtly lover, will give her his belt, purse and buckle. He dances for Marion, then goes to fetch their friends for a country picnic feast.

The knight returns; this time he is looking for his falcon. Once again rebuffed by Marion, he sees Robin manhandling his bird (another likely double entendre – just what is Robin handling?) and strikes him. More forceful and direct (in tune with the *pastourelle* tradition), the knight carries Marion off on his horse. She calls for Robin to help her, but the presence of his social superior appears to render Robin powerless, as it does all the male peasants.[37] They hide in a hedge, leaving Marion to her fate. This might be expected of the *pastourelle* peasant Robin, a bit of a wimp who needs the help of burly friends with clubs and mastiffs to overcome one knight.[38] Aubert stresses his wealth and social power over Marion, offering her some of the meat that his falcon has caught. We are not told whether this is cooked or raw, but it is, of course, not the only 'meat' he is offering her. The other offer is much more intimate; *he* is the one who wishes to do the consuming. If Marion accepts his meat offering, he will consume her – personally and sexually:

LI CHEVALIERS
Prendés cest oisel de riviere
Que j'ai pris; si en mengeras.
MARION
J'ai plus chier mon froumage cras
Et men pain et mes bonnes poumes . . .

KNIGHT
Take this river fowl
That I have caught: eat some of it.
MARION
I prefer my rich cheese,
And my bread, and my good apples . . .[39]

The audience (already primed by the initial 'leather-headed falcon' references) might be expecting rape at this point, but Adam's shepherdess saves herself once again – by means of her verbal power, her persistence and her personal courage.

Finally the knight leaves, and does not return. At this point the underlying form changes to that of a *bergerie*; freed from fear of their lords and masters, the peasants do what they are supposed to do in *bergeries*: they eat, drink and play games.[40] They also argue, show off and generally jostle for position in their own little hierarchy. Adam gives us a glimpse of personalities – the vulnerable young woman, Peronelle, and the thrusting, upwardly mobile Gautier, the self-proclaimed 'lord' of the village:

. . . j'ai au mains ronchi traiant,
bon harnas et herche et carue,
et si sui sires de no rue.

I have in my possession a draught mare,
A good harness, harrow and plough,
And I am the lord of our road.[41]

He also has a tunic and an overcoat cut from the same cloth, and he will inherit a valuable goblet, a cow and the income (in grain) from his mother's mill when she dies. Gautier is acquisitive and worldly, pinning his future hopes on his possessions. Other vices are associated with Gautier's avarice – he is proud, lustful and dirty-minded with a mouth to match, and a glutton. When the group plays 'kings and queens' he wants to take precedence, and he suggests a farting game, to Robin's horror:

Savés si bele esbanoiier
Que devant Marote, m'amie,
Avés dit si grant vilenie?

How can you think it so funny,
That [you], in front of Marie my lover,
Have said such a disgusting thing?[42]

The comic games are interrupted with an episode in which a wolf carries off one of Marion's sheep and Robin saves it, thereby redeeming his earlier ineffectual bragging and cowardly behaviour with the knight – and leading to more comedy as Robin manhandles the sheep, showing off its genitalia to the audience. The story ends with Robin, at Marion's request, leading the peasants in a dance along the edge of the wood. This may also have been a cue for the audience to participate:

ROBINS
Or sus, biau segneur, levés vous
Si vous tenés; g'irai devant.
Marote, preste-moi ton gant –
S'irai de plus grant volenté.
. . .
Venés apres moi, venés le sentele,
Le sentele, le sentele, lès le bos.

Come, fair lords, stand up!
Take your places; I will go in front.
Marote, lend me your glove –
I will go with great goodwill.
. . .

Come after me, come down the path,
The path, the path, beside the wood.[43]

In the *Jeu de Robin et Marion*, Adam de la Halle brilliantly exploits both the courtly and the coarse elements of his genres to produce an entertainment that would appeal to an audience of mixed age, gender and social class. In a situation where morale boosting was required, his technique works very well indeed. So much for morale – but why does the satirical element point the finger at status-based power that callously disrespects and abuses those of a lower social class? Adam's Marion has conquered the genre: she has overturned both the *pastourelle*'s and the *bergerie*'s traditional expectations.[44] Given that not only the knight but the upwardly mobile peasant Gautier is portrayed as a potential abuser of women, Adam appears to be equating wealth and social power with the abuse of lower-class women and girls. This is certainly the case, but why would Adam turn what was supposed to be a reinforcement of French authority into a critical satire on class in French society? There may be an explanation for this, in a religious element that is grounded in the persona, literary and performed, of the Virgin Mary, mother of Christ and Queen of Heaven.

As an increasing number of studies are now pointing out, the language, imagery and syntax of many cultural and literary forms were employed in praise of 'Our Lady'.[45] Poems and songs in her honour drew heavily on the courtly love poems addressed to earthly mistresses, as well as on the Song of Songs, the most erotic book in the biblical canon. In the spiritual context of Marian liturgies, the motets sung in her honour might feature counterpoints (different voices singing a variety of lyrics at the same time, intersecting with the main lyric at critical points) drawn from *pastourelles*. While the main tenor sang in honour of the Virgin, a supplementary voice might sing lines taken from a *pastourelle*.[46] The allegorical way in which people were taught to 'read' and to interpret word and image meant that alternative images, sometimes coarse or blasphemous ones, could be used to increase the likelihood that an audience would remember the teaching associated with the original.[47] A link, therefore, between *Marie*/Mary and Marion ('little Mary') was already present in the lived cultural experience of Adam and his audience. Marion is a mirror image of the Virgin Mary, the other side of the same coin. What may seem to us the blasphemy of presenting the Blessed Virgin in the form of a peasant girl would not have occurred to a medieval audience. The Mary of medieval art was generally depicted as a Western European lady rather than the wife of a Middle Eastern artisan. In the same way, the shepherdess of the *pastourelles* has the features of a noble European lady, rather than the sun- and wind-burned skin and musculature of a peasant's daughter. In a manner similar to the *pastourelles*, descriptions of Mary's body odour were meant to arouse devotion in her worshippers – despite, or even because of, their erotic associations.

There is evidence to support this view in the work of another great French author, Gautier de Coinci, the thirteenth-century Benedictine monk who adopted the persona of the Virgin Mary's *trouvère* in composing his poems, songs and *Miracles of the Virgin* in her honour. The Virgin Mary was the spiritual love of Gautier's life, and he tells his audience how, in the manner of the *pastourelles*, he 'found' this *flourete* / 'little flower' while ambling along at leisure through a meadow. In response, he says:

Qui que chant de Marïete
Je chant de Marie
Chascun an li doi par dete
Une raverdie.
C'est la fleurs, la vïolete,
La rose espanie,
Qui tele odeur done et jete
Toz noz rasasie.
. . .
Chant Robins des robardeles,
Chant li sos des sotes,
Mais tu, clers, qui chantez d'eles,
Certes tu rasotes!
Laissons ces viés pastoreles
Ces vielles riotes,
Si chantons chançons novelles
Biax dis, beles notes
De la fleur
Dont sanz sejor
Chantent angele nuit et jor.

Whoever sings of Mariete,
I sing of Mary,
Every year I owe her by obligation
A spring song.
She is the flower, the violet,
The rose in bloom,
Who releases and spreads such fragrance
That it saturates us all.
. . .
Let Robin sing of fashionable girls,
Let the fool sing of fool women,
But you, clerk, who sing of them,
Truly, you are rambling!
Let us leave those old *pastourelles*,
Those old babblings,
And let us sing new songs,
Beautiful words, beautiful melodies
Of the flower
About whom, without rest,
Angels sing night and day.[48]

Gautier tells us several things here: that Mariete (or Marion) was part of the same thought process as the Virgin Mary, that a tension was seen – by some but not all clergy – to exist between them, that both relationships were based on openly erotic love lyrics and imagery, and that Robin was a fool, a singer and a dancer in relation to Marion/Mary in both literature and in performance. In fact, Gautier implies that some of the composer/performers *were* clergy.[49]

On the one hand, Adam de la Halle's Marion is a *pastourelle* shepherdess, even if she is endowed with a greatly developed personality and is quick-witted enough to talk her way out of the seduction/rape scenario that is usual for the genre. On the other hand (the other side of the same coin, if you will), she is an image of the Virgin Mary, chaste and powerful. She is untouchable to both knight and peasant without her permission. The fact that Marion gains dominance over the knight in *Robin et Marion* is a depiction of Mary's superiority over the sinful, irrespective of their class status. Of all the characters in the *Jeu*, it is the knight, the representative of the ruling class, who will not, who cannot, be 'saved' by her;

although in awe of Marion, he leaves in disgust and anger when he cannot have what he wants, perhaps to return another day or to seek alternative prey.[50] As in biblical examples such as that of Dives and Lazarus – a well-known theme in medieval theology and art – the poor and the powerless have equal claim to Paradise as the rich and powerful, perhaps more so.[51] Adam's knight presents sins that are castigated and punished in medieval comic stories and in trickster tales: jealousy (of Marion's lover, Robin), greed/gluttony (he wants to consume without limit), anger (he becomes overwhelmingly angry when his desires are thwarted, and he leaves with a barrage of very uncourtly insults) and pride (in his unearned social status). Leisure is presented as the idleness (another deadly sin) of someone who has nothing better to do than molest shepherdesses minding their sheep and their own business, in contrast to the peasants who have earned their leisure by working hard; and lust – treated as natural, even God-given, in the *pastourelles* and as both natural and a joke in comic and trickster tales – is presented as evil. Like Lucifer, Aubert's attractiveness and his nobility are all surface. Marion even compares her two would-be lovers; ennobling her lover by referring to him as Robert, she contrasts him with the knight Aubert, noble in status but not in character.[52]

There is a confessional element to the story, and this is no accident. The Virgin stood at the centre of religious practice that, for the laity, involved a regular round of penance. After failing to help her, and finding that he is still loved, Robin follows the medieval path of confession; he examines himself, becomes convinced (or 'convicted') of his own sin, confesses it, and Mary/Marion reaffirms her love for him. Robin (the sinner) demonstrates the cleansing of his relationship with God, through Marion/Mary, as he performs good works, such as rescuing one of her sheep from a wolf. The wolf and sheep are, allegorically, the knight and Marion. The sheep's rescue is a redemptive act in which Robin can do what he did not do before when he failed to protect Marion from the knight. He is then allowed to participate fully in the feast (now a Eucharistic supper, before which – in the form of the Mass – all sinners should undergo priestly confession) with the rest, including Marion.

In the first half of *Robin et Marion*, Marion's part is largely that of a *pastourelle* shepherdess, resisting the advances of a courtly suitor. In the second half, however, she is inserted among the usual *bergerie* subject matter of peasants showing off, laughing, playing, arguing and generally enjoying themselves in an unthinking, peasant-like way. In fact, she dominates this part of *Robin et Marion*. She is the image of spiritual, moral and social virtue. Although she may not approve of the games they want to play, Marion is adept at playing, and at winning, them all. She protects the vulnerable young girl, Peronelle, from the men's bad language and innuendo, and from Gautier's lustful suggestions. She prevents a fight from breaking out, and encourages the peasants to live in harmony through food, play, music and dancing. Her relationship with Robin is affirmed by handfasting, and she does everything with his help and support. They are ideal companions, but he is still her servant; he leads the final dance only after she has given him her permission. As he continues in a close and harmonious relationship with Marion, Robin is transformed. He ceases to be the cowed, and cowardly, young man who hides behind a hedge, and becomes a noble person who behaves in a courtly manner towards the women and distances himself from the coarse language and behaviour of the men. Although Robin is the most favoured and the most devoted of her friends, Marion brings out everyone's inner nobility – even in the case of Gautier, who, unlike the knight, is shown to be redeemable by altering his behaviour at Marion's request. Everyone, except the Devil and his minions and those who reject God, can be saved. This is Mary/Marion as the friend of sinners, the Mother of Mercy, traditionally depicted in medieval art with her human 'sheep' gathered under the shelter of her skirts.[53]

In this way, while entertaining them with a delightful love story and some pretty coarse fun, Adam de la Halle is reminding his audience of their need to be good Christians, and of their special association with the Virgin Mary. In French national legend, it was the Virgin Mary who had given the vial of holy oil to Clovis, their ancestor, with which the Capetian kings of France were still being anointed at their coronations. Mary was both the patroness and the special protector of France. Therefore, Adam's work was designed not only to bolster the morale of the Franco-Sicilian community and their troops, but to reinforce their self-identity and their confidence – in addition to being in itself an offering of worship to the Virgin.[54] This offering was not just about community building and general morale boosting, it also functioned at a personal level: Adam was a composer, a performer, a musician – just like Robin in the *Jeu*. Robin is, in this sense, Adam himself, a servant – the most important servant – of the Virgin Mary. Because of his special skills and the strength of his devotion, she gives the *trouvère* the task of leading the rest of her 'household'.

The *pastourelles* are important for the Robin Hood tradition because they illustrate what was probably the origin of his stories. They also demonstrate the origins of Robin as the lover/servant of the Virgin Mary, who was associated from an early stage with the shepherdess Marion. This was acknowledged by poets such as Gautier de Coinci, and would have been recognized by medieval audiences.

There is a postscript to this story. When Edward I, who was married to the half-sister of King Philippe IV of France, held a great feast at Pentecost in 1306, French *trouvères* visited England in order to take part. Among the list of visitors is one Adam le Bossu: *le Bossu* (the hunchback) was the family name of Adam de la Halle.[55] This might, of course, have been a relative, but that seems unlikely in view of Adam's reputation and position in the cultural world of Arras. Unfortunately, there is no record of what he might have performed. This being Pentecost, later the traditional time for Robin Hood performances, he could have presented a *pastourelle* story – perhaps even one of Robin and Marion?

FOUR

Robin Hood and the Virgin Mary

Who was this Virgin Mary who was so very important to Robin Hood? How did his early audiences understand her? In the Bible Mary was, of course, the wife of Joseph the carpenter and the mother of Jesus Christ. In the biblical narratives she was present at the Annunciation, the Visitation, the Nativity, the marriage at Cana, the Crucifixion, the Resurrection and the coming of the Holy Spirit at Pentecost, and the Church celebrated her at its festivals for these events. They also celebrated her birth and her death (more accurately, her 'dormition' or 'falling asleep', as it was believed that Mary could not have died a natural death). Instead, the Western Church taught that she had not died but had been taken up into heaven during her final hours, at which point her virginity had been miraculously restored as it had been at the conception of Jesus. Then her son crowned her the Queen of Heaven, a subject that was very popular in medieval Christian art. From this position she was said to intercede for those who reverenced her and asked her for aid in their troubles, and to work miracles on their behalf. People frequently approached Christ through his mother, so these ideas were not seen as heretical or unbiblical. As ownership of Books of Hours, in particular those that featured the 'Little Hours' of the Virgin, spread widely (aided by the advent of printing in the mid-fifteenth century), so Mary's popularity became ubiquitous, nowhere more so than in England during the fifteenth century.

The Marian *Miracle* stories existed alongside a broader collection of the lives and the miracles of the medieval Church's saints;

they existed in verse and prose, literature, performed drama, sermon *exempla* (short stories offering moral examples), pictorial and sculptural artwork. The engaging thing about miracles of the saints, in particular the performed versions, was their materiality; the efficacy of prayer, confession and a good life was demonstrated in benefits that were physically present and believably 'real'.[1] They made plain before people's eyes and under their noses that 'good prayer' worked, at a time when prayers were valued for their efficacy, utility and longevity.[2] Although viewed by different audiences, including what we might call 'the masses', miracle plays were usually written by clerics, and so were a product of the social and educational elites (like Pilkington – an educated cleric from a gentry family).[3] Their popularity was a Europe-wide phenomenon; stories originally written in Latin were reworked in vernacular languages and art forms across the Continent. In terms of English versions, most have been lost, although records show – in terms of performances, at least – that there were many.

All manner of saints were commemorated on stage; St Thomas Becket seems to have been especially popular, and St George made many appearances. None of these was as frequently performed as the Virgin Mary, and 'Mary plays' seem to have been widspread all over Europe in the later Middle Ages. Lincoln held its annual Mary play at Pentecost, although she was useful at almost any time of the year. It may be that his association with the Virgin accounted for Robin Hood's appearances in performance at that time of the year. William Copland offered May as a time for his Robin Hood games, because Robin Hood events almost always took place at Whitsuntide.

Whitsun, also the important Church festival of Pentecost, took place annually on the seventh Sunday after Easter. It celebrated the outpouring of the Holy Spirit on the followers of Christ after his ascent into heaven. Whitsuntide was a time of processions, and also the time when most of the payments to 'Robin Hoods' were made; donations to the outlaw, or events for giving in general, reflected God's gift of the Holy Spirit at Pentecost. The biblical account of the story notes particularly that the Virgin Mary was present. Given that contemporaries were used to visualizing the life of Christ through the eyes and experiences of his mother, it would have been seen as appropriate to venerate her as well at this time. Pentecost usually fell in late May, and therefore coincided both with the beginning of summer and with the feast of the Visitation, the celebration of the pregnant Mary's visit to her cousin Elizabeth, also pregnant; this was an important event in the life of Mary, and one of the Virgin's traditional 'Joys'. The liturgical year ended at Pentecost, and the new one began with this event, the first acknowledgement of the incarnation of God's son as a human being by another human being – the unborn John the Baptist, who 'leapt in his mother's womb' when he felt the presence of the divine foetus. This coincided with older festive events for the beginning of summer; Mary plays and saint plays also featured at this time, as did Corpus Christi plays and miracle cycles. The important Church festival of Corpus Christi, at which the miracle of transubstantiation (the transformation of the bread and wine into Christ's actual body and blood when the priest said the prayer of consecration over them during the Mass) happened on the Thursday after Trinity Sunday, which was the first Sunday after Pentecost. It normally fell shortly after Pentecost, in the first two weeks of June.[4]

Plays and games were usually commissioned, financed, organized and staged by confraternities (often known by the slightly misleading term 'guild'), attached to a local church or to craft guilds. There were very many of these, in all areas from major cities to rural village communities. Some had an exclusive, wealthy membership; the Norwich Guild of St George included members and ex-members of the city government, for example – in fact, they eventually became synonymous with it.[5] On the other hand, some confraternities were local and relatively cheap to join, and were inclusive of any poor residents who could afford a matter of pennies for the subscription fee. Some might have been free to join; there has been relatively little work on this type of local organization so far.[6] There was no guarantee of longevity for a confraternity, either; some had short lives. Confraternities offered their members funeral and burial rights, and the right to have salvific prayers said for the dead. They also kept chapels or lights in the church, had social and religious meetings, and put on social events such as plays. In major cities and towns, there might be many guilds and confraternities. The guild and the confraternity were not always the same; guild members would usually belong to the confraternity associated with their guild, but members of other guilds, or members of the non-guild public, might also be involved.[7] The confraternities also had charitable motivations; the Paris confraternity (*confrérie*) of St Étienne, associated with the Guild of Goldsmiths, held a dinner for paupers on Easter

Sunday in the Hôtel-Dieu, at which the members themselves performed the service.[8] Similar arrangements, with variations, could be found in other European cities. London had confraternities and there are records of a *puy*, or competition for the arts: from 1384 onwards, the Guild of Parish Clerks met annually at Skinner's Well, or Clerkenwell, and Richard II, Henry IV and Henry V attended the performances, which lasted four to five days.[9]

Many more of the short miracle plays depicting saints' lives, deaths and miracles exist in Old French than in English. Of about fifty surviving Old French plays, forty exist in a single manuscript book (now split into two manuscripts, Bibliothèque Nationale, Paris, MSS fr. 819–20). Together, these are often known as the Cangé manuscript after the duc de Cangé, who donated them to the French royal library in the early eighteenth century.[10] The forty plays are usually referred to by scholars as the *Miracles de Nostre Dame par personnages* (Miracles of Our Lady [performed] by actors). One play was performed each year, at the annual general meeting and social gathering, or *siège*, of the Goldsmiths' Company of Paris, between the years 1340 and 1382. The plays were performed continually, with breaks in 1354 and 1358–60.[11] Each year's performed play – which was then kept on record – was the winning entry in an annual *puy*, a competition arranged by the confraternity of St Étienne (or St Loy – the patron saint of goldsmiths, by whom Chaucer's Prioress was wont to swear in *The Canterbury Tales*), in advance of the gathering.[12] Although they were grocers and not goldsmiths, members of the Calle family, including the Pastons' former steward, would have belonged to a similar confraternity grouping – or perhaps more than one – in fifteenth- and early sixteenth-century London. The world of the Cangé plays has many points of similarity to that of Robin Hood.

In keeping with the nature of the Goldsmiths' Company of Paris (and similar groups in English cities), the world of the *Miracles* is very aspirational, bourgeois and mercantile in its values. Although some of the stories feature merchants, most of the major protagonists are members of the clergy or the upper classes. Many of these, however, are not viewed in a good light. It is a world in which monetary value matters more than aesthetics, and even ideals are measured in cash, or in terms of their economic or 'opportunity' cost. In terms also seen in Robin Hood stories, economic profit is relatable to moral and spiritual worth. It is entirely legitimate to be counted as religious and yet to worry about what will happen to your possessions when you are dead, as well as to ask God for help in passing them on:

> *Car, Dieu mercy, je scay et voy*
> *que nous avons de biâus menages*
> *et avons de grands heritages*
> *et foison de beins temporiex.*
> *si que s'a Dieu pleust c'un fiex*
> *Ou une fille nous donnast*
> *qui apré nous les possessast*
>
> Because, by God's grace, I know and see
> That we have a lovely home
> And we have a large inheritance
> And wealth in worldly goods.
> May it please God to give us
> A son or a daughter
> Who will own them after us.[13]

Material possessions and comforts matter a great deal to the characters, who have little difficulty in reconciling such care for material wealth with their faith. Subsistence, profit and loss underlie all areas of physical life. Religious devotion also has a price. When a papal servant asks the pope to relieve him of the burden of having to burn sacred oil before the altar of St Peter every day, the pope agrees to do this, but demands a payment of 200 *besants* in return.[14] St Peter is annoyed and he reprimands the pope, but it is for his avarice in overcharging, not specifically for buying or selling the sacred duty. He orders the pope to pray to the Virgin Mary for forgiveness. She is reluctant but agrees to pardon him. The grateful pope buys two splendid carbuncles for St Peter's altar from a merchant, but the saint tells the pope to give them to the Virgin instead. Like a *pastourelle* shepherdess, Mary is very pleased indeed with the jewels, and no judgement is offered on the buying and selling of spiritual credit, or the part played by the merchant, which is legitimate trade. Nobody is judged for buying material objects to prove their faith and there is no inquiry into the methods used to obtain them. Devotion is measured in hard currency in this case, just as it is in the Robin Hood tales. If spirituality is an accumulation of personal spiritual credit, salvation is frequently measured in terms of profit and loss, and the Virgin always pays her debts. In the plays, this is well demonstrated in the miracle of *Le Marchand et le Juif* (The Merchant and the Jew), a play in which the Virgin's payment of financial debt is as miraculous as the way in which she manipulates money in the *Lytell Geste.* A merchant has run himself into debt by being generous, giving alms and charity until his money is gone. Pending the return of his cargo, he borrows money from a Jew, swearing in front of a statue of the Virgin and Child that he will pay his debt. As soon as the merchant's fortune returns, he goes to pay back the Jew. He puts the money into a box, which he releases on to the river so that God can guide the floating box to the Jew's house. The Jew's servant draws it from the water, and he finds the money inside. However, conforming to the received stereotype that Jews were liable to sly deception and avarice, the moneylender denies receiving the money. The merchant makes him swear to the truth of his denial in front of the same statue of the Virgin and Child, at which point the enlivened statue itself reveals the Jew's duplicity. The merchant is saved, and the Jew is converted.[15]

What the stories also show is a more general exteriorization of an individual's internal, spiritual life. Religious observance is seen in terms of activity and giving material objects – *realia*, or 'things'. Just as Robin Hood is obsessed with his need to attend Mass and is prepared to put his life on the line to do it, devotion is measured in terms of physical effort as well as money. Penance usually takes the form of going on pilgrimage, giving up material wealth, making donations or (as in the case of the emperor Clovis) founding religious institutions. The Virgin herself, like Marion in the *pastourelles*, likes pretty things. In a *pastourelle* touch, she is particularly pleased with one young man, a merchant's son, who spends his time making her garlands of flowers. His uncle objects to his neglect of more practical, entrepreneurial concerns, and so, under this pressure, the young man agrees to go on a business trip. When he stops en route to pray, a highway robber sees him and plans an attack. Seeing this, the Virgin Mary steps in; she comes down from heaven and places a garland of her own on the young man's head.[16] The thief is astonished and is converted on the spot. This characteristic also underlies the value system of the Robin Hood *rymes* and sets them apart from the 'money no object' gift-based economy of the high aristocracy – the world of the *pastourelles*. Money is not bad in itself – it is what you do with it that counts. The impoverished merchant in *Le Marchand et le Juif* has given away his wealth, just as Robin Hood does at the king's court in the *Lytell Geste*:

Had Robyn dwelled in the kynges courte
But .xii. monethes and thre
That spent an hondred pounde
And all his mennes fe
In every place where Robyn came
Ever more he layde downe
Both for knyghtes and for squyres
To gete hym grete renowne

When Robin had lived in the king's court
only fifteen months [twelve months and three]
He'd spent a hundred pounds
And all his servant's fee.
In every place where Robin came
Ever more he laid out
Both to knights and squires
To get himself great renown.[17]

Having enough money to live according to one's social status (not simply enough to survive on) was important to these audiences, although it is not clear what that status actually was. The difference between what is necessary and what is excessive is the same as that set out by Robin Hood when he robs the monks from St Mary's. Being rich is not a problem, as long as one's priorities are correct. The virtue of Sir Richard atte Lee is set against the vice of the monks who love their money so well that they attempt to conceal it, not only from Robin Hood but from the Virgin herself. Being wealthy is not a sin; avarice (loving your wealth for its own sake) is. Giving is of prime importance, even if it is unintentional, as in the case of the Scrooge-like *Pierre le Changeur* (Peter the Money-changer), whose soul is saved by the Virgin after his death, because he once threw a loaf of bread at a beggar to make him stop being a nuisance and go away.[18] The audience of Robin Hood, like the audience of the *Miracles*, might have some cause to be anxious about the means by which they had gained their wealth. The Church taught that usury was a sin (Robin is not guilty of this – he lends but does not charge interest), and in some cases the boundary between trade and robbery might be pretty thin. It must have been a comfort to know that the Virgin Mary was prepared to overlook these things. Interestingly, when considering the violence of the Robin Hood stories, she is prepared to forgive, even to overlook, a very great deal – even premeditated murder, especially if the murderers are women.

The Virgin's particular preoccupation with the fate of women in society echoes Robin Hood's own priorities. There are several instances in the *Miracles* where she answers the prayers of murderers. In the *Miracle de la femme du Roy de Portugal* (Miracle of the Wife of the King of Portugal), a nobleman's daughter is tricked into spending the night with the king's seneschal rather than the king himself. The intended royal bride, on discovering what has happened, persuades her female cousin to help her decapitate the rapist. After the crime has been carried out, she prays to the Virgin Mary for forgiveness:

> *. . . vous savez le voir,*
> *Dame, q'il m'a deshonnorée;*
> *Car par lui sui depucellée*

> . . . you can see,
> Lady, that he has dishonoured me;
> Because I have been deflowered by him [he has taken
> my virginity][19]

She was, however, not unhappy for the king to deflower her himself, having given him the key to her room. The king marries the girl, thinking her to be a virgin. She must keep up the deception, and so she persuades her cousin to take her place on her wedding night. However, when she comes to claim her husband back again, the cousin refuses to give way. Another murder follows: the queen ties her cousin to the bed, sets fire to the room, then saves her husband, leaving the cousin to burn alive. Overcome by a sense of her own guilt, the queen confesses her '*deux folies*' (two foolish acts) to her confessor, who is so shocked that he tells the king. Condemned to burn by her husband, the queen (although she realizes that she deserves to die) calls on the Virgin Mary for help. The Virgin forgives her and sends a hermit to the king to order her release and restitution. The confessor is not so lucky – he is burned alive, presumably for violating the confessional. His fate seems somewhat unfair, but this is the storyworld of the Virgin's miracles, and Mary's values are not always what we might assume them to be. The point here is that the Virgin is reversing the unfairness of society's values and paradigms, and the vague and often serendipitous nature of justice and law. Many of the heroes of the *Miracles* are unjustly accused or trapped by a society that disadvantages them because of their gender or their age.

In the *Miracle de l'Empereris de Rome* (Miracle of the Empress of Rome), an emperor goes on pilgrimage to the Holy Land to fulfil a vow, leaving his wife and empire in the care of his brother. The brother becomes infatuated with the empress, but she rejects his advances. Filled with jealous rage, the brother denounces his sister-in-law as an adulteress, and she is condemned to death. However, the two soldiers entrusted with the deed take pity on their captive, and leave her on a rock in the sea instead. There she prays to the Virgin Mary, who comes to comfort and nourish her. Mary arranges a passing ship to take the empress to shore, where she is cared for and healed by a 'wise' woman. Meanwhile, the emperor's brother has become a leper as a punishment for his malicious lies. The emperor, seeking a cure for him, sends for the same woman who has, unbeknown to himself, been caring for his wife. The woman declares that the man will only be cured if he confesses his sin. The crime is revealed in confession, and the empress is reunited with her husband. The story of the empress was very well known; as well as literary examples, there are scenes from the story in the roof bosses of the fourteenth-century Bauchon Chapel in Norwich Cathedral, and in the famous fifteenth-century series of miracles painted on the walls of Eton College Chapel.[20] The Virgin is, in this guise, an equalizer, and it is in precisely this guise that she appears – or rather does not appear in person – in the Robin Hood stories. She works, rather, through Robin Hood and his outlaws, for example in the case of Sir Richard, whose son is just such a victim, trapped by his lowly social status in relation to his accuser.

I had a sone forsoth, Robyn,
that shulde hav ben myn ayre.
Whanne he was twenty wynter olde
In felde wolde just full fayre.

Strength and sweetness: the Virgin Mary in her double guise. A roof boss in York Minster features Mary as she would have been seen by the audiences of 'Mary' plays, surrounded by worshipping angels. Her sweetness is indicated by the garland of red roses (one of her special flowers) which surrounds her, and her virginity by her crown of daisies. She makes a gesture of obedience and submission, but the sunburst around her indicates majesty, glory and power.

He slewe a knyght of Lancaster
And asquyer bolde.
For to save him in his ryght
My godes beth sette and solde.

Truly, I had a son, Robin,
Who should have been my heir.
When he was twenty winters old
He wanted to joust well in the field.
He killed a knight of Lancaster
And a very bold squire.

In order to keep his inheritance
My possessions were put up and sold.[21]

Sir Richard himself reverses a similar situation when he helps the yeomen wrestlers.

The overall attitude of the *Miracles* to men in authority, ranging from husbands to kings and emperors (who are often also husbands), is an interesting one. They are presented in a less than favourable light most of the time. This is particularly true of the attitude to rulers, which is comparable to the relationship of Robin Hood and his outlaws to kings and their representatives, such as the sheriff of Nottingham. These men are violent and victims of their own passions, willing to condemn and believe the worst, especially of their women. King Thierry is even willing to believe that his wife, Osanne, has given birth to three puppies. He is then prepared to imprison her and to kill the children; the Virgin Mary has to step in to save them all.[22] The king of Hungary wants to marry his daughter incestuously, causing the girl to cut off her own hand in an attempt to thwart him.[23] The power society gives to kings, and to men in general, makes them all potential tyrants as far as their female dependents, and those of lesser status, are concerned, and there is little remedy except divine intervention for such injustices. This is the injustice that also rules the world of Robin Hood. It is a world in which not all offenders are solely to blame for the atrocities they commit. In this world, the innocent suffer, even children and babies. When the knight Amis is struck down with leprosy for lying in order to save his best friend Amille, God tells him that he can only be cured by bathing in the blood of Amille's young children. Amille loves his friend so much that he kills his children in order to save him.[24] The Virgin and her son take pity on the two men because of their pure friendship, and the Virgin appears in order to restore the children to life. St Jehan de Paulu offers shelter to a king's daughter when she is lost in the forest, but devils tempt him to rape and kill her. He repents at once and calls to the Virgin for help. At her bidding, he embarks on a life of hard penance in the wilderness, and the Virgin restores the girl to life.[25]

Only one woman and her baby owe their lives to a loving, caring husband. In the *Miracle de l'enfant que Nostre Dame resuscita* (Miracle of the Baby that Our Lady Resuscitated), a couple are granted a much longed-for child by the Virgin Mary.[26] The woman, feeling tired, takes a bath with her baby, but falls asleep and lets the child drown. She is imprisoned and condemned to death for murdering her baby, but her distraught husband calls to Mary for help. Allowed to hold her child just one more time before she dies, the woman cuddles her baby's body, and the Virgin makes it come to life in her arms. Nobody has sinned or done anything wrong (although perhaps bathing with your small baby when you are likely to fall asleep may be criminally stupid), but without Mary's help the child and the woman will pay society's price. The weak and innocent may, or may not, be restored to life in the end, but the choice is not necessarily theirs – nor is it dependent upon their own faith or innocence.

Justice, then, is an issue with which the Virgin Mary is very concerned. In legal terms, she is an equitable judge, more interested in the spirit rather than the letter of the law. In the *Miracles*, she often appears as an advocate on behalf of her devotees, at a spiritual tribunal of some kind in which her son is the judge. In these scenes she is revealed to be combative, forceful (even thrusting), loud, disruptive, even less than entirely truthful, in pleading their cause. This side of Mary also appears in contemporary *Avocacie de Nostre Dame* literature, where she acts as a defence lawyer, putting the case of her children, the human race, against the Devil's arguments – correct according to the letter of God's law – that their souls are forfeit to him because of their sins. She reassures them:

bien vous povez asseürer
jamès ne pourroie endure
l'Umain Lignage à desconfire:
tant fery qu'il devra souffire.

You may be well assured
That I could never suffer
The Human Race to be destroyed:
I will do whatever it takes.[27]

In a cruel world where right, wrong, justice and injustice may be treated indiscriminately by both society and the law, the outcome is determined by the fact that the Virgin as advocate will protect the innocent, even after death. If she cannot prevent the death of innocents, the Virgin can be relied upon to protect them in the next world. Sometimes she revives their mortal bodies, sometimes not.

Clergy are treated with some ambivalence in the *Miracles*. Popes pay others to do their devotions, archdeacons fry in purgatory for being avaricious and corrupt, and clergy even resort to murder to achieve promotion. Others become monks and hermits (a particularly popular choice) in response to the Virgin's goodness, or to expiate their sins. A fugitive nun returns to her convent, and yet a hermit happily returns to the world to become a bishop. The pregnant abbess in *Le Miracle de l'Abbesse Grosse* (The Miracle of the Pregnant Abbess) seems to have stepped straight out of the world of *fabliau* stories. Having weighed her options of being found out, she seduces a young clerk who works as her secretary. She has miscalculated, however; her young nuns gossip viciously about her. When they tell the bishop and he comes on a visitation, the Virgin spirits her away, delivers her child in the forest and then replaces her, no longer pregnant, in the convent. It does seem, however, that in the world of the *Miracles*, as in the world of Robin Hood, clerical sinfulness draws greater condemnation, and stronger punishment, than the sins of the ordinary laity. One avaricious archdeacon, condemned to purgatory, is saved by the repentance and penance of his lay cousin.[28] In only one story, that of an archdeacon's murder by his rival for a bishopric, does the Virgin hold out for the death penalty. She rejects any idea of forgiveness for a bishop who has murdered his rival, a pious man, her own devoted servant and doer of her will, whom she describes as 'mon serjeant' (my man-at-arms).[29] This close, personal service is how the Virgin interprets her relationship with the archdeacon, the same kind of relationship that she has with Robin Hood. Although a man of peace, she refers to the archdeacon as her *serjeant*, a personal servant with a protective, military role. The archdeacon's devotion, prayer and virtuous acts are her weapons in the war against evil, and he is her soldier. Robin, too, is the Virgin Mary's *serjeant*, a trusted servant, or *yeman*, for the killing of whom she will accept no repentance. This may help to explain some of the casualties in the Robin Hood stories. The sheriff and the monk are guilty of trying to kill her *serjeant*, or of trying to have him killed, which in her eyes is an unforgivable sin. The Virgin protects her own with the ultimate sanctions available to her; these men deserve everything they get.

The Virgin Mary of the *Miracles* – tough, legalistic, sly, loud, practical, realistic, even apparently amoral and vengeful at times – is recognizable as the Virgin Mary of the Robin Hood stories, and the world of the *Miracles* is also their world. Sometimes in the *Miracles*, as in the Robin Hood stories, she hardly appears at all, and some stories (for example, *Amis et Amille*) have few openly religious references. This begs a question – were the early Robin Hood plays actually Mary plays, and do the stories as we have them enshrine the content of lost popular religious performances? None of the surviving stories has any appearance by the Virgin, however confected, although the protagonists call on her regularly, and the narrator may mention Robin's devotion. *Robin Hood and the Monk* has a story largely based around Robin's devotion to her. In the *Miracles*, the Virgin usually appears personally in spaces created in the narrative for her, accompanied by music and the singing of angels; her train may also include some saints, or on the odd occasion her son. There are places in the text of the existing Robin Hood stories where this might be done, but there is no evidence that this was the case. The adaptability of the Robin Hood stories (or *dits*) and the close relationship between different types of text as demonstrated in the Sloane manuscript imply this, too. Their mix of moral, religious, secular and (sometimes very) naughty material sits quite happily alongside some lovely carols in honour of the Virgin.[30]

Another French group of medieval *Miracles of Our Lady* (now Bibliothèque Nationale, Paris, MS fr. 12483) is commonly known as the *Rosarius* because of its close links with the Virgin Mary, the 'Rose'.[31] Produced in northern France around 1330, its author was a member of the Dominican order of friars. The book is arranged in fifty sections, each beginning with a description of an animal, plant, mineral or other natural object, stressing the qualities shared by that thing with the Virgin Mary. This is followed by a miracle of the Virgin, then a link that leads to a poem, song or story somehow associated with the theme of that section. These stories are usually quite short, but vary in length. They may not necessarily be entirely what we would think of as appropriate. The *Dit de la Queue de Renart* (Tale of the Tail of Reynard) is a satirical poem, making a sly social comment about those who secretly want to 'wear Reynard's tail', that is, a deceiver, a liar and an all-round sinner, as Reynard the Fox was known to be in the popular beast fables. The poem is entirely secular in its content, apart from a few lines at the end where Reynard's evil nature is denounced, and the poet prays that God will guard and keep 'nostre roy et ses amis' (our king and his friends), and that He will keep us all from evil.[32] It is placed in the section on heaven. The story that accompanies the section on lettuce is actually a mildly rude *fabliau*, *Du Prestre qui fu mis au lardier* (Of the Priest who Was Put in the Larder).[33] A priest is having an affair with the wife of a shoemaker, but is surprised in the bath when the husband returns unexpectedly. The wife tells the priest to hide (naked) in the larder while she entertains her husband in the bath. As the priest listens, the husband says that he is going to take the old larder away in order to sell it. As the crowd gathers round to look, a rich friar who knows the priest spies him through a crack in the larder. The priest calls to him from inside (in a blasphemous liturgical reference), 'Frater, pro Deo, delibera me' (Brother, for God's sake, get me out of here) but the seller hears the larder speaking Latin, announces a miracle, and puts up the price. The friar has to pay twenty *livres parisis* to buy the larder and free the priest. Lettuce was supposed to extinguish the fires of lust, so the moral is simply 'don't let lust get you put in a larder'. The section on 'ointment of mallow' (a section on sweet smells) ends with the *fabliau* of the *Vilain asnier* (Peasant Assdriver), which is built around smell.[34]

There is little to connect such stories with the material that surrounds them, let alone to the Virgin Mary, and yet they appear in a context entirely devoted to her worship. It would be much easier to associate a short Robin Hood story with Marian verses or miracles. Shorter, *dit* versions of romance stories were easier to adapt than long narratives, and they might have a more moral, or religious, focus than the original. This is true of *Amis et Amille* in the *Miracles de Nostre Dame par personnages*, which was adapted from the shorter version rather than the full-length narrative. The shorter story has a religious basis, and was read more like a saint's life in the later Middle Ages.[35] There was also a *dit* of *Robert le Diable*, but the content of the miracle play of that name is not similar enough to conclude that this was the source, rather than the full-length narrative.

It is also easy to see how stories of, or inspired by, the Virgin Mary could become political and socially dangerous. Robin Hood serves a very unruly, dangerous, female lord. Theirs is, potentially at least, a 'radical pastoral' world.[36] This can be seen in the history of the *Miracles de Nostre Dame par personnages*. That the plays were not held in the years 1358–60 was no accident. In September 1356 King Jean II of France was taken prisoner at the Battle of Poitiers, and the English government demanded a huge ransom for his release. His son, the Duke of Normandy, devalued the currency and imposed new taxation in order to raise the ransom money. The middle classes of Paris rose in revolt, led by King Charles of Navarre, newly escaped from Jean's prison, and by the provost of Paris, Étienne Marcel, who was also a prominent goldsmith and a member of the confraternity of St Étienne. With King Edward III of England attacking Paris, Marcel was killed, prompting the return of the duke and the arrest of several leading goldsmiths. Some were executed. Goldsmiths also took part in the Paris revolts of 1380–83 against the taxation of Charles VI. In order to quell discontent and unrest, Charles issued letters patent forbidding public meetings of guilds and confraternities.[37] The plays ended in 1383. Charles VI was no hater of plays; he founded his own confraternity of the Passion, which presented dramatic performances but was outside the control of powerful guilds. Although festivals and public performances all over Europe were popular and stimulated or expressed loyalty and religious beliefs, in troubled times they could have the opposite effect, when they could also be a major public order issue.

Thus Robin Hood is political, although he is neither a freedom fighter nor a social bandit, ways in which he is frequently interpreted today.[38] Robin is just a servant; it is his lord, the Virgin Mary, who is potentially dangerous in a socio-political sense. Mary is the lord of a great household whose 'seat' lies in, or possibly just beyond, the forest. This is, as in the *Miracles*, where her greatest power is located. Like Venus in John Gower's *Confessio Amantis*, she presents an ideal of reciprocal lordship between herself and her retainers, or clients.[39] Mary's livery, the rosary/livery in the *Confessio*, equates to the green and scarlet clothing handed out by Robin Hood. The outlaws are not poachers because the forest is Mary's own park, and the food they eat is her provision. The guests Robin invites to meals are being offered the Virgin's hospitality, not stolen goods. The truth tests Robin applies are a form of secularized confession, as is required of Amans by Genius in the *Confessio*. Robin plays a part similar to that of Genius, described by Venus as her 'oghne clerc', or private chaplain, not only administering confession but requiring his guests to swear to their own honesty. Mary requires reciprocity from those to whom she offers her lordship; they must give her a gift (from their money) and she, in return, guarantees an environment in which they, her clients, are able to exercise their own good lordship.[40] In this way, she changes highway robbery into productive labour. She does not wait for petitioners to come to her in the way that Amans, the lover, approaches Venus in Gower's *Confessio*, but sends out her servants to find them on the highway. When Sir Richard atte Lee saves the wrestlers in the *Lytell Geste*, and when he shelters the outlaws from the sheriff of Nottingham, he is not simply being a good man, but performing the reciprocity of lord/client relations between himself and the Virgin Mary. When King Edward asks for green cloth for himself and his men he is becoming the Virgin's client, not Robin Hood's. He performs reciprocity by returning peace, order and natural justice to the people of Nottingham. This structure reflects the political ideals of the gentry and aristocratic classes in the later fourteenth and fifteenth centuries, when it was usual for government in the provinces to be carried out by local lords and their client families in the king's name.

This was the model of government and society in the 'Robin Hood lands' of the northwest and the northwest Midlands. It was a highly contested model in the fourteenth century, when Richard II (r. 1377–99) attempted to subvert it by the use of direct royal intervention in governmental and legal processes. It lay behind the acts of the Merciless Parliament of 1388, at which Richard II's closest supporters were condemned for treason and summarily executed, and ultimately to the revolt led by Henry Bolingbroke and the deposition of the king in 1399. This is the system presented by the Robin Hood stories, although they also show the tensions inherent in it. The king can only restore order by direct intervention, and his lordship of his own court is less than desirable. At his court, the king seeks to keep Robin captive (he may not leave without permission, and the king demands his return in a matter of days), and in the end Robin simply runs away. He cannot be, as the Bible reminds his audience, the servant of two masters.[41] The lordship of the king offers physical sustenance, money and material goods, but the reciprocal lordship of the Virgin Mary offers him subjectivity (the ability to be himself) and the freedom of self-determination.

FIVE

Robin Hood and Romance Narratives

The *Miracles* of the Virgin in their varied forms draw on a wide range of existing genres (romance narratives, hagiographies or lives of saints, histories, comic stories, Bible stories and liturgical practice) for their materials, and Robin Hood stories share this characteristic with them. Indeed, one possible generic interpretation of the surviving Robin Hood tales is that they are reminders in text and performance of lost Marian *Miracles*. Robin's closeness to Mary before the Reformation exists in form and genre, as well as in their religious and societal relationship.

Robin's role as Mary's servant and a transmitter of her divine agency is enough in itself to dictate that he must exist outside of society. The permanency of his residence in the greenwood begs an explanation. If he is neither a madman (see below) nor a hermit, then he needs to be a forester or an outlaw. As a forester, in societal terms he would need to serve a human lord, as foresters were employees. This may be why he needed to become an outlaw. There was also a cultural, generic reason; the themes of exile and outlawry were already present in romance narratives. Stories told and performed through the medium of romance were ubiquitous in medieval Europe; it was one of the major languages in which the social elite, the educated and the aspirational created, absorbed and understood their world, then passed the stories down to those below them in society. Romance encompassed history, such as Geoffrey of Monmouth's *Historia Regum Britannie* (History of the Kings of Britain) and other Arthurian material, the related historical world of the *chansons de geste* (songs of deeds), and the fantasy worlds of *chansons d'aventure* (songs of chance or destiny). The *pastourelle* storyworld of peasants and shepherdesses was a romance one, and (as we have seen) the Virgin Mary was often referred to in terms applicable to a romance love mistress. It is hardly surprising, therefore, that the early storyworld of Robin Hood has romance elements.

It would be an understatement to simply say that outlawry and exile are common themes in romance narratives, although they are older than the romances themselves. 'Outlaw' is an Old Norse word, meaning someone placed outside the protection of society and its laws. Old Norse sagas in which outlawry was a recurrent theme would have been well known in the Danelaw (the area of England north of the River Trent that had once been in the hands of Scandinavian rulers), where Robin Hood (probably) had his English origin. Along with its female equivalent of 'waiving', outlawry remained an alternative to the death penalty in the north into the fifteenth century.[1] The language used to describe outlaws and exiles in literature is similar, but two different ideas are at play.[2] In Old English and beyond, the outlaw is also termed 'wolfshead', and like the wolf, s/he inhabits the wilderness just beyond society's boundary, visiting the socially included world only to wreak havoc. This is the concept evoked in the Old English poem commonly known as *Wulf and Eadwacer*, where a woman laments the loss of her lover and imagines the devastating consequences of his return:

Wulf is on iege, ic on oρerre.
Faest is ρaet eglond, fenne biworpen.
Sindon waelreowe weras ρer on ige
Willaδ hy hine aρecgan gif he on ρreat cymeδ . . .
. . .
Wulf, min Wulf, wena me ρine
Seoce gedydon, ρine sedcymas,
Murnende mod, nales meteliste.

Wulf is on an island, I on another.
The island is secure, surrounded by a fen.
There are bloodthirsty men on the island
They will consume him if he comes among them . . .
. . .
Wulf, my Wulf, my hopes of you

Have made me sick, your rare visits,
A mournful spirit, not food-longing.[3]

Exile may be a consequence of invasion, jealous lovers or (most frequently) the animosity of close relatives, especially parents or step parents. Self-exile may be undertaken for love, loss of love or religious reasons. The romance outlaw, like the romance exile, is usually the noble victim of either injustice or circumstance. Generally speaking, outlawry in sagas and *chansons* is a precursor to exile and to exotic adventures in other lands. Although he is mainly known as the fierce warrior-king of Norway defeated at Stamford Bridge in 1066, Harald 'Hardrada' Sigurdsson's saga tells of his adventures in the eastern Mediterranean with the Byzantine emperor's Varangian Guard, whereas Fouke FitzWaryn sails the northern seas, fighting dragons and other monsters while also saving Saracen princesses from a fate worse than death. Castile's Rodrigo Díaz de Vivar 'the Cid' serves Muslim warlords, fighting the Moors of North Africa and winning himself a kingdom in Valencia.[4]

It is often hard to tell where exile becomes outlawry, as the two are easily confused. Outlawry is always a form of exile, even when the outlaw is the 'other within' his or her own land, living on the margins of their own community, as Robin Hood does. It differs from exile in being a state that has been legally (or illegally) imposed by authority figures, whether that is a prince or a court of law. King John, being a bad king and a bad man, outlaws Fouke FitzWaryn for purely personal reasons (one of the signs of a tyrant), because there has been 'bad blood' between them since their childhood together:

> *Avint qe Johan e Fouke tut souls sistrent en une chamber juauntz a escheks. Johan prist le eschelker, si fery Fouke grant coupe. Fouke se senti blescé, leval le piee, si fery Johan enmy le pys qe sa teste vola contre la pareye, qu'il devynt tut mat, e se palmea. Fouke fust esbay . . . Si frota les oryles Johan, e revynt de palmesoun, e s'en ala al roy, son piere, e fist une grant pleynte.*
>
> At one time, John and Fouke were sitting all alone in a room playing chess. John picked up the chessboard and struck Fouke a great blow with it. Fouke felt himself wounded, lifted his foot and kicked him in the chest so that his head struck

> against the wall; he was checkmated and passed out. Fouke was scared . . . he rubbed John's ears, and he recovered from his faint, and went to the king, his father, and complained greatly.

John's father, Henry II, tells him he must have deserved it and has him whipped. The audience is told that 'Johan fust molt corocee a Fouke, quar unqe pus ne le poeit amer de cuer' (John was very angry with Fouke, and from then on never again had any heartfelt love for him.)[5] None of the outlaws in romance stories, or in the Norse sagas, are portrayed as essentially bad, even if they have killed someone and done things they should not have. In a few cases there may be good reason for the sentence: Sir Gowther, for example, is demonically driven and extremely violent until he discerns the reason for his nature, does penance, and is redeemed.[6]

Of the *Miracles de Nostre Dame* based on romance narratives, the story of *Robert le Diable* (Robert the Devil) has many similarities with the Robin Hood tales. *Robert le Diable* was a very popular story. The earliest remaining version dates from the early 1200s, with another still extant from the second half of the next century. This makes the text roughly contemporary with *Fouke le Fitz Waryn*, *Eustace the Monk* and *Richard Coer de Lyon*. Regarded as history, it was added to the *Grande chronique de Normandie* in the fourteenth century. A shortened version, or *dit*, was created in the early 1300s, and another short prose version was created and published in Lyon in 1496.[7] Wynkyn de Worde published a translation into English at the sign of the Sun in London around 1500. There were no fewer than eleven French publications between 1496 and 1580.[8] Given its appeal, it is possible that *Robert le Diable* had some influence on the formation of Robin Hood. The story is closely linked to northern France; its most recent editor believes that it may have been loosely founded on the life of William the Conqueror's father.[9] The Anglo-Norman nobility and gentry loved to hear stories of both British/English and Norman history; they were proud of their joint heritage, and so a story like this would have been very popular in courts all over Britain.

Robert is the only son and heir of the Duke of Normandy, born after many painful years of childless marriage. Unknown to his father, however, Robert's conception was the result of his mother's desperate prayer to the Devil for a baby. In consequence, Robert is not like other children:

Toute jour crie et brait et pleure;
. . .
Moult durement s'en esmerveillent
Les norrices qui por luy veillent,
Qui sont taintes, pales et maigres . . .

Every day he yelled and shrieked and wept
. . .
They marvelled very much,
The wetnurses who looked after him;
They were wan, pale and thin . . .[10]

Robert develops teeth while still on the breast, and uses them to bite off the nipples of his most beautiful nurse. As Robert grows, he becomes ungovernably violent, killing his tutor and hating the sacraments of the Church in particular. As a knight, Robert loves tournaments, because they give him an occasion for killing and maiming as many people as possible. He roams around his father's duchy, robbing, raping and killing, until the people complain to the duke. Sorrowfully, the duke agrees his son must die. After blinding the men sent by his father to arrest him, Robert takes to the forest with a band of murderous thugs. From there, they ambush, rob, rape, kill and burn. Seeing how people hate and fear him, Robert goes to seek some answers from his mother, who admits that she committed him to the Devil before he was born.[11] Robert goes to see the pope to find out how he can be saved. On the way he visits his gang in their forest hideout, and exhorts them also to repent and go with him. When they refuse, he kills them. The pope is unable to tell Robert what to do, so he sends the young man to his own confessor, a hermit who lives in a nearby forest. Divinely guided, the hermit says that Robert must pretend to be mute, take up the person of a fool, and live with dogs, eating only their food, until he is told otherwise. Robert does this and becomes the emperor of Rome's prized servant – but he only sleeps and eats with the emperor's dogs.

Rome is being threatened by a Saracen invasion, and Robert wants desperately to help, but he cannot give up his fool's persona. However, he is given divine help: a divine voice tells him to go to the fountain in the emperor's garden, where he is given miraculous white armour and a white horse. He rides out incognito to save the day, no fewer than three times. Although everyone wants to know the identity of the mysterious knight, Robert cannot tell; and neither can the only other person who knows, the emperor's beautiful, but also mute, daughter, who has watched Robert in the garden from her nearby window. Eventually, the emperor attempts to flush out the hero by offering him his daughter in marriage, and half his empire, if he comes forward. The emperor's evil seneschal, who covets the girl, gives himself a wound just like Robert's and turns up at court on a white horse, claiming to be the unknown knight. The emperor is delighted, and the imposter is betrothed to his daughter. The horrified girl is given the power to speak. She tells the whole story, and the emperor offers the prize to his fool. Both pope and hermit realize that Robert is now forgiven, and he is allowed to become himself again. He is reconciled with his father, too. In some versions of the story Robert marries the emperor's daughter, ultimately becoming a ruler in his own right, and in others he rejects all earthly reward.

Like Robin Hood (who shares his given name), Robert of Normandy is a greenwood outlaw before he understands the reason for his inability to control himself. His violence, however, is less targeted than Hood's, and his attitude to women is very different:

Venus est a une abeïe,
O ses barons, o sa maisnie,
Ou avoit soissante nonains:
Robers en ochist de ses mains
Plus de cinquante des plus beles;
. . .
Puis prent le feu, par tout le rue,
S'art le dortoir et les estables,
Si com li fist faire diables.

He came to an abbey
With his barons, with his company,
Where there were sixty nuns:
Robert killed with his own hands
More than fifty of the most beautiful;
. . .
Then he set fire to the whole place,

He burned the dormitory and the stables,
He acted as if he were a devil.[12]

The emphasis here is on the diabolical nature of Robert's violence, as it is in other romance stories, such as the tale of Sir Gowther (which is very similar) and the epic *chanson* of *Richard Coer de Lyon*, in which the king (whose nature is half demonic owing to his mother being a demon) pulls out a lion's beating heart with his bare hands, and eats the bodies of his Saracen enemies. In the adaptation of one of the shorter stories for performance in the *Miracles de Nostre Dame par personnages*, the relationship between Robert and his merry men is more developed, as they have names and discuss their exploits together.[13] On hearing that his father has outlawed him, he encourages them:

Seigneurs, ne vous desconfortez!
Nous sommes en bonne forest,
Et si avons fort qui bon est
Et s'avons des vivres assez.

Lords, do not despair!
We are in a good forest,
And we have a lot of what is good [a lot of good things]
And we have enough to live on.[14]

Unlike those for whom the forest is an alien place or a place of wilderness and hardship, for Robert – as for Robin Hood – the forest is a source of plentiful provision. He welcomes his exile and says that his father will soon be made to pay for his decision. After his conversion, Robert is depicted (very briefly) asking his men to join him, although he still kills them all when they refuse to repent and change their ways. He presents himself as God's avenging angel:

Puis que vous estes touz d'accort
D'ainsi en mal perseverer,
Diex ne vous laira point durer.
Car je, pour li, sanz plus attendre,
Vueil de vous touz venjance prendre.

Since you are all in agreement
To continue thus in evil,
God will not allow you to live any longer,
So I, on his behalf, without any more waiting,
Intend to take vengeance on you all.[15]

He may have just begun to turn his life around, but Robert has not changed much, yet. In his fool's persona, Robert is referred to by the lower-class diminutive 'Robinet', as he has become a servant. In de Worde's English version, there is a description of the woodland lodge where Robert takes up his abode:

> he [Robert] lete make in a thycke wylde foreste a stronge house, wherein he made his dwellynge place, and this place was wylde and strong, and more meter for wylde beestes, than for any people to abyde in, and there Robert assembled and gadered for his company, all the moost myscheuouste and falsest theues that he coude fynde or heere of in his faders lande, to wete morderers, theues, streterobers, rebelles, brenners of chyrches and houses, forsers of women, robbers of chyrches, and the moost wyckest and curseste theues that were under the sone. Robert had gadered to doo hym seruyce wherof he was Capytayne . . .
>
> He ordered a fortified house to be made in the thick, wild forest, wherein he made his dwelling place, and this place was wild and strong, and better suited to wild beasts than for any people to live in, and there Robert assembled and gathered to be his company the most mischievous and falsest thieves that he could find or hear of in his father's land; to wit murderers, thieves, highwaymen, rebels, burners of churches and houses, rapers of women, robbers of churches, and the most wicked and cursed thieves under the sun. Robert had gathered [them] to serve him, and he was their Captain . . .[16]

We are not told what Robin Hood's lodge looks like, but in the *Lytell Geste* we are told that he has one. On sending his men out to find someone to ambush, Robin tells them to 'Bringhe hym to lodge to me,' and Sir Richard having been taken, 'they brought hym to the lodge dore.'[17]

Not only does Robert, in his unredeemed state, live with his men in the forest, in some versions of the story he returns to it, rejecting the offer of an empire and a duchy, and of the emperor's beautiful daughter as his wife. He becomes a hermit (a different type of self-exile) in the forest, and he dies there.

> *En la fin morut el boscage,*
> *La u il ert en l'ermitage*
>
> In the end he died in the woods
> In the place where he had his hermitage.[18]

In the same way, of course, Robin leaves the royal court in the *Lytell Geste* to return to the greenwood, where he tests the Virgin's favour by shooting a great deer with his bow and arrows, and is gladdened by the sight of an outlaw band of young men drawn to him by his reputation:

> And gadred them to gyder
> In a lytell throwe
> Seuen score of wyght yonge men . . .
>
> And there met together
> In a little while
> Seven score [140] fit young men . . .[19]

At the very least, these similarities indicate that Robin's greenwood/forest is a 'romance' space. They may also result from a more direct intertextual relationship between *Robert le Diable* and Robin Hood.

In reality, forests were rapidly diminishing during the later Middle Ages, even in the northwest of England, where drainage and assarting (clearing the woodland for agriculture) were pushing back the trees. By the fifteenth century most of England's woodland was managed.[20] The term 'forest' had always referred to a legal-geographical space, in particular the royal forest, which was ruled by punitive, even cruel, forest laws. Emparkment, or the enclosing of woodland as private space for keeping and hunting deer, was increasing rapidly, too.[21] It is the *romance* idea of the forest that is celebrated in the Robin Hood stories. The romance forest is a place of encounter between the human and the spiritual, or the supernatural, for good or ill. It is here that Sir Orfeo encounters the wild hunt, where Marie de France's Bisclavret turns into a werewolf, where Chrétien de Troyes' Perceval first sees a knight, and where the Wife of Bath's knight-rapist sees the fairy dance and meets the 'hag' who tells him what women want.[22] In the forest, or the deep wood, a human being becomes lost and disorientated; frighteningly, they lose their agency. Orfeo is reunited with his wife 'by chance'; he does not find her himself. Sir Gawain comes upon the Green Chapel with its Green Knight rather than actually finding it. The 'king lost in the forest' is a popular romance trope. It is when lost in the forest that King Solomon comes to the house of the peasant Marcolf, and it is when he is lost while hunting that King John falls into the hands of Fouke FitzWaryn and his gang. This is not good for either of them: Solomon's wisdom and his authority will be challenged, bested even, by the wily peasant, and John will be forced to back down and restore Fouke's lands. Getting lost in the forest or the woods can also be beneficial, if scary: Thomas of Erceldoune is lost when he meets the fairy lady who will eventually give him the gift of prophecy and song, and (in a story widely popular in medieval Europe) Partenope of Blois is lost on a hunting trip when he falls into the power of his fairy lover.[23] Thomas and Partenope are found worthy: the judgement of the forest, like that of the sea, is a true and a fair one, because it is divine. Women and children tend to fare better, as the forest is more merciful to the powerless than is the social world. In the *Miracle de Nostre Dame de l'abbesse grosse* (The Miracle of Our Lady of the Pregnant Abbess), the Virgin Mary herself delivers the abbess's baby in the woods. In another of the *Miracles*, it is in the woods that the beleaguered princess Berthe prays to the Virgin, and is helped to triumph over her enemies.[24]

As a result of this loss of agency or control, going to the woods could also be a type of shorthand for losing one's mind. This may derive from Platonic ideas concerning the mind, in which the *silva* (wood), without pathways, is a metaphor for a chaotic memory or mind.[25] In the *Morte Darthur*, both Lancelot and Tristan go to the woods and live like 'wildmen' when rejected by their respective lovers, Guinevere and Isolde. With his wife in the hands of the fairy king, Sir Orfeo leaves his kingdom to his steward and takes to the woods, where 'ever he liveth in gret malais'.[26] It is in the woods that Merlin the prophet goes crazy in the *Vita Merlini*.[27] The speaker of one of the lyrics in the 'Harley' manuscript, considering that he may not be able to find a lover, contemplates the alternative with desperation:

> Yef me shal wonte wille of on,
> This wunne weole y wole forgon
> Ant wyht in wode be fleme.
>
> If I don't get my way with one [a woman]
> This happy joy I will forgo
> And right now [I'll] become a fugitive in the woods.[28]

For most people in the medieval world, the woods marked the boundaries of their communities. Medieval people were, of course, more mobile than was once thought. They were used to travelling, especially around their local area. They travelled by known roads and tracks, and knew where the boundaries of their community were. These boundaries might be marked by stones, ancient trees, streams, or by other natural or artificial landmarks. Towns and cities often had walls and ditches, and within them streets, alleyways, buildings or garden walls could mark the boundaries of parishes. Parishioners traversed their boundaries in procession every year, hitting them with sticks, 'bumping' children's bottoms on them, praying over them.[29] Their sense of personal and communal identity was grounded in this geography. The wood lay just outside these boundaries, like the sea and the prison, familiar in its continued everyday presence, but mysterious and therefore dangerous in its depths.[30] For the elite hunter, who had absorbed romance tales of the woods and forests, it was a place of adventure where he could pit his wits against both the nature of wild animals and the forces of darkness. The hunt, therefore, was as much spiritual and moral as it was practical. Not to catch one's quarry, or as in the case of the king in the *Lytell Geste of Robyn Hode*, not to find anything to chase, was to fail morally and spiritually. Just as the demonic fairy king in *Sir Orfeo* catches nothing from his hunting, so the king who goes to Plumpton Park and 'fails of his deer' is confronted with his own moral and spiritual failings. That he catches nothing or has nothing to catch (we are not sure which) is a sign of the Virgin Mary's, and therefore of God's, disfavour. Being a king, he is unlikely to go hungry, but he will lose face dramatically in the eyes of his noble guests, and his kingship will be diminished. The poacher, on the other hand, is like the fox: he moves silently and alone, and he knows his way in the pathless wilderness, just as dangerous people, such as outlaws, do. And the poacher, like them, is a criminal.

In romance stories, the woods are a frightening place; they are timeless and yet in time, unstable, mutable, *female*. To enter the forest, to hunt, kill your prey and survive, or to meet Robin Hood and survive (at least, with your purse and your dignity intact), was like entering the body of a woman and coming out again – it both threatened moral dissolution and enhanced the masculine power of those who could negotiate it, obtain its benefits, and return to the world within their own boundary.[31] It is no accident that Arthurian knights, when on quests, spend much of their time going round and round, getting lost in forests. Robert of Normandy, like so many romance heroes, is young, learning how to rule well before he becomes a ruler in his own right. Social human beings who become lost, or are abandoned in the forest (or on the sea), are in danger according to their deserts, because the forest (like the sea) is governed by divine rather than by human authority. Divine authority is often exercised through the Virgin Mary, as in the *Miracles*. This is particularly dangerous, as both the *Miracles* and Robin Hood stories demonstrate, for people of power. The penitent, the deserving, the young and the weak are saved, while the powerful learn valuable but often very painful lessons about themselves and the nature of their authority.

The nature of authority is important in the Robin Hood stories, as in all romance stories. Romance rulers may be ill informed, duped, deluded and poorly advised, but they are not usually evil. It *is* tough being a king, as these stories accept: rulers must recognize and hold in balance the opposing forces that surround them in order to provide peace and stable government. Besides, supporters who are clever and skilled in arms are no mean assets. Heroes such as Robin Hood are loyal to a king who actually wants to pardon them and obtain their services, but needs the occasion and the excuse to do so. The 'comely king' Edward admires what he has heard of Robin Hood, and sets out to meet him in the forest. When he learns of the outlaws' loyalty, he is quick to offer pardon, food and fee. In dressing as one of Robin's favourite potential victims – an abbot – and in going to the greenwood, he places himself voluntarily in Robin's hands. He very willingly dons Robin's livery of green cloth: in fact, he himself asks to buy some. The threat from the outlaws in this scenario is a real one, however, and the king (like the elite hunter – and in the *Geste* Robin becomes a 'green hart' for the sheriff to hunt) is demonstrating both his leadership and his courage. The citizens of Nottingham have suffered violence before at the hands of these outlaws, and they are quite willing to believe that their city will be taken, and they and their families killed.

> All the people of Notyngham
> They stode and behelde
> They sawe nothynge but mantels of grene
> That covered all the felde
> Than euery man to other gan say,
> 'I drede our kynge be slone.
> Come Robyn hode to the towne, I wys,
> On lyve he left never one.'
> Full hastily they be gan to fle
> Both yemen and knaves
> And old wyves that myght evyll goo,
> They hypped on theyr staves . . .

> All the people of Nottingham
> they stood and watched;
> they saw nothing but cloaks of green
> that covered the whole field.
> Then everyone began to say to the other,
> 'I fear our king is slain.
> If Robin Hood comes into town, I believe,
> He'll not leave anyone alive.'
> They began to flee as quickly as they could,
> Both yeomen and boys,
> And old women who found it hard to run,
> They hopped along on their sticks . . .

The king laughs (which is somewhat ungenerous of him, given the panic the townsfolk are in) and takes control, reassuring the citizens (somewhat) by revealing that he is in Robin's company.

Hunting had a continuous presence in the medieval world, as aristocratic entertainment and as employment, on a regular (within the household) and a casual basis. This hunter, on a misericord in Gloucester Cathedral, is dressed in a similar costume to the Antwerp 'Robin Hood'.

When they se our comly kynge
I wys they were full fayne
They ete and dranke and made them glad
And sange with notes hye

When they saw our comely king
I believe they were very relieved,
They ate and drank and were very glad
And sang loudly[32]

A tense situation is soothed, and a settlement brokered by the king in much the same way as Henry II steps in to end the private wars between the FitzWaryns and their Welsh neighbours:

Le roy Henri dona a Lewys le fitz Yervard, enfant de .vii. anz Jonette, sa fyle, e en mariage lur dona Ellesmere e autres terres plusours; si men Lewys a Loundres ou ly. Le prince Yervard ou sa meyné prist congié du roy, e s'en ala vers Gales, si dona a Rogier de Powys Blauncheville e Maylour.

King Henry gave to Lewis [Llewellyn] FitzYervard, a child of seven years, little Joan, his daughter, and gave them on their

> marriage Ellesmere and much other land; he took Lewis [Llewellyn] to London with him. Prince Yervard and his following took leave of the king, and went towards Wales; he [Henry] gave Blancheville and Mylor to Roger of Powys.[33]

This contrasts with King John, who seems to have been particularly problematic as a ruler, and who is depicted in the *chanson* of Fouke FitzWaryn as a bad king and a bad man. Having been captured by Fouke, he has to be pressured to do the right thing:

> *'Sire roy', fet Fouke, 'ore je vous ay en mon bandon. Tel jugement foi je de vous come vous vodrez de moy, si vous me ussez pris.' Le roy trembla de pour, quar il avoit grant doute de Fouke.*
>
> 'Lord king,' said Fouke, 'Now I have you in my power. Shall I pass the same sentence on you as you wanted to do to me, if you had taken me?' The king trembled with fear, because he had a great distrust of Fouke.[34]

In a similar situation to the comely King Edward but unlike him, John responds in a less than kingly manner:

> *Fouke jura qu'il morreit pur le grant damage e la desheritesoun qu'il avoit fet a ly e a meint prodhome d'Engleterre. Le roy ly cria mercy, e ly pria pur amour Dieu la vie, e yl ly rendreyt Fouke jura qu'il morreit pur le grant damage e la desheritesoun qu'il avoit fet a ly e a meint prodhome d'Engleterre. Le roy ly cria mercy, e ly pria pur amour Dieu la vie, e yl ly rendreyt enterement tou[t] son heritage . . .*
>
> Fouke swore that he should die on account of the great harm and the disinheritance he had carried out against him and many worthy men of England. The king cried out for mercy, and begged for his life, for the love of God, and he would restore the whole of his inheritance to him . . .[35]

The generous aristocratic hero gives ground, and shows mercy to the beleaguered but cowardly king. The poor old Duke of Normandy has no chance with his terrible son Robert 'the Devil', however. On being chastized for his behaviour, the son simply tells his father:

Vous avez tort, pére, de moy
Blasmer, et perdez vostre paine.
Ne cuidez point que je me paine
De bien faire: n'en ay talent.

You are wrong, father, to
Reproach me, and are wasting your time.
Don't imagine that I can be bothered
To turn good: I just don't have the will.[36]

In the *Lytell Geste* the comely King Edward is happy, it seems, to allow Robin Hood to have sovereignty over his own 'kingdom' in the greenwood. All these outlaws want, ultimately, is to submit to royal authority and the king's law. What they really want is a good king and just laws – in their own eyes – which work in their own interests. What the king wants is local leaders who will be loyal and who will rule their 'countries' on his behalf, above all keeping the peace. The situation in *Robin Hood and the Monk* is somewhat different, though. The king in this story has failed to balance and control the opposing forces within his kingdom. He fears loss of face, and the loss of authority that accompanies it. His response to being tricked by Little John is a wistful one; his only course of action is to accept defeat and the death of his officer, the sheriff, then to cover it up. This is a canny decision, but it could have been avoided by knowing, and choosing, his servants better.[37]

Even the wisest of kings suffers from being lost in the forest. This happens to the wisest king of all (according to the Old Testament) in the *Solomon and Marcolf* stories, which seem to have been especially popular in central Europe during the fifteenth century, although they were more widely known than this.[38] Interestingly, Marcolf's name may have been derived from the Old English *marc wulf*, a wolf who prowls the boundaries, and therefore he can be classified as an outlaw in the sense of Wulf in *Wulf and Eadwacer*.[39] Marcolf is a wily peasant who counters the legendary (biblical) wisdom of King Solomon with his own practical wit. He embodies the challenging voice of practical wisdom versus the learned, philosophical ideas of Solomon, whose wisdom is a special gift from God.[40] The *Dialogue*, in its printed version, consists of at least three elements: a visit to Solomon by Marcolf and his wife with an exchange of proverbial sayings, an encounter in the forest at Marcolf's home, and a return visit to Solomon's court by Marcolf, where the king finally loses his temper with his visitor and Marcolf is sentenced to death. The second and third elements, in which the king visits Marcolf and Marcolf visits the king in turn, have similarities with the so-called 'king and commoner' stories represented by the texts of *King Edward and the Shepherd* and *The Kynge and the Barker*.

In the second element, Solomon is out hunting when he comes upon a house. Without dismounting from his horse, the king looks in at the door and asks who is inside. From inside, the peasant Marcolf says, 'Wythin is an hool man, and an half, and an horse hede, and the more that they ascende, the more they downe falle.'[41] He explains that he is the 'entire' man, Solomon is the half man (because he's only partly inside, as is the horse's head), and the rising and falling things are the beans boiling in the cooking pot. After another series of riddles, which the king again fails to solve, Solomon has to leave, but before leaving he sets a riddle of his own: Marcolf's mother should send him the next day a pot of milk from her best cow, covered by material from the same cow. She is equal to the task, filling the pot and covering it with a caul made of the same cow's milk. On his way to deliver the milk, Marcolf grows hungry. So he eats the caul and covers the pot with a cowpat from the field. When Solomon demands to know why the pot is covered with cow turd, Marcolf replies that the king simply said it should be covered 'of the same cow' – and so it is.[42]

Marcolf remains with the king, making proverbial statements ('men may not trust women', 'nature is more powerful than learning') and proving them; Marcolf tells his sister the 'secret' that he intends to kill the king, then picks a quarrel with her in front of the king, during the course of which she reveals what was told her in confidence. Marcolf releases three mice in front of the king's cat, which cannot resist chasing the third. The king, who has threatened Marcolf with death if he cannot prove his statements, becomes angrier and angrier with each of his guest's 'proofs'. He tells Marcolf to leave or he will set the hounds on him, but Marcolf releases a live hare from underneath his clothes to distract them, and works his way back into the king's presence. Told to be careful how he behaves or else – 'Beware that thys daye thou spytte not but upon the bare grownde' (Beware that you don't spit except on the bare ground today) – Marcolf spits on a bald man's head and is brought before the king again. The aggrieved bald man challenges Solomon's authority: 'Wherto is this moost vyle rybaulde sufferyd in the kings presence us to rebuke and shame? Lete hym be kast out!' (Why is this coarse man suffered to be in the king's presence to rebuke and shame us? Let him be cast out!)[43]

Eventually, King Solomon flies into a rage and commands Marcolf to leave on pain of death: 'Go from hens out of my sight, and I charge thee that I se thee no more betwixt the eyes' (Get out of my sight, and I order you not to let me see you again between my eyes). So, Marcolf leaves the palace with his shoes on backwards and backward-facing bear's feet on his hands (the origin of the 'backwards' horseshoes trope as found in *Fouke* and *Eustace the Monk*?). The next morning Solomon hears reports of a fantastic beast's footprints, and he sets out to hunt it. Just outside of town, he finds an old oven, in which Marcolf has taken refuge, and peers into it – to find himself face to face with the peasant's bare backside, which Marcolf has left facing out of the oven. His defence for this huge insult is that Solomon is no more looking at him 'betwixt the eyes', but into the crack of his ass instead. Solomon flies into a rage and orders Marcolf to be hanged. The wily peasant escapes his fate by being allowed to choose the tree from which he will hang. Of course, he never finds a suitable tree, so in the end everyone gets fed up and goes home. Solomon's 'rage beyond reason' is similar to the unreasoning rage that characterizes rulers in other trickster stories and the sheriff in Robin Hood tales. Enraging rulers, therefore, seems to be one of the outlaw/trickster's main aims. It adds weight to William Caxton's suggestion that stories such as this, including those of Robin Hood, are actually more about the victims than the perpetrators. They may have been seen as warnings against the consequences of allowing oneself to be consumed with unreasoning anger, whatever the provocation.[44] Generally speaking, medieval advice, even to kings and princes, would be, 'Don't go down to the woods, you can get seriously lost.' If you do get lost, it will help if you are in the good offices of the Blessed Virgin. Then perhaps she – or perhaps her *yeman* Robin Hood – will help you.

SIX

Robin Hood and Other Tricksters

The *Solomon and Marcolf* tradition does not have a parallel in the existing Robin Hood stories per se, but it does appear in the same manuscripts as *Robin Hood and the Potter* (Cambridge, University Library, MS Ee.4.35) and *Robin Hood and the Monk* (Cambridge University Library, MS Ff.5.48) in the form of *The Kynge and the Barker* and *A Tale of King Edward and the Shepherd* respectively. In both of these stories a king wanders off by himself, gets lost and meets a member of the lower classes. Not recognizing the king (why would he?), the 'churl' freely offers his companion a piece of his mind, on the state of government and the impact of the king's officers on his local community.

In *King Edward the Third and the Shepherd*, the king meets a shepherd called Adam while wandering by a river (as in *pastourelles*).[1] They talk, and Adam tells the incognito king about the abuses of purveyance (providing for the court's needs by purchasing goods and services from local resources) by the king's officials. Edward says that he is a merchant whose son serves the queen; as a result he can help obtain payment. Adam demands four pounds and two pence, and offers the 'merchant' seven shillings – a considerable sum – for his trouble. The shepherd must come to court the next day, and ask at the door for 'Joly Robyn' the merchant. Adam takes the merchant home, where he plays a drinking game (a recurring motif in this type of story, equivalent to the 'pluck buffet' game of the *Lytell Geste*), then offers his guest poached venison and cony (rabbit). He shows his new friend his basement store of poached meat and wines. The next day Adam goes to court and asks for 'Joly Robyn' at the entrance.

He is admitted, and asked to be Robyn's honoured guest at dinner. On being told that his host is the king, Adam is terrified; he kneels and begs forgiveness. The rest is missing; it is unlikely that the king's mercy was not forthcoming, but the detail surrounding his forgiveness might have been interesting to compare with other examples. The names here are interesting, too, as Edward is the name given to the king in the *Lytell Geste* episode, and of course the name Robin is used for the king's alter ego.[2] There may be some cross-fertilization, although Robin is regularly used as a 'peasant' name in medieval literature. Edward III had a magnificent reputation in the fifteenth century as a model king, which is very likely the reason why his name is adopted by the author of this story about enlightened kingship, although it could just as easily refer to his father, Edward II, or even his grandfather Edward I. 'Edward' just implies a king of the recent, but not too recent, past, because every king of England between 1272 and 1377 had that name, anyway, along with two Princes of Wales who did not succeed to the throne. The element of political satire is strong here, with both the king and the shepherd the object of criticism. The king, a personage to be feared, allows his officers to abuse his subjects in his name, and Adam is a flawed individual, a criminal and a braggart who is a little too sure of himself and a wee bit too clever for his own good. The king remains in control, as he does not in the *Lytell Geste*, and Robin Hood does not display similar character flaws to those of Adam the peasant (who is more like Gautier in *Robin et Marion*) – not in the *Lytell Geste* story, anyway.

In the other Cambridge manuscript, *The Kynge and the Barker* also features the romance trope of the king lost in the forest while hunting. This king meets a tanner riding along on his horse. The tanner is sitting on 'blake kow heydes', with the cows' horns still hanging from them. The king greets the strange apparition: he asks the way to Drayton Bassett, and the tanner obliges but refuses to ride with the king, as he has not yet had his dinner. The king offers to feed him well, but the tanner scorns his offer, saying, 'Y trow Y hafe more money yn mey pors [purse] / nar [than] thow hast yn theyne.'[3] Seeing the king's men approach, the tanner decides that caution is required, so he agrees to travel with the 'wayfarer'. When they meet Lord Basset, he and his servants kneel to the traveller, and the tanner realizes with whom he is travelling. He thinks he will be hanged. When they reach the King's Chase, the king asks the tanner to change horses, and he does so, but he removes his hides with the horned heads in case the king rides away with them. The king's horse sees the horns, thinks the Devil is on his back, and runs like mad. The tanner hits his head on an overhanging oak branch and is unhorsed, but the king 'had god game / and seyde, "Ser, thou rydyst to ffast"' (enjoyed himself a lot / and said, 'Sir, you ride too fast.')[4] The horses are changed again, and the two travellers swear friendship; no real harm is done, and everything is back where it should be. It is a short, funny story – any moral message appears to be about the value of keeping quiet about one's wealth, and of keeping one's mouth shut and being prepared to look like an idiot rather than insult the king. The artisan, rather than the (rather smug) king, is the butt of the joke. This is similar to the 'joke' that the king plays on Robin Hood in the *Lytell Geste*, and yet in that scenario the king finds himself in the outlaw's power, nonetheless. Kings, because of their nature, must be noble, and therefore cannot succeed in games of low cunning, where the churl outmatches them. This is not a bad thing, as it demonstrates the superiority of nobility. The game of 'pluck buffet' that the king plays with Robin Hood is like the avowal of friendship in the *Barker* story, but with added menace: the outlaws could overcome the fake abbot and his men at any time, and kill them out of hand. It is only their loyalty to the king that prevents them. In that respect, the story of the king in the forest in the *Lytell Geste* is closer to *King Edward and the Shepherd* than *The Kynge and the Barker*. What this shows is that stories may be generically similar, but the themes and particular elements they contain, along with their impact and their meaning, may vary considerably – the Robin Hood stories behave in this way, too.

The type of humour represented by these two stories, and possibly in the 'feast in the forest' trope from the *Lytell Geste*, can also be seen in stories of the German trickster Till Eulenspiegel.[5] *The Adventures of Till Eulenspiegel* – or *Howlglas* (Owl Mirror) in English, a translation of *Eulenspiegel* – were first printed in Strasbourg around the year 1500. Like the *Lytell Geste* of Robin Hood and the stories of Reynard the Fox, they were republished in the middle years of the sixteenth century. The *Till* stories, like those of the *Lytell Geste*, are individual texts that could be told as discrete units but have been arranged to give the appearance of happening in sequence, in chronological time. They begin with Till's birth and end with his death. The tales in between have both similarities and differences in relation to northwestern European trickster tales, but they are, like them, part of a pan-European culture of short moral stories that hammer home their point by making people laugh.[6]

Till, we are told, was born on a farm in the countryside, although on the edge of a forest, not in it. He is, therefore, an outsider by birth. Although his father is comfortably off, this makes Till a peasant. Unlike Robin Hood but like many noble outlaws and heroes of romance, Till travels, or wanders. He does not actually seek out victims, unlike Robin, nor does he send others to do so, as Robin does. He simply reacts to the situations in which he finds himself. He makes his own living, too, as an entertainer and an itinerant labourer inside the German states and on occasion outside. He is said to have visited the kings of both Denmark and Poland, travelling the trade routes of the Baltic, at this time dominated by the merchants of the powerful and wealthy Hanseatic League. Of course, he gets the better of both men, who nevertheless develop a liking, even affection, for him (as the emperor of Rome does for the 'fool' Robert of Normandy in *Robert le Diable*). Although he begins his life in the countryside, Till's exploits almost all take place in an urban setting. His victims are usually what might be described as of the middling sort: artisans, merchants and professionals of some kind. They usually have an inflated sense of their own importance and treat their servants badly. Till, like the other tricksters, tends to succeed by generating unreasoning anger in his hosts, whose pride, avarice and pretensions expose their soft underbellies and make them vulnerable. The anger exacerbates their vices; they turn on Till, and come to grief as a result. Working as a baker's boy, Till asks his master to improve his poor working conditions by giving him some light to work by, as bakers often work in the dark hours. The master, who is rather pompous and very mean, tells Till that he has never had to give his employees any light to work by; they worked by moonlight, and he must do the same. Till, then, does precisely as he is told; using the light of the moon to work by, he sifts the flour out of the window into the moonlit yard. Told by a furrier to make 'wolves' (a type of coat) out of valuable skins for some important court clients, he makes the fur into stuffed wolves. In both cases, Till has simply interpreted the instructions he has been given literally: 'You told me to make wolves. If you'd said, "Make me some wolf-coats," I'd have done that, too. And if I'd known I wasn't to earn any more gratitude, I wouldn't have used up so much energy.' Both masters bear a certain amount of guilt for the outcome, but neither really wants to admit it.[7]

Till is employed as a 'fool' and entertainer by the king of Denmark, who is pleased with his performance and values him highly. As a reward, he says that Till may have his horse shod with the very best horseshoes by his royal blacksmith. As a result, Till gets the blacksmith to shoe his horse with gold horseshoes held by silver nails. The king is shocked, but he realizes his own mistake, too, and his affection for Till is not diminished. Kings are more generous than tradesmen – but then kings are in far less danger of losing their social position along with their cash. When a priest is served much better than himself but the innkeeper and his wife make Till pay the same, Till waits until the priest has left, then defecates in his empty bed. When the lady of the house is shocked by the way in which the priest has apparently behaved, Till tells her that's what happens – he who gets food in greater quantity and of better quality can be expected to shit more as a result. Thus, although Till might be termed a trickster and was seen as such, his actions are not really 'tricks' in the same sense as those of Reynard, Eustace, Trubert or Robin Hood. He mostly reacts to what he is told to do by following the letter, rather than the spirit, of what he has been told. In this way he reveals the social and personal injustices suffered by the powerless at the hands of the powerful in all social degrees. The master is as powerful and as unjust in the eyes of the employee as princes can be in the eyes of their subjects.[8] He also reveals the absurdity of this situation and of the discourses – the forms and uses of language – that uphold it. By challenging the language of the social world, he also challenges its accepted norms and values. Robin Hood also does this when he challenges the discursive and social meaning of loans, of hospitality, of theft and of rulership. Till is a 'wise fool' who by his actions expresses the foibles, failings and frailties of social communities and of those who inhabit them – which is really the function of all great tricksters.

The stories do not tell us what Till Eulenspiegel looks like, as this is not important for the action. What is surmised of his appearance, like that of Robin Hood and Reynard, has been influenced by the woodcut images that accompanied the early editions. In Till's case, the images were designed by the great German engraver Albrecht Dürer, specifically to illustrate these stories. Like the Robin Hood image of Pynson's 1492 edition (copied by Leeu), images of Till are of a man in 'ordinary' late medieval riding dress. Both figures are defined by what they carry. Pynson's 'Robin' has a forester's bow and arrows, whereas Dürer's Till carries the owl and the mirror which became his iconic trademarks. The text tells us that Till left his identifying 'tag' drawn over the door of any building where he had played a trick. This was an owl and a mirror, under which he wrote in Latin, *Hic fuit* (he was here). When he was buried, we are told, a stone was placed over his grave depicting an owl grasping a mirror in its talons. *Eulenspiegel* literally means 'owl mirror', and, as stated, the English version of Till was entitled *Howlglas*. This demonstrates Till's dual nature; the owl, *bubo* in Latin, was associated with the Devil, but was also the familiar of the Greek goddess Athena, and therefore a creature of wisdom.[9] The mirror was part of guides to good rulership, as in the popular 'mirrors of princes' genre, but as well as truth, it also denoted vanity. In addition, the term *Eulenspiegel* is similar to Old Dutch/Flemish words meaning 'arse-wipe'.[10] As he encompasses all of these functions, Till is the complete and perfect 'fool'.

It is important for the early Robin Hood tradition that the challenge to authority in these stories, as in *Solomon and Marcolf*, comes from a non-elite person, a 'churl'. Most of the heroes who challenge authority are of high social status, even when they seem not to be. Even the slave girl Nicolette, in the French story of *Aucassin and Nicolette*, turns out to have been a princess, captured, enslaved and converted.[11] This is apparent, most of all, in the way they look. They will, regardless of sex or gender, be beautiful or handsome – in French, *bel* (male) or *bele* (female). Even the dreadful Robert of Normandy is good-looking. Lower-class people, peasants or churls – *vilains* in French – were supposed, at least in literature, to look physically different from their social betters. In the *Solomon and Marcolf* stories, the social status of Marcolf and his wife is obvious:

> This Marcolf was of short stature and thick. The head had he great, a broad forehead red and full of wrinkles or frouncys, his ears hairy and to the middys of chekes hanging, great eyes and running, his nether lyppe hanging like a horse, a beard hard and foul like unto a goat, the hands short and

blockish, his fingers great and thick, round feet, the nose thick and crooked, a face like an ass, and the hair of his head like the hair of a goat . . .

His wife was of short stature, and she was out of measure thick with great breasts, and the hair of her head clustered like thistles. She had long wide brows like the bristles of a swine, long ears like an ass, running eyes, bearded like a goat; her visage and skin black and full of wrinkles, and upon her great breasts she had, of a span broad, a brooch of lead.[12]

In the *Morte Darthur* Sir Tor is brought to Camelot by his 'father' Aries, a cowherd. That Tor is really not this man's son would be immediately obvious to Malory's audience by his appearance and his preferences. Aries says that he has thirteen sons, 'and all they will fall to what labour I put them and will be right glad to do labour, but this child will not labour for nothing that my wife and I may do, but always he will be shooting or casting darts, and glad for to see battles and to behold knights.' Aries's sons are all 'shaped much like the poor man', but Tor is fit and handsome. It is no surprise at all when his mother reveals that she was raped, *pastourelle*-style, by a knight (now King Pellinore) and that Tor is his son.[13] The hierarchical order is thereby rendered natural and ordained by God. Nature will reflect this order, even if nurture does not support it.

The difference between high and low was exacerbated by education and upbringing – *noriture* – which taught the young aristocrat to be *courtois*, both in nature and in behaviour. The difference between *courtois* and *vilain* was crucially important in later medieval society – hence the proliferation of deportment books or books of manners, in English, produced for the aspirational professional and middle/merchant classes in the fifteenth century. This was not just being 'courteous'; it was vitally important to behave according to one's position (or one's desired position) in the world. *Vilain* designates people of lower-class status or peasants, rural landscapes where manual labour is carried out, the moral sphere of the base and vile, crude words and expressions, and genres such as *fabliau* and 'trickster' tales.[14] These meanings are never far from the surface in Robin Hood stories. While on an exotic adventure in the northern seas, Fouke FitzWaryn encounters a group of outlaws. He and his companions are looking for supplies to restock their ship when they meet a young shepherd, who 's'en ala vers eux, e les salua de un latyn corumpus. Fouke ly demanda s'il savoit nulle viande a vendre en le pais' (approached them, and greeted them in corrupt Latin. Fouke asked if he knew of any food for sale in the land). The shepherd takes them into a cave, where he asks them to wait while he summons a servant from a nearby hill. He blows six blasts on his horn, ostensibly to summon the servant, and then things take a different turn:

> *Bien tost vindrent sis gros e grantz vilaynz e fers, vestuz de grosse e vyls tabertz, e chescu avoit en sa meyn un gros bastoun dir e fort, e, quant Fouke les vist, si avoit suspecion de mavesté. Les sis vyleinz entrerent une chamber, e osterent lur tabeertz, e se vestirent de un scarlet vert e sodliés d'orfreez, e de tous atirs furent auxi richement atireez come nul roy poeit estre . . .*
>
> Very soon six big, tall and fierce peasants arrived, wearing coarse and dirty tabards; each one had in his hand a large club, hard and strong, and when Fouke saw them he suspected trouble. The six churls went into a chamber, took off their tabards, and dressed themselves in scarlet and green cloth, with shoes embroidered with gold: costumed in this attire they were as richly dressed as any king might be . . .[15]

The men demand that Fouke and his men play chess with them, and each man in turn loses, until Fouke refuses to play. Told to play or fight, Fouke draws his sword, and he and his friends 'ocistrent tous les vilyenz glotouns' (killed all of the *vilain* scum).[16] The author makes clear to his audience that these men are *vilains*, churls, and that they are also violent, cunning and generally 'peasant scum'. Their weapons are *bastouns*, large clubs often studded with nails. These are churls' weapons, unlike the sword with which Fouke dispatches them. These outlaws live in a cave, and yet they have stores of food and of rich cloth, together with other luxury items such as chessboards and pieces. They can also ape their betters by speaking Latin (albeit corrupted) and playing the aristocratic game of chess. In addition, they wear scarlet and green. These men make Robin Hood and his outlaws look very civilized, but they also have much in common with them. Is this how a truly noble outlaw like Fouke would see Robin and his men? They are brutish, living in a beast-like habitat, dangerous and thuggish, making their social betters welcome with a meal before making a mockery of them and then robbing (and most likely killing) them.

One of the most dangerous and reprehensible things about these cave dwellers, from a noble or 'official' point of view, is the way in which they conceal their true nature behind a facade of noble dress and manners. You were what you appeared to be, and so it was desirable to demonstrate one's character and status by means of one's appearance. This is the reason why Robin Hood, on learning of Sir Richard atte Lee's financial problems, gives Sir Richard new clothing and attendants commensurate with his status as a knight:

'Moche wonder thinketh me
Thy clotynge is so thine . . .'
. . .
'Master,' than sayde lityll John,
'His clothing is full thynne.
Ye must gyue the knight a lyueray
To helpe his body therin.'

'I wonder greatly that
Your clothing is so thin . . .'
. . .
'Master,' said Little John then,
'His clothing is very thin.
You must give the knight a suit of clothes
To help his body in.'[17]

By the end of the fourteenth century, the fundamental nature of 'noblesse' was a matter for debate, as Chaucer's Wife of Bath points out, when her ugly, dirty old woman asserts the superior value of her own nobility of nature over that of her rapist knight:

But, for ye speken of swich gentillesse
As is descended out of old richesse,
That therefore sholden ye be gentil men
Swich arrogance is nat worth an hen.
Looke who that is moost virtuous always,
Pryvee and apert, and moost entendeth ay

To do the gentil deedes that he kan;
Taak hym for the grettest gentil man.
Crist wole we clayme of hym oure gentillesse,
Nat of oure eldres for hire old richesse.

But, as you speak of such nobility
As is descended from ancient riches,
And that therefore you should be gentlemen –
Such arrogance isn't worth a hen!
In private and public, who tries the hardest
To do all the noble deeds that he can,
I take him for the greatest gentleman.
We should claim our nobility from Christ,
Not from our ancestors because of their inherited wealth.[18]

The rise of a wealthy, aspirational middle class challenged and changed the perception of *vilain* and *courtois*. Robin Hood and his men are definitely not noble in status, as the poems stress over and over again. The Middle English term *yeman* does not refer to an aristocrat; it relates either to a wealthy, high-ranking non-noble or to a servant.[19] Yet Robin Hood in particular, and his men generally, exhibit *courtois* behaviour. This is not intended to be a joke; Robin and his men are not making themselves look ridiculous. Like Chaucer's hag, the poet may be delivering a rebuke to members of the higher, *gentil*, class. In the *Lytell Geste* the abbot of St Mary's is a member of the clergy, the First Estate, and would probably come from a noble, or at least a gentry, family. Yet his speech and his behaviour are noticeably *vilain*:

The abbot sware a full grete othe
By god that dyed on a tree
Get the londe where thou may
For thou getest none of me . . .
. . .
The abbot lithely on hym gan loke
And *vylaynesly* hym gan loke [my italics]

The Abbot swore a great big oath,
By God that died on a tree,

> Get yourself land where you can,
> For you'll get none from me . . .
> The abbot quickly began to look at him
> and looked at him in a churl's manner.[20]

Class divisions are here turned on their heads; the outlaws are noble in both dress and behaviour, while the higher clergy and their monks speak and behave like a load of churls. This makes the clergy's speech and behaviour all the more shocking and all the more reprehensible. They are acting against what should be their God-given nature, or *kynde* to use the medieval term, and thus against the will of their Maker. It could be a joke, as in the mock romance *Audigier*, where what is base is exalted at the expense of the courtly and the 'high'.[21] An ill-equipped, poorly dressed knight would arouse suspicions of cowardice and ineptitude, as in *Audigier*; this is what Robin Hood sees when Sir Richard atte Lee is brought to him, and why he asks cheeky questions about how the knight got to be so poor.[22]

The audiences of romance stories seem to have expected outlawry situations to require a funny story of trickery and/or disguise. Little sections of humour are regularly inserted into otherwise serious-minded, violent stories: Fouke FitzWaryn escapes from his pursuers by turning his horse's shoes back to front in the snow; Hereward the Wake (in the *Liber Eliensis*) disguises himself as both a potter and a fisherman; Robert of Normandy, because of the crusading, anti-Semitic nature of his background, plays nasty, unnecessary tricks on Jews. On one occasion, he makes a Jew fall into a muddy puddle in his wedding clothes, and in another he makes a Jew kiss his dog's ass. In both cases Robert is acting in his fool's identity, and the action makes everybody laugh. Disguising one's true identity, and exercising the cunning of the trickster, is a low-born, *vilain* form of behaviour. In the story of *Witasse le Moine* (Eustace the Monk), Eustace is a real master of disguise who becomes so many different characters that his enemy, the Count of Boulogne, exclaims in desperation that he has begun to think everyone he meets is Eustace.[23] Outlaws like Fouke FitzWaryn and Hereward the Wake are noble, *courtois*, and only exhibit such behaviour in very few, very extreme circumstances – if they really have to. Even arch-disguiser Eustace the Monk has a just cause; his father has been murdered and his inheritance unjustly confiscated. The writer refers to Eustace's works as 'vile', and yet his characterization is very appealing in its exuberance. The unlawful loss of his family's possessions also raises the sympathy of the audience for Eustace, and offers a reason for his later actions. What he does is partly a quest for revenge and justice, and partly trickery for its own sake, for the sheer love of it. In this Eustace is comparable to Robin Hood. Robin cannot resist the urge to dupe the sheriff – why else would he dress as a potter and infiltrate the sheriff's home when he has no need to? This sense of 'play', which is central to the Robin Hood stories, can be found to some extent in Eustace the Monk. Eustace cannot resist making fun of his fellow monks at Saumer:

Il faisoit les moignes juner
Quant se devoient ester desjuner;
Il les faisoit aler nus piés
Quant devoient ester cauchiés.
Wistasce lor faisoit mesdire
Quant devoient lor eures dire;
Wistasce lor faisoit mesprendre
Quant devoient lor grasces rendre.

He made the monks fast
When they ought to have been breaking their fast;
He made them walk around in bare feet
When they should have been in bed.
Eustace had them gossiping
When they were supposed to be saying their Hours;
Eustace had them up to no good
When they should have been giving thanks.[24]

His deliberate playfulness makes Eustace as much a trickster as he is a heroic victim attempting to right the wrongs that have been done to himself and his family. Eustace's inclination towards deception and trickery is explained by making him a student of experimental science and the demonic:

Puis ke de Toulete revint
Ou il ot apris nigremanche,
N'ot home el roiaume de Franche

Ki tant seüst ars ne caraudes;
A maintes gens first maintes caudes.
Il avoit a Toulete esté
Tout .I. ivier et .I. esté
Aval sous terre en .I. abisme
Ou parloit au malfé meïsme
Qui li aprist l'enghine et l'art
Qui tout le mont dechoit et art.

After he returned from Toledo,
Where he had learned necromancy,
There was not a person in the kingdom of France
Who knew so much about magic and spells.
He cast many spells on many people.
At Toledo, he had been
A whole winter and summer
Under the ground in a cave
Where he communed with the Devil himself
Who taught him the skill and the knowledge
By which everyone is deceived and tricked.[25]

For part of his internal exile, Eustace lives in the woods as a temporary 'greenwood outlaw' – like Fouke FitzWaryn and Robert the Devil. A permanent greenwood-dwelling trickster was Reynard the Fox, the hero – or anti-hero – of beast fables in which King Noble the lion and his courtiers parody King Arthur and his Knights of the Round Table.[26] The stories are based on classical beast fables (especially those of Aesop); they developed in a Latin, clerical milieu in the middle of the twelfth century. As far as we know, the fox first raped the wolf's wife in the *Ysengrimus* (*c.* 1148–9); this act became the basis for the famous episode of 'Reynard's Trial', around which William Caxton's later (Dutch/Flemish) version is based.[27] The Reynard stories spread far and wide through the late 1100s and early 1200s, forming over twenty different 'branches' by around 1250. As well as the Low Countries, where he was Reynaerde, he became Reinhart in the German states and Rainaldo in the Italian states, all before 1250. Interestingly, there are no extant Reynard stories in English, although *The Fox and the Wolf* is a known Reynard episode ('Reynard traps Isengrin down a Well') derived from Branch IV of the Old French stories.[28] Of course, there is also a mention of Reynard's son, Russell, by Geoffrey Chaucer in his 'Nun's Priest's Tale' from *The Canterbury Tales*. As Kenneth Varty has shown, there are many likely references to a variety of Reynard stories in English medieval church art.[29]

Reynard's motivations for his 'crimes' – which include the wholesale murder of other animals, rape and serious bodily harm – are also those of human peasants: namely hunger and lust, in that order. He shares a secondary motive with the likes of Robin Hood and Eustace the Monk, though; he enjoys making others look stupid, and he also enjoys the simple act of getting what he wants from them. There are times when he comes close to looking like a fool, although he is both cunning and sly. This is not, however, a sign that he is necessarily intelligent in an educational sense. His intelligence is that of a cunning and streetwise *vilain*, a churl, although socially he is depicted as a noble. In Reynard's case, it is his animal nature that allows him, as a member of the high-class social elite, to behave like a *vilain*.[30] Reynard's streetwise guile and craft is, therefore, his chief attribute. As Eustace's enemy is the Count of Boulogne, Fouke's is Prince John, and Robin Hood's is the sheriff of Nottingham, so Reynard's nemesis is Isengrin the wolf. Like these others, Isengrin always comes off worse, but in an even more extreme way – he is flayed, tonsured, trapped down a well, stuck in ice, and in at least one variant of Reynard's duel (as in the Dutch example translated by Caxton) he is humiliated, beaten up and treated to mouthfuls of his opponent's pee, with which Reynard has filled his bushy tail. Reynard also cuckolds Isengrin; the fox commits adultery with Lady Hersent, Isengrin's wife, on several occasions, and on at least one occasion Reynard rapes her. In addition to publicly insulting his wife and his mistress, as well as other females such as Pinte the hen (whose daughters he has killed), and raping Hersent and Queen Fière, Reynard beats his own wife, the lady Erméline, black and blue on discovering that she plans to remarry after his supposed death. This is similar behaviour to that of Robert 'the Devil' of Normandy, but in Reynard's case is excused, or condoned, because of his fox's nature (and the fox symbolized the Devil in bestiary literature). Reynard has some features which are interesting in terms of the Robin Hood stories: he lives in the forest, he leaves it to steal (although Reynard's mission to assuage his perpetual hunger is not shared by the well-fed and watered outlaws of Sherwood), to play tricks on his enemies and on the unwary, and to create havoc. Like Robin Hood, Reynard patrols the boundaries of the woodland, relying on chance for the arrival of his victims. Also like Robin, he seizes opportunities as they arise, using his wit and his ability to dissemble and disguise to get what he wants from his victims. Reynard the fox is the prey-turned-hunter who is also a poacher and a thief, but unlike Robin Hood he has no higher motive than his own needs and pleasures.

Likewise, poaching and highway robbery are the activities of *vilains*, as references to Robin Hood in medieval court cases show.[31] It was not an easy decision for someone of gentle rank to take up such a life, as the author of a well-known poem on the abuses of Edward I's Trailbaston laws makes clear:

Ytel devendra leres que ne fust unque mès,
Que pur doute de prisone ne ose venir à pes;
Vivre covient avoir chescum jour adès;
Qy ceste chose comenca, yl emprist grant fes.

He will become a thief who was never one before,
Who for fear of prison dare not bring hostilities to an end;
One needs the means to live every day;
Whoever begins this thing, he has taken on a great task.[32]

This speaker, like Robert of Normandy and Robin Hood, sees the woods as a place of ease and of safety:

Vus qy estes endité, je lou, venez à moy,
*Al vert bois de Belregard, là n'y a nul ploy,**
Forque beste savage e jolyf umbroy;
Car trop est dotouse la commune loy.

You who have been indicted, I counsel you, come to me,
To the green wood of Belregard [beautiful aspect],
 where there is no plea
Only the wild beast and the lovely shade;
As the common law is too untrustworthy.[33]

In cases of deprivation, necessity for survival and unjust disinheritance, it was allowable for a *gentil* person, who should always be *courtois*, to speak and act in a *vilain* manner, but never to become so *within* themselves. To be *vilain* inside is the social sin of Robin Hood's opponents, but not of the man himself. Robin Hood, like the Robin character of Adam de la Halle, displays *courtois* manners and behaviour, and a noble nature, whatever his own class background.

It *is* possible for the medieval trickster to display courteous behaviour without being (overly) noble in mind, however, as is demonstrated by the French trickster Trubert. The only surviving medieval version, of collected stories arranged to seem chronological (like the *Lytell Geste* but contemporary with *Eustace* and *Fouke*), was written sometime in the first half of the thirteenth century by a writer who names himself as Douin (possibly Hardouin or Baudouin) de L'Avesne. The date of the manuscript is circa 1270, so a date earlier in the thirteenth century is most likely. The surviving version has been located by means of its dialect to the Picardy region of northern France.[34]

Trubert is undoubtedly amoral (or immoral); his exploits are, on one level, pure entertainment, intended to make an audience laugh. Like Reynard and Robin Hood, Trubert comes out of the woods, where he lives with his mother and sister. For a medieval audience, this would be easily identifiable as a parody of Chrétien de Troyes' *Conte du Graal* (Story of the Grail), in which the *naïf* hero, Perceval, is raised alone in his mother's house, with so little understanding of his late father's world that he thinks chain mail is ladies' finger rings sewn together. The family is poor, and although this makes Trubert a churl, a *vilain* character, he is neither a peasant nor an artisan. His trade, rather, is what we might call service provision; his widowed mother owns and runs a lodging house:

En la forest de Pontalie
Ote une fame herbergie
Vueve fame fu, sanz seigneur . . .

In the forest of Pontalie
Lived a female innkeeper
She was a widow, without a lord . . .[35]

This serves to identify Trubert more closely with those who made their living travelling the roads, those who lived on and around the margins of the social world, who moved in, out and through the dark woods that are also Robin Hood's environment. We are told that one day Trubert notices the threadbare condition of his sister's clothing, and determines to help by making some money. In a recognizable folktale trope, he takes the family cow and sells it, in Trubert's case for six sous. With five of these he buys a goat. Stumbling on some workmen in a church, he pays them to paint his goat in their bright, rainbow colours. Having nothing left apart from his goat, Trubert just happens to walk past the castle where the local lord, the aristocratic and super-rich Duke of Burgundy (also referred to in the story as the count), lives. The duke, whose name is (erroneously) Garnier, is not at home. His countess, however, is. Called by her maid to see Trubert's goat, she thinks it a marvel and determines to possess it. She sends the maid, called Aude (who has the same name as the ill-fated fiancée of the *chanson de geste* hero, Roland), to ask the price.[36] Trubert, like other trickster-heroes, is not greedy for money – he asks only for the going rate, plus a little bit extra 'in kind' for his trouble:

'Amis, la chievre nos vendez
S'il vos plet, et si en prenez
De nos deniers ce qu'elle vaut.'
'Dame,' fet il, 'se Deus me saut,
Je la vos vandrez volontiers:
Un foutre et cinc sous de deniers
La faz . . .'

'Friend, sell us the goat
If you please, and take
Of our coin what it's worth.'
'Lady,' he said, 'God keep me,
I will sell it to you willingly.
A fuck and five sous in cash
Will do it . . .'[37]

The horrified countess offers to pay as much money as Trubert wants, but he sticks to his price. Aude, like many of the female servants of romance stories, offers a down-to-earth solution:

Ne vous chaut, Dame, c'est uns fos,
Meintenant que sera montez
Descendra, et puis si avrez
La chievre qui tant par est bele.

Don't distress yourself, Lady, he's an idiot
No sooner has he got on than
He'll get off again, and then you'll have
The goat, which is so very lovely.[38]

Her opinion of Trubert is obvious, and will be proved wrong, of course. So the deal is done, and our hero gets into bed with the countess. Alas, as ever in such tales, her husband turns up prematurely, and the countess panics, urging Trubert to take his goat and go, while pressing large amounts of coin into his hands:

La dame a pris un cofinel
A son chevez, ou si joel
Estoient, et si ert toz plains
Du parisis et du charteins.
La dame en done au bachelor,
A ses jointiees, sanz conter . . .

The lady took a little chest
From the head of the bed, where her jewels
Were, and without further ado
She grabbed parisis and chartreins [coins of Paris
  and Chartres, 'good' money]
The lady gave them to the young man,
Into his open hands, without counting . . .[39]

Trubert walks away with his goat and handfuls of cash. On the way, he meets the duke, who also wants to possess the marvellous goat. Trubert asks for the same amount of money as he requested from the countess, once again with a little 'in kind':

. . . quatre peus du cul en avrai
Et cinc sous, ou point n'en vendrai . . .

... four hairs from your anus
And five sous, or I won't sell it at all.[40]

The duke is similarly horrified, but eventually he is prepared to swallow his pride and bend over in order to get the goat. The first extraction is so painful that it makes the duke bellow, and he offers Trubert the princely sum of one hundred marks to stop. Trubert once again accepts the money, and gives up the goat. When the duke gets home, his wife sees the goat and confesses all, in the mistaken belief that Trubert must have told him already. The duke forgives her readily, in a manner reminiscent of the way in which Noble the lion dismissed the adultery alleged against Reynard by Isengrin:

Ne vous chaut, dame, or vos levez,
Que ja por moi mal n'I avrez:
Bien puet une fame enginier
Cil qui decoit un chevalier!

Don't distress yourself, lady, now get up,
I cannot be angry with you.
He is well able to trick a woman
Who can deceive a knight![41]

Trubert goes back to the woods and gives the money to his mother, who is delighted. His sister gets some good new clothes.

The remaining stories follow a similar pattern. The duke decides to build a great hall to demonstrate his wealth and power. Trubert disguises himself as a master builder. He is well paid and lodged in good rooms in the castle, but he cannot sleep because his accommodation is too comfortable. Restless, he visits the duchess's room in the dark, pretending to be the duke, and 'serves' his hostess no fewer than thirteen times before returning to his room to sleep like a baby. When the real duke turns up, he is turned away by his wife who is, understandably, exhausted.[42] This nocturnal rejection makes Garnier very angry and very restless; it is he who cannot sleep. Trubert persuades the duke to accompany him into the woods to look for timbers for the new hall. He persuades Garnier to help him measure a large tree by embracing the trunk, then attaches him, painfully, to the trunk by tying his thumbs together with a piece of cord. Trubert beats the duke black and blue and steals his horses, only to sell them to some horse traders on the road. The same dealers try to sell the (now sore and untied) Garnier his own horses, and are soundly beaten by the duke's men until they identify Trubert as the culprit.

The duke becomes very sick after this ill treatment, and a doctor is sought from Montpellier. Trubert disguises himself as a doctor, carrying a pack full of herbs he has picked on the way. He picks up a handful of dog faeces in similar fashion, and adds them to his doctor's bag. Admitted to the duke's sickroom, he persuades the duchess and the servants that they must not disturb the cure by attending the duke, even if he cries out for them. This done, Trubert proceeds to truss up the duke in a peasant's basket and rub his skin with dog shit, including his face. Everyone ignores Garnier's impassioned cries, and Trubert leaves, ironically, with their thanks. In the morning, the duke's men go looking for Trubert, who is pointed out for them by the duchess in the castle grounds. Unfortunately, Trubert has exchanged clothes with the duke's nephew, and it is Garnier's nephew who is left 'dangling'. In the nephew's rusty armour, Trubert then saves the kingdom from invasion by convincing the invading king, Golias (another evocative name), that the duke's army are all madmen.[43] A truce is signed, and Golias agrees to marry Garnier's youngest daughter, Rosette ('little rose').

When the duke finds out about his nephew he is mad with sorrow and beside himself with rage, so he sends his men-at-arms into the woods to arrest Trubert at his mother's house. With no means of escape, Trubert puts on his sister's clothing, adopts a high-pitched voice and pretends to be a girl. There is muffled laughter when he says 'her' name – Coillebaude, or 'Scrotum-bawd' (or perhaps 'StrumpetBalls', or 'LaughingBalls' on the basis that a *bawde* is also a joke – all these meanings would have been perfectly obvious to Douin's audience). The pretty newcomer is accepted into the duke's family circle, becoming the companion of his naive and innocent youngest daughter, the same Rosette who is engaged to marry King Golias. Needless to say, Rosette does not remain very innocent with Coillebaude in her bed, and her mother the duchess soon begins to notice the telltale signs of pregnancy:

Roseite a la couleur changi:
Toute pale en son vis devint.

Rosette's complexion has altered
Her countenance has become very pale.[44]

Trubert saves him/herself by claiming to have had a dream vision in which Rosette has been left 'plaine d'angeloz' (full of angels) on account of an (blasphemous) immaculate conception.[45] Rosette's mother persuades Duke Garnier that his daughter cannot be married to the king after all, and her companion is suggested as a substitute bride. So Trubert, as Coillebaude, marries King Golias. S/he successfully navigates the wedding night by means of the darkness and the deft handling of a small drawstring purse hidden between her/his legs. During the night s/he pretends a need to get up for a pee in order to get out of the room, but her/his husband ties a piece of cord to her/his toe in order to make sure that s/he returns. Outside the room at last, Trubert finds a servant girl, and asks her if she would like to be a queen. Of course she would, and so he rapes her (because she's meant to be a recently deflowered bride), then takes the string from his toe and puts it on to hers. The servant returns to the king's bed as his wife. It is here that the stories run out, as does Trubert – slipping away into the darkness, leaving a servant-queen asleep in the arms of a king.

The stories of Trubert offer some interesting insights into the Old French/Anglo-French culture surrounding the Robin Hood tales. First, the Trubert stories have been influenced, often directly, by a wide variety of sources. There are the Arthurian romances. Trubert is a marginal figure, a young man who lives on the far edge of society, who is described in the text as 'nonsachent et nice' (unknowing and simple).[46] His family is maternal, and his world is dominated by women, in this case his mother and his sister. We are not told anything about his father. From here, the hero travels through and out of the wood to make his fortune at the region's greatest court, that of the Duke of Burgundy. He is an obvious parody of Perceval. Perceval, also a *naïf* living with his mother, seeks his fame and fortune at the court of King Arthur. From there, he learns to become a paragon of chivalry and eventually becomes the Grail Knight. Trubert learns about court, too, and becomes adept at his own line of 'chivalric' endeavour, seeking and finding plenty of money, food and sex. He does not desire money for its own sake, however. Like Robin Hood, he is motivated less by the cash than by what it can do, and revels in the success of his own 'play'. He may be lower class, but Trubert is not a peasant in his behaviour, and he is by no means mercenary. His mother is an innkeeper, and we might logically assume, therefore, that he is occupied in helping at the inn. This means that he is able to be *courtois*, while in class terms he is a *vilain*. As there is no mention of how Trubert's family eat or stock the inn while they are so poor, it might logically have been assumed by Douin's audience that he trapped and shot animals in the woods. Robin Hood also possesses sufficient courtly manners and general chivalric qualities for questions to have been raised about whether or not he was already seen as a dispossessed or outlawed nobleman in the fifteenth century, before Anthony Munday portrayed him as the dispossessed Earl of Huntingdon at the end of the sixteenth century. By looking at the way in which Trubert operates, we can see that such a link is not necessary. Robin and his men are courtly, but this does not mean that they cannot be of lower status and servile. Robin and his men are, after all, service providers themselves, offering hospitality in the woods at a price – as do Trubert's mother and her family.

Trubert initially sets out to relieve his family's financial need. When he beats the count and leaves him tied to his tree in the forest, Trubert alleges that he is motivated by revenge at the count's failure to pay what he has promised: 'c'est por le seurquot et la quote / que me feïstes ier doner' (it's on account of the surcoat and the coat / which should have been given to me yesterday).[47] This is quite a thin premise, although not out of keeping with Trubert's lower-class status and consequently practical aims. Similarly, Robin Hood poaches the king's deer because he and his men need to eat, and they may carry out robbery to meet other needs, but Robin also seems to play tricks on the sheriff because it's fun and because he *can*. A saga outlaw such as Egil Skalagrimsson wants his victims to know who tricked them as a matter of honour and refuses to make his escape until he has told them, but these French tricksters enjoy rubbing it in for their own amusement, as does Robin Hood, sending a white palfrey to the sheriff's wife:

> And gret well they weyffe at home
> The woman ys ffoll godde
> Y schall her sende a wheyt palfrey . . .

Images of fools are common in medieval church art, representing the fool 'who says in his heart, "There is no God"' from Psalm 14:1/53:1. This misericord from Gloucester is interesting in that it depicts the huntsman, with bow and arrows and sword, in fool's costume. It may have allegorical meaning (the stag can also be Christ or the Church), but fools and minstrels were also employed – as Sir John Paston's William Woods was – in keeping horses, and as huntsmen.

> And greet well your wife at home
> She's a very good woman.
> I shall send her a white palfrey . . .[48]

These words of Robin's resemble Trubert's admission to Burgundy that he has screwed the duke's wife thirteen times in one night. Unlike her unchivalrous husband, he tells the duke, his wife is 'debonaire et courtoise' (noble-spirited and courteous).[49]

In several places Trubert is described as a *fol*. When he first turns up at the castle, the unsuspecting Aude mistakes this for a stupid fool – a *foubert* or an idiot. The true *fol*, on the other hand, is the character that speaks and acts fearlessly, holding up a mirror to power and its representatives. This type was familiar to medieval audiences, particularly in dramatic form.[50] Robin Hood can also be described as a fool of this type. Just as Burgundy's pride in his own situation makes him vulnerable to Trubert's trickery, so does that of the sheriff blind him to Robin Hood's devices. Robin disrupts his congenial existence, takes his wealth and his goods (representative of greed, lust and avarice), and provides him with an example of success and lordship, leading him into uncontrollable rage (wrath) and to his downfall. Medieval audiences were thoroughly practised at seeking out the Seven Deadly Sins, and would have seen warnings about these sins and their consequences in trickster stories. Just as with Caxton's Reynard, so with Robin Hood, Trubert and *fabliaux* in general, the stories are hugely entertaining, but they are also meant – like *fabliaux* – to teach moral lessons. The victims are sinful rather than simply stupid. In fact, their stupidity is a result of their sinfulness in a personal sense.

Not only is there no indication that either man is a bad ruler on a day-to-day basis, but the evidence suggests that, like the kings in romances of deeds and adventure, both the duke and the sheriff do their jobs well. In fact, Trubert's duke is quite genial, and as well as being generous in forgiving his wife her adulterous bargain with a *vilain*, he also takes her rejection of his nighttime visit on the chin. He is angry but without rancour. He is generous and loving, even indulgent, when his youngest daughter becomes pregnant. Does he really believe that she is full of angels? We cannot tell, although, like the sheriff chasing a hart at Little John's suggestion in the *Geste*, he is apparently easily duped. His grief at the death of his nephew is genuine, although his own anger was the ultimate cause. The main problem with the duke, as far as Douin is concerned, is that he is simply accepting of his power and wealth. He takes it for granted, and does not appear to respond to it with a sense of social (or any other) responsibility. He certainly does not treat the needs of his poor subjects with the generosity demanded by God of his exalted status. His main concern seems to be with the display of power. The duke loses his temper when pushed far enough by a lower-class 'fool' who is cleverer than he is. His sins, stemming from pride in his (inherited) status and office, make him vulnerable and lead to his shaming.

The sheriff of Nottingham is similarly genial, especially in *Robin Hood and the Potter*. He is wealthy and powerful, happy to make room for a gullible 'potter' in his hall and his household, to give him food and shelter and to offer him a job when he proves his skill at archery. There is no suggestion that the sheriff's men are evil or that they are stupid, either. They seem to be well paid, housed, fed, clothed and armed, and the archery contest is carried out in a spirit of camaraderie:

All they schot a bowthe agen
The Screffes men & he

Off the marke he welde not ffayle
He cleffed the preke on iij.
The Screffes men thowt gret schame
The potter the mastry wan
The Screffe lowe & made good game . . .

They all shout a round again,
The sheriff's men and he,
He would not fail to hit the mark,
He split the stick in three.
The sheriff's men felt really ashamed
That the Potter won the mastery.
The sheriff laughed and made fun of it . . .[51]

It is when the name of Robin Hood is mentioned that the sheriff changes:

'Knowest thow Robyn hode?' seyde the Screffe,
'Potter, y prey tell thow me.'
'A C torne y haffe schot with hem,
Under hes tortyll tre.'
'Y had lever nar a C ponde,' seyde the Screffe,
'& sware by the trenite,
That the ffals owtelawe stod be me.'

'Do you know Robin Hood?' said the sheriff,
'Potter, I pray you tell me.'
'A hundred rounds have I shot with him,
Under his trysting tree.'
'I'd rather go without a hundred pounds,' said the sheriff,
'And swore by the Trinity,
Than that false outlaw stood by me.'[52]

The irony, of course, is that he *is* standing right next to Robin Hood. Up to this point the sheriff is a reasoned and a pleasant host, but he begins to lose control and become sinister as his anger takes over. It is evident, also, when he is woken in the night in *Robin Hood and the Monk*, and in the *Lytell Geste*:

Up then rose this prowde Schereff
And radly made hym yare
Many was the moder son
To the kyrk with hym can fare.
In at the durres þei throly thrast
With staves ful gode wone

Up then rose this proud sheriff,
And quickly got him hence.
Many was the mother's son
Who went with him to the church.
In at the doors they violently burst,
With a goodly load of staves . . .[53]

In this context, there is no incongruity that the man who gives generous hospitality to a stranger is also prepared to break into a church with an armed mob and to cause death and mayhem in the streets of Nottingham in order to take and kill an outlaw – not just *any* outlaw, but this particular one.

All the schemes of the great fall apart when Trubert and Robin Hood show up. It also happens – as in comic *fabliau* stories – when the great men's women interfere. If anything, both men are guilty of the social sin of uxoriousness, of allowing themselves to be subject to their women, which the medieval Church taught was a form of lust and had been the sin of Adam. Like Robin Hood (who serves both the Virgin Mary and the courageous Lady Lee, who plunges into the forest to save her husband), Trubert serves the women in his life – his mother and his sister. He takes the financial rewards from his first two adventures to his mother. His successes are the result of an alliance, whether complicit or not, between the two classes at the bottom of the medieval social pile, women and *vilains*. On the other hand, Duke Garnier is uxorious, giving way to his wife rather easily. The duchess is the means of the hero's initial entry into the court, just as the sheriff's wife invites the 'potter' into her husband's house. The sheriff's wife may not be buying a painted goat for a fuck and five sous, but she *is* beguiled by five free pots, things of little real value that turn out to cost a great deal. Female servants also play important roles. The servant Aude not only carries the name of a great romance lady: it is she who persuades her mistress to pay Trubert's price for his goat. We do not know if it is Aude who ends up married to King Golias at the end, but it would provide a very satisfactory ending if she did. These are gutsy women who stand up to men and are able to manipulate them by their clever words if they cannot. Unfortunately, but entirely in keeping with the cultural imperatives of the period, their men come to grief as a result. Through these women, who often work knowingly or unknowingly in concert with the tricksy outsider, the world is turned upside down, a common theme of medieval comic stories. The men are outwardly strong but inwardly weak, and they collapse when pressure is carefully applied to the weaker parts of their personal armour.

Stories like those of Trubert and Robin Hood can, and do, enshrine an element of social protest. The duke may not be a bad person, but he is entitled by birth and made noble and wealthy by inheritance, not necessarily covetous but with a sense that he has a right to get whatever he desires from his subjects. Otherwise, he is a genial man, generous and apparently loyally served by his people. There is no reason for Trubert to target him personally as he does, except that the duke is rich and Trubert's family are poor. We are not told that Trubert and his family lack food, but that they lack the money to buy 'made' goods such as fabric and clothing. In these stories we see the state of the poor, and a poor man getting his own back on the rich for his poverty, taking with interest what they have not received but – by implication – should have been given. Not only does Trubert steal from the rich, he steals from the highest authority in his country, his region. Trubert's Burgundy is hardly a minor aristocrat, as (potentially) is Robin Hood's sheriff – although it does raise the question of what Robin Hood's medieval audiences understood by a sheriff. Sheriffs would usually be nobles, and might be drawn from among the highest nobility in the land. The sheriff's status is frequently downplayed in modern recreations of the Robin Hood stories, as is the courtliness of the man and of his courtiers. It is common to underestimate the function of wealth and power in this medieval world: Robin Hood and Trubert are facing off against very daunting people in whose presence they were expected to doff their hats, kneel, lower their eyes and speak only when spoken to. In taking on such enemies, both of them display courage, daring and rashness equal to any Arthurian knight. In the twenty-first century, when tabloid newspapers frequently refer to royal princes by their given names and use or invent nicknames for them, it is easy to lose sight of a time in which such familiarity might lead to serious punishments – from a fine and/or a slit tongue to accusations of treason and the most horrific of deaths.[54] Trubert commits treason many times over, not least in inserting his *vilain* semen into the body of the duke's wife, and hence potentially into the ducal bloodline, and by physically assaulting the duke. Although the sheriff may pursue Robin Hood for treason, Robin is careful not to actually *be* a traitor. He is, however, an outlaw and a felon, and guilty of capital crimes such as theft and murder. As such, representatives of the king's law and justice must pursue him in order to face trial and hanging, or they might pay the penalty themselves. This is what the sheriff is afraid of in *Robin Hood and the Monk* when he seeks to cover up the death of the king's messengers.

We do not know why Robin Hood was outlawed, but Trubert's original motive is altruistic: to clothe his sister decently. Douin is setting up a comparison between the poverty and misery of a poor family and the excessive wealth of a family who can afford to pay large amounts of money for luxuries and the satisfaction of their own whimsical desires, from great halls to multi-coloured goats. This is both social and political comment. At the end of the story, the rich remain rich and the world's resources remain unequally distributed, as the will of God and divinely instituted social hierarchies dictate. In spite of this, two or more people have risen higher up the social scale by their own efforts. At least in one little corner of the world there has been a more equitable redistribution of fortune. For the aspirational, wealthy peasant, the professional, the upwardly mobile servant and the merchant entrepreneur, this would have been a satisfying development.[55] Robin Hood offers a similar redistribution. If he did not take from the rich to give to the poor (in the sense in which it is understood today), his taking and giving is not simply anodyne wish fulfilment. It is a similar redistribution from the less to the more deserving, from the prosperous to the needy, whatever their social status. Trubert's duke and Robin Hood's sheriff are rich but ultimately undeserving, rather than corrupt.

Although a *vilain*, Trubert does not conform to the literary norms for a lower-class character. He is a pretty youth and a *courtois* one. Robin Hood is not the only cultured churl in the medieval greenwood. Perhaps because he derives from a service economy,

Trubert understands how to behave in different situations and settings. He is not a courtier but can act like one. His manners are such that he can pass as a knight, a learned doctor and a young lady. He is none of those things, any more than Little John is a squire to Sir Richard atte Lee or the sheriff of Nottingham, but he is able to display the correct behaviour by copying those who are. *Noriture*, courtly education, is once again seen to be a behaviour only, something that can be replicated without accompanying fine feelings or knightly status. Some people's *noblesse* is only skin deep; it is the inner qualities that really matter. As with names, so with beauty: Trubert does not look servile or lower class, any more than Robin Hood does. On the contrary, he is pretty enough to pass as a young woman. Inside, however, he thinks like a *vilain*. Trubert demonstrates that churls do not have to look or behave like churls, but fine behaviour and appearance do not guarantee that there are fine feelings on the inside. Neither Robin Hood nor his men are anything like the cave dwellers encountered by Fouke FitzWaryn, even if they may resemble them outwardly – or are they? The noble outlaw thinks and acts like a churl only when, and because, his situation requires it. Trubert has a *vilain*'s character (permanently) inside a *courtois* body in order to perform the requirements of his position, his social situation. In other words, they are part of how he does his job. So it is with court servants, actors and performers of all kinds – and it makes them, in the eyes of their social betters, dangerous. In the case of Robin Hood and his men, the outlaws' appearance disguises finer feelings on the inside.[56] They are, however, at times violent, sly, quarrelsome and coarse – typical *vilain* qualities. Robin Hood is (strangely) socially ambiguous and, like Trubert, dangerous as a result.

SEVEN

Robin Hood and the Comic Tale

Robin Hood stories can also be related to the comic tales often referred to by modern scholars as *fabliaux*. These stories could be found all over Europe in the Middle Ages – although they survive in only a few examples in English.[1] Their humour ranges from intermittent to ubiquitous, from deadpan through wry smile to belly laugh, and from mildly rude and suggestive to crudely obscene. The lack of examples in English may be because educated English audiences could understand French anyway, but it could equally well be a result of simple luck. These stories, like the May games with which Robin Hood became associated, were ever-changing, ephemeral and disposable literature. They varied from teller to teller, they were of the moment, unobtrusive and everyday, and would hardly have seemed – apart from to those who composed and performed them – to be worth keeping. The early audiences of Robin Hood stories would have loved them. In fact, one of the few remaining English-language *fabliaux* is in Cambridge (Gilbert Pilkington's manuscript, University Library, MS Ff.5.48), alongside *Robin Hood and the Monk*.

The Tale of the Basyn (or 'The Story of the Chamber Pot', fols 58r–61v) is typical of the association of mild rudeness, sex and adultery found in many *fabliau* stories.[2] A feckless husband, under the thumb of his lazy, adulterous wife, allows her to waste most of his money. She sends him to ask for more from his brother, a prosperous and wise clergyman. The brother advises him to steal the chamber pot from the bedroom and bring it to the priest's house. When he has control of the pot, the brother takes it to his room and puts a secret 'prayer spell' on it, then gives it back, with instructions to replace it just as it was. Having obeyed the instructions, the other brother leaves home, leaving his wife alone. She immediately makes a feast and invites her lover, the local parson. After the meal they go to bed. When the lover wants to pee, he reaches for the pot. His hands stick firm. The wife tries to help, and her hands stick firm, too. They shout for the maid, who also sticks to the pot. In the morning, the parish clerk finds them all dancing, stark naked, around the pot. A carter, shovelling earth from the door, goes in to find that his own lover, the maid, is one of the idiots stuck to the pot. He strikes her across the buttocks with his shovel, which then sticks fast. The two brothers then come in to see them all. The cuckolded husband threatens to cut off the parson's balls unless he pays him one hundred pounds. When he agrees, the brother-priest releases the spell. The parson leaves town, and everyone is silent out of shame. The wife remains faithful and obedient to her husband, whose debts are relieved. The story ends with an invocation to the Virgin Mary to save us all from trouble. The story would undoubtedly enliven a sermon, or could even be performed as mime or acted. The moral meaning is clear in this case. The Virgin Mary provides another link to Robin Hood, one that Pilkington, as a priest, might well have exploited.

Stories like this were very well travelled, often the same story in different versions. The close relationship between the *fabliaux* and the 'trickster' and 'fool' stories is demonstrated by *Trubert* and by *Till Eulenspiegel*.[3] In the scene where Trubert, in the person of Coillebaude, persuades the innocent, chaste Rosette to have sex with her/him, Trubert begins playing with her/himself, and Rosette asks what s/he is holding. Trubert replies that it is a pet:

Ce est un petit connetiaus
Il est petiz, mais molt es biaus

It's a little bunny rabbit;
He's small, but very pretty[4]

S/he proceeds to invite Rosette to first play with the little rabbit, and then insert it into her warm 'nest'. Rosette loves this game, and wants to play with the baby rabbit often. This use of euphemism and coarse allegory to describe the sex act is evident in other *fabliaux*, such as in *L'Esquiriel* (The Squirrel), where it is described as feeding a young man's 'squirrel' on an innocent girl's pre-digested food, and in the story of *La Saineresse* (The Lady Doctor), where an unfaithful wife describes the sexual act in terms of strange (and yet somehow familiar) medical treatments administered to her by a visiting 'lady doctor', who is of course neither a lady nor a doctor. The wife describes her 'treatment' to her husband – it was harsh but salved with 'ointment', which 'issoit d'un tuiel / et si descendoit d'un forel / d'une pel molt noir et hideuse / mais molt par estoit savoreuse' (came out of a pipe / which descended from a forest / with a very black and ugly skin / but was really delicious).[5]

There is more evidence of pan-European material in Till Eulenspiegel's engagement with comic stories. In one story Till gives twelve blind men twelve non-existent guilders, then sends them to an inn to have a really good meal. Each of the men thinks that one of the others has the money. The innkeeper is only too eager to provide for them; in his desire for the cash he forgets to ask to see it. When the trick is discovered, the innkeeper locks the blind men in his pigsty, hoping to gain some recompense for them. Till returns to the inn, and assures the innkeeper he will find a pledge for them. He then visits a priest, telling him that a friend has an evil spirit and needs exorcism. The priest agrees to do the man a favour and exorcise his demons. Till brings the innkeeper's wife to the priest, who repeats the offer of help to her; completely misunderstanding, the wife believes that the priest is offering to stand surety for the innkeeper's money. She returns to her husband, to reassure him that this has been arranged, and the priest will give him what he needs in two days' time. In the meantime, Till leaves town. When the innkeeper's wife returns and asks the priest to pay twelve guilders, he tells her that he was only asked to release her husband from an evil spirit. The innkeeper believes that the priest is lying in order to escape the debt. He goes to the priest's house, in arms, to get the money. The priest sees him coming and raises the neighbours; an impasse ensues. For the rest of their lives, the composer of the story tells us, the innkeeper and the priest were hostile to one another, the former believing he was owed money and the latter believing that the innkeeper was possessed by demons. This story is a version of another comic tale entitled in French *Les Trois Avugles de Compiègne* (The Three Blind Men of Compiègne), in which a clerk 'gives' a *besant* to three blind beggars.[6] The story is basically the same, except that the blind men are not put in a pigsty, and the clerk himself offers the priest as a pledge to the innkeeper – there is no wife involved. The innkeeper goes to the priest for his money, and the priest exorcises him while the neighbours hold the man down. The innkeeper goes quickly back home ashamed at having been deceived. The French *fabliau* is recorded in a thirteenth-century manuscript in the Bibliothèque Nationale in Paris.[7]

Similarly, on his deathbed Till is pestered for a legacy by a greedy priest. He promises, in return for money, to hold vigils and say masses for Till's soul for the rest of his life. Till tells him to come back later, when Till will put a piece of silver into his hands. The delighted priest leaves. Till takes a jug and half fills it with human faeces, then puts some money on top of this. When the priest returns, Till offers him the jug on the condition that he is not greedy and just takes a little. The priest, of course, cannot resist the lure of the coins, and thrusts his hand deep into the jug. When the priest complains, Till replies that he would not be – literally – in the shit, if he had not been so greedy; he had been warned. This story will be familiar to anyone who knows the 'Summoner's Tale' from Chaucer's *Canterbury Tales*, where the sick peasant Thomas tricks a greedy friar into feeling under his body for money, only to be repaid with a large fart:

'A' thought this frere, 'that schal go with me.'
And doun his hond he launched to the clifte,
In hope for to fynde ther a gifte;
And whan this syke man felte this frere
Aboute his tuel grope, ther and heere,
Amyd his hond he leet the frère a fart.

'Ah,' thought this friar, 'that shall go with me.'
And he launched his hand down into the cleft [of the backside]
In the hope of finding a gift there.
And when this sick man felt this friar
Groping around his anus, here and there,
Into his hand he let fly a fart.[8]

Such tales travelled far and wide across the European continent, finding expression in localized tales of local heroes, or were adapted and related to local situations and conditions. It is no surprise to find that some of them may be related to the Robin Hood stories. There were probably more which no longer exist.

Fabliaux vary in length, but on the whole they are – again, in the manner of the Robin Hood stories – short and punchy. Because they are efficient and full of impact, *fabliaux* are built around action and feature quite sparse, direct dialogue; they rarely describe emotion or offer any depth of character. Characters are usually 'types': the unfaithful wife, the jealous husband, the lusty and daring (or desperate) lover, and the conniving (usually female) servant. Peasants, or *vilains*, are usually well built, lumbering and stupid; in other words, they are stereotyped in the same way as in romance stories. This is well demonstrated in *Le Vilain asnier* (The Peasant Ass Driver), in which a peasant drives his ass into a part of town where there are many spicers' stalls. The lovely perfume of the rich and valuable spices overcomes the peasant, who falls to the ground in a dead faint. One of the onlookers offers a handsome cash reward to anyone who can make the man get up and move on, but nobody can revive him. A quick-thinking passer-by takes a fork and scoops up a forkful of manure from a nearby heap, which he then waves under the peasant's nose. Immediately the man is revived by the lovely smell of shit, which is sweeter to him (being a peasant) than the spices of the wealthy and the cultured.[9]

The trick of the composer/performer is to make the characters, however stereotypical, seem quotidian and believable. This is mostly achieved by the use of everyday settings and of situations with an element of plausibility – what we might term 'realism'.[10] If the format insists that the mere mention of a rich merchant or farmer's wife means that her lover/s will not be far behind, the everyday need of merchants and farmers to travel to markets or go out into fields and exchanges makes the ensuing deceptions possible. Husbands do unexpected things, like coming home early or sometimes just not really leaving at all. Settings are usually domestic: the interiors of houses are frequently used. In the upmarket 'middle-class' home, the existence of a fashionable upper storey can enable the plot, as in *La Borgoise d'Orlians* (The Bourgeoise of Orleans) and *La Saineresse*, where women entertain lovers on the upper floor while their husbands remain, entirely ignorant, downstairs.[11] The action may spill over into outbuildings or into a barn, garden or farmyard. Encounters may also happen in the street or on the highway.[12] It is this realism that Robin Hood shares with the *fabliau* world. It is easy to see in the storyworld of the Robin Hood tales the real world of their time, as most of the action takes place in a realistic setting – where travellers have to pay road and bridge taxes, where housewives look for bargains, where abbots can curse as well as poachers, and Nottingham's walls have weak spots:

> He gaf hym a good swerd in his hond
> His hed with for to kepe
> And ther as the wallis were lowyst
> Anon down can thei lepe.
>
> He gave him a good sword in his hand,
> To keep his head safe,
> And where the walls were lowest
> Immediately they lept down.[13]

The highway where Robin looks for travellers, the streets of Nottingham where he walks, fights and is pursued, the window from which Little John watches for the monk: all have the air of being real places. The towns, parks and villages in Robin Hood stories, as in *fabliaux*, usually have real names. This is the *fableor*'s sleight of hand, however – there is a decided lack of description of any of these settings or landscapes, or indeed of any of the characters involved, unless this is required for the internal logistics of the plot. The audience must supply the scenery from its own experience. What it supplies will be current, so the story always takes place in the present as well as in the past.

Robin sells 'pots' outside the sheriff's door. Is this a house or a castle, a marketplace or a courtyard? What are the pots like? We are not told about this, although sheriffs were usually stationed in castles and markets were frequently situated outside the gates of castles or in the main streets of towns. We are told that Robin Hood's clothing is 'green' because the king's demand for outlaw livery prompts a vague description of its colour, and because the clothing of Sir Richard in the *Lytell Geste* prompts a comic measuring of cloth:

Lytell Johan toke none other mesure
But his bowe tree.
And at every handful that he met
He leped footes three
'What devylls drapar,' sayid litell muche,
'thinkest thou for to be?'

Little John used no other measure
But his bow tree.
And at every handful that he met
He leapt three feet.
'What devil's draper,' said little Much,
'Do you think you are?'[14]

We know that the outlaws use bows and arrows and that some, like Robin, also carry swords or knives. Who makes the 'good whytebrede' that the outlaws serve to the king in the *Lytell Geste*, and who makes the clothing? At one moment the king is buying cloth, and in the next he is approaching the walls of Nottingham dressed in a green 'outlaw' outfit. Perhaps the merry men include bakers, cooks and tailors. They may well have done both in medieval fact and in the medieval imagination, but we are not given precise information to confirm this. The action moves on, and the audience's attention is supposed to move with it. Disbelief is suspended; the audience is left to make assumptions while the composer/performer concentrates on the action and on the dialogue that supports it. It is the everyday language of the dialogue, the everyday actions of the characters (eating, drinking, attending to their clothes and their equipment, counting their money), and the recognizable ordinariness of the props and features (furniture, utensils, coins, bows and arrows, horses and carts) that convey the credible 'actuality' of the stories. The setting can be, within the parameters set (wood, road, kitchen, bedroom, church, hall), anything members of the audience care to imagine. In this way, they make the stories their own, as do the audience of Robin Hood tales. It is a very powerful storytelling style.

A focus on objects (things) and actions (the human and animal body) has the effect of making the world of the *fabliaux* appear very materialistic. Characters with strong inner beliefs or attitudes, particularly if they are female, are made to look ridiculous. In the realist world of the *fabliaux*, religion is more a matter of superstition, ritual or fetishized objects and outward practice than of inner faith. On the one hand, this reflects the nature of late medieval Christianity, where salvation and mitigation of time in purgatory could be gained by saying certain prayers for a fixed number of times, or by buying candles and giving money to images, or visiting shrines on pilgrimages. On the other hand, the concentration on the artefacts of religion makes comedy and criticism sharper and more effective. It may seem that religion is being mocked, especially stories about the gullibility of fanatically devoted young women. Blind to the realities of the world around them, they are easily gulled. This ranges from the religious and devoted young wife Margery in the Middle English story of *Dame Sirith*, who is tricked into committing adultery by the old woman of the title, who has been promised large amounts of cash by her would-be seducer, to the proud, deluded young girl who believed she could learn to fly. She is tricked by a wily (and lusty) priest, whose methods of teaching, involving kissing to grow a bird's beak and having sex to grow a bird's tail, only help her to get pregnant.[15]

However, these are very moral stories, and even if in more extreme cases where we would think that the treatment of characters (female ones in particular) is unfair or even cruel, the moral given reveals that a medieval audience may have 'read' the story differently. The composers expect their audiences to act as judges on the moral meaning of the story, and may direct them to do so. At the end of this story, the narrator offers the audience a moral reading:

se grosse iestes, ce est nature
mes ce estoit grant desmesure
que par l'air voliez voler

becoming pregnant is natural,
but it is really outrageous
to want to fly through the air.[16]

The story of *Cele qui se fist foutre sur la fosse de son mari* (The Woman who Was Fucked on the Grave of her Husband) tells of a heartbroken young widow who refuses to be comforted after her husband's death and wishes to die herself. As she will not leave his graveside, her friends leave her there to grieve. A passing knight, with his squire, is sympathetic, but the squire tells his master that he is wasting his sympathy; he (the squire) will easily be able to persuade the woman into having sex. They make a bet, and the knight conceals himself in order to watch. The squire approaches the woman and listens sympathetically as she tells him of her grief. He says that he, too, is grieving for his dead wife. He was guilty of killing her as a result of his violent sexuality. The widow confides that she wishes to die and asks the squire to kill her, too – and so he fucks her on her husband's grave. The watching knight is overcome with laughter. By way of moral, the author says that he is foolish who trusts a woman: 'de noiant rit, de noiant plore' (they laugh over nothing at all, cry over nothing at all).[17] This seems hardly fair, but is a reading that the *fabliau* audience may well have made, especially as they knew the format really well. They may, or may not, have felt that this was a valid outcome in the real world, but in the world of comic stories it was the kind of reading they probably expected to make. The comic world had its own moral imperatives, whether that applied outside, in the real world, or not. Even when members of the upper classes, such as knights, are involved, the action of *fabliaux* usually centres on sex, food and material gain. Motivations are likewise basic and without much nuance – greed, lust, anger, jealousy, covetousness and pride – and the ability to achieve the object of these desires is usually praised, whether it is morally righteous or not. In the world of *fabliaux*, it is usually not.

Fabliau morality punishes jealousy, greed and avarice rather than adultery or gluttony. Many of the deceived husbands are jealous of their wives, or they are proud and overly concerned about their possessions and their social standing. Immoral types in *fabliaux* include the husband who boasts of his wife's fidelity, or the knight who prides himself on having a uniquely virtuous lady. The former is cuckolded, while the latter discovers the history of his model wife's extramarital sexual encounters when she inadvertently confesses them to him.[18] As the *fableor* says about Aloul (who is about to be cuckolded by a lusty priest):

Deniers amoit seur tote rien
En ce metoit toute s'entente.
. . .

Ce dist l'escripture qu'Alous
Garde sa fame com jalous.
Male chose a en jalousie!
Trop a Alous mauvese vie,
Quar ne puet estre asseürez.
Or est Alous toz sos provez,
Qui s'entremet de tel afere.

He loved cash above everything else
And dedicated all his effort to it.
. . .
Written stories say that Aloul
Kept his wife like a jealous man.
He suffered very badly from jealousy!
Aloul had a really hard life,
Because he could never be sure
Now Aloul was shown to be a complete idiot
For meddling in such a business.[19]

Avarice and jealousy are manifestations of the same vice. When Chaucer's Wife of Bath calls her husband a *niggard*, a miser, for his unwillingness to share her sexually with his apprentice, she is giving the judgement of *fabliau*:

He is to gret a nygard that wold werne
A man to light a candel at his lantern

He is far too great a miser who would forbid
A man to light a candle at his lantern[20]

Avarice and greed are particularly well punished in these stories, as in the Robin Hood tales, whether the perpetrators are secular or religious. The clergy, in particular the abbot of St Mary's and the Monk (his cellarer?) in the *Lytell Geste*, represent avarice in its most aggressive form. The 'truth test' imposed by Robin Hood on his dinner guests is a test of their avarice rather than their honesty.[21] The point is not that people lie, but that their love of money causes them to do so. It may be that the Church's reputation for greed (fuelled by its great possessions and the fact that every household had to pay a tenth – the tithe – of their income to the priest) leads Robin to urge his men to *bete and binde* bishops and archbishops, and other clergy. Robin Hood may be anticlerical not in the sense of objecting to the clergy per se, but because they were seen as obvious practitioners of this particular vice, which was hated by everyone. This included the merchant classes, those increasingly important consumers of literature and performance, because they themselves were potentially tainted by it; methods of wealth creation among the merchant community were not all exactly blessed by the Church, usury and excessive profit-making in particular. Given his likely mercantile associations and his predilection for theft, perhaps Robin Hood protests too much. This strict morality does not always apply to what might be called sexual sins. In *fabliaux*, lusty priests may often get away with their escapades, especially if they happen to be young or still clerks in training. The *fabliau* wife's lover is often a priest, using worldly wisdom to outwit her stupid husband.[22] In the story of *Le Moigne* (The Monk), a priest's 'wet dreams' are treated sympathetically, as an object of fun, although he is 'brought up sharp' when they cause him to do himself physical harm.[23]

Fabliau priests sometimes suffer in gruesome fashion. The fact that they were celibates, institutionally castrated men, was too good a joke to miss. There are no hard feelings involved in this, though. In *Le Prestre crucifie* (The Crucified Priest), a priest has an affair with the wife of a sculptor of crucifixes. Escaping her husband, he flees into the man's workshop, where he hides in plain sight by climbing on to a cross. The husband sees the priest's genitalia and pronounces the crucifix a poor piece of workmanship. He then cuts off the offending elements, making the metaphorical castration a reality.[24] A priest's genitals were taboo objects, and this made them – along with all pricks, in fact – particularly useful for comic inversion. In *Le Pescheor de Pont seur Saine* (The Fisherman of Pont-sur-Seine), a dead priest's erect penis becomes the means by which a husband forces the truth about 'what women want' from his wife. The priest 'blesses' the young couple *after* his death.[25] Priests may be liable to lust, avarice and anger, but no more so than other men. They have a privileged position, supplied by the confessional and private access to women, that makes the temptation greater.[26] The point is that they are simply men like all the others, but with a special calling that not only demands more of them, but lays them more open to attack than their lay counterparts. If Friar Tuck was a creature of lusts in the Middle Ages, as he is portrayed in William Copland's 1560 play, and possibly also in morris dances, this would be entirely in keeping with the morality of the priests and friars we see in *fabliau* stories. Their lust is acceptable as long as they are engaged in punishing the vain, the avaricious and the mean-spirited.

Priests could also be 'collateral damage'. In the story of *Estormi*, an impoverished couple extort money from three prelates who lust after the wife, by making a false promise to each that he may enjoy her favours in return. To the wife's chagrin, her husband gets mad and kills each one. They call their nephew Estormi to dispose of the first body, which he does. Each time he comes back to the house, Estormi is confronted by another body, and told that devils brought it back from the grave. After three bodies have been disposed of – with great effort – Estormi meets a priest on his way home from Matins 'par sa male aventure' (through his [the priest's] bad luck). Estormi kills the priest and buries him, then goes back to report that he has killed all four. Everyone keeps silent, and the couple is saved from penury. The husband remarks on the fourth priest:

A molt grant tort perdi la vie
Li prestres qu'Estormis tua,
Mes deables grant vertu a
De genz engingner et sousprendre

Very unjustly did he lose his life,
The priest that Estormi killed.
But the devil is very capable
Of tricking and trapping people.

The moral, says the composer (one Hues Piaucele), is that:

folie est de covoitier
autrui fame, ne acointier

it is folly to covet someone else's wife,
or to woo her[27]

In passing, he also notes that people should look after a poor relative 's'il n'est ou trahitres ou lerres' (if he isn't a traitor or a thief), because (as in the case of Estormi) they may need them sometime.

The deaths of the monk and his little page in *Robin Hood and the Monk* could be seen in this context, too. What we see as extreme violence against an innocent does not seem to have troubled a medieval audience. The child as collateral damage can be seen in the well-known tale of *The Snow Child*, in which a merchant returns from a long journey to find that his wife has recently had a baby. The woman swears that the child was conceived as a result of snowflakes falling on her body, and her husband appears to accept her explanation. He says nothing and raises the boy. Some years later, he goes on another business trip, taking the child, now a young man, with him. Down by the quayside, he causes the young man to fall into the water and drown. Returning to his horrified wife, he simply tells her that, as the boy was made of snow, the sun shone so brightly that it melted him. The woman must accept his explanation.[28] The child in the story may be innocent, but he is so closely associated with the mother's sin and lies that he becomes a justifiable target for the husband's violent revenge against her. Likewise, the monk's little page may have no part in his master's sins, but he is closely enough associated with them both to suffer the same fate. Both the monk and page die, eventually, for the sake of the monk's avaricious obsession over his original loss of 100 pounds to Robin Hood, which, as he tells the sheriff, 'shalle neuer out of my mynde'.[29] Like the boy's mother in the *fabliau,* the monk is more concerned with his own life and well-being than with that of the child who depends on him. He pleads for his own life, not the boy's: 'the Munke saw *he* shulde be ded / lowd mercy can he crye' (the monk saw *he* was going to die, loud 'mercy' he began to cry (my italics)). For a medieval audience, death was not the end of the story, so they might expect the Blessed Virgin to step in afterwards to 'save' the innocent victim for Paradise, as she does in Chaucer's 'Prioress's Tale', where a murdered child is kept alive by the Virgin Mary for long enough to ensure that his killers are found and brought to justice. He then goes straight to heaven.[30]

Morality and money are often intertwined in *fabliaux*, as they are in the Robin Hood stories. Cash, and portable 'high ticket' items, such as rich cloth, are used to measure moral worth and, in a similar way to food, as a means of negotiating social and spiritual power relationships. The tropes of the impoverished knight, the loan and the lady's payment (which is also the subject of a miracle of the Virgin Mary), which we see in the story of Robin Hood and Sir Richard atte Lee, appear in comic form in *Le Chevalier qui fit parler les cons* (The Knight Who Could Make Cunts Talk). A shorter, variant version of this French *fabliau* can be found in a famous trilingual English manuscript (British Library, London, MS Harley 2253).[31] In this story, a 'hardi, pruz bel bachiler' (bold, worthy, handsome knight) is nonetheless very much down on his luck, as 'il ne auoit rente ne terre' (he had neither rents nor lands). He sets off to seek his fortune at a tournament, accompanied by his squire, Huet, whose name means 'little Hugh'. On the way, they come to a fountain where three naked nymphs are bathing. Huet rides on ahead, steals the girls' clothing, and takes it to his master; it will raise some funds if they sell it. The knight is angry and demands that they return the clothes. The nymphs are delighted, and each offers the knight a gift in return. The first says that the knight will always be welcome wherever he goes. The second offers a stranger gift: if the knight speaks to the vagina of any female animal, it will reply. The third says that if the vagina will not reply, then the anus will speak on its behalf. In the Anglo-Norman (Harley) version, the second says that no woman the knight wants to love him will refuse, and the third gift is the gift of the speaking cunt and anus:

Ne est dame ne damoisele
Ne seit ele ia si bele
Si sa amour desirrez
E de vous amer la prierez
qe s'amour ne vous grantera
e tous vos pleysirs en fra
. . .
Je vous dorroi le poer
De fere cul e coun parler.

There is no lady or girl
Be she never so lovely,
If you desire her love
And you ask her for love
Who will not grant you her love

And do all your pleasure
. . .
I grant you the power
To make anus and cunt speak.[32]

On their way again, the pair meet a priest riding his mare. As predicted by the first nymph, the priest is very glad to see the knight, although he is a complete stranger. Huet suggests that they try out the other gift, so the knight asks the mare's vagina where the priest is going. It answers him immediately:

'Sir ie porte a mesoun; le prestre a s'amie.'
'Ad yl amie verroiement?'
'Oil sire certeignement,
E dis marcz en s'almonere
Qu'il dorra a sa amie chere'

'Sir, I'm taking him home; the priest to his lover.'
'Has he got a lover, honestly?'
'Yes, sir, for sure,
And ten marks in his almspurse
That he's going to give to his dear love.'[33]

The priest is so terrified – not to mention embarrassed – that he jumps on the horse and rides off, leaving behind a valuable cloak and the purse containing the ten marks. The knight uses the money to pay his bill at the inn. He and Huet travel on until they reach a fine castle. Once again, everyone rushes out to greet them although they are complete strangers, and they are taken inside. They are welcomed by the count, the lord of the castle, and his countess, who feed the knight royally. In the French versions, the countess desires to go to the knight's bed, but for fear of her husband she sends her maid instead. In the English version, the knight employs his second gift, ingratiating himself with 'une demoiselle' (a young lady) and asking her to accompany him to bed. As the knight feels all over the girl's body, he comes to her genitalia. In the French version, he asks her vagina why she is sleeping with him, while in the English version he asks it to tell him 'si vostre dammoisele / seit uncore pucele' (if your lady is still a virgin). The English reply is somewhat coarser than the French (which simply tells the knight that the girl's mistress has sent her):

'Nanyl syre certeignement
Ele ad eu plus que cent
Coillouns a soun derere
Que ount purfendu sa banere'.

'Not at all, sir, truly
She has had more than a hundred
Scrotums at her backside
That have breached/penetrated her banner.'[34]

In both versions, the girl is frightened and runs to tell the countess. The next day the lady refuses to let the knight leave without a meal. During the course of this, she loudly announces that she has heard that her guest can make cunts talk. The knight admits to his gift, and the lady promptly offers him a wager of a hundred pounds cash (sixty *livres* in the French version) if he can make hers speak. The knight has nothing to offer in return except his horse, but she is so confident that she accepts his terms. The lady goes to her chamber, where she stuffs a cotton tampon into her vagina, filling it completely. Then she demands that the knight make it speak. He is devastated to find that he cannot. At this point Huet reminds him of the third (or in the English version, the other part of the third) gift, so the knight addresses the lady's anus instead. The anus tells all. The embarrassed countess is forced to pay up: the knight goes home with a fortune and is able to live comfortably thereafter.

In the *Lytell Geste*, Sir Richard is also down on his luck and poorly attired, although he has no squire or other attendants. He meets an intermediary who gives him a divinely inspired gift (or a loan, in his case). He has to face up to an insanely avaricious cheat who wants to strip him of everything; he uses his gift/loan to overcome this, and is able to live according to his station in future. Neither the countess in the *fabliau* nor the abbot in the Robin Hood story needs the money – let alone the large amount of money – that they want to take from a man who has nothing. Both victims are saved by supernatural intervention, the knight by naiads and Sir Richard by the Virgin Mary, who 'repays' Robin by means of the cellarer's four hundred pounds. In each case the cash represents a negotiation of moral worth and a transfer of spiritual capital from the avaricious aggressor to the impoverished knight. That one is coarse, verging on the obscene, and the other high-minded, would not separate their purpose overmuch in the eyes of a medieval audience; both have a similar moral trajectory, and much of the material in the Harley manuscript is of a religious nature. It was once thought to have belonged to the household of a bishop, Adam Orleton of Hereford and Worcester, but has since been convincingly demonstrated to have belonged to an aristocratic household in Shropshire or Staffordshire.[35] Interestingly, this is the same area that is associated with some of the early Robin Hood stories. The Harley manuscript is dated around 1340, the most likely time for early development of Robin Hood tales, although there is no direct extra-textual link. There is, however, the thematic similarity which suggests that when Robin Hood sees the poorly dressed and ill-attended Sir Richard, he is meeting a comic trope which was popular not only in the northwest Midlands, but in French-speaking Europe as a whole.

The name 'Robin' occurs in several *fabliau* stories. In the *Borgoise d'Orlians*, Robin is the name of one of the household servants, not too bright but very strong, who is used by the wife to beat her husband. In *Jouglet*, Robin is the name of a wealthy young man with learning difficulties and no nobility, who is married (by his aspirational mother) to the daughter of an impecunious knight. When the mischievous *trouvère* Jouglet tricks the impressionable young groom into eating large quantities of ripe pears on his wedding night (in order to improve his virility), his wily young wife induces Robin to defecate all over Jouglet's room, in his clothing, and in the case where he keeps his *vieille* (a viola-like musical instrument). Robin is also the name of the lusty young man who invites the maiden to stroke his pet in *L'Esquiriel*, and of a valet in one version of *Le Sacristan*, another story of 'body disposal' similar to *Estormi*. In *Le Vilain de Farbu* (The Peasant of Farbu) he is the son of a stupid peasant. When his ignorant father sees Robin spitting on a hot horseshoe to cool it, he spits in his hot soup to the same effect, but it still burns his mouth. The name 'Robin' in these contexts, therefore, implies a *vilain*, or peasant, although not necessarily financially poor or of the lowest social class. He may be a servant, he may not be overly intelligent or bright, but on the other hand he may be wily, strong, dangerous, even challenging. In whichever of these guises he appears, naming a character 'Robin' is not, certainly in social terms, paying them a compliment.

Was Robin Hood always as *clean* as he appears in the early stories that remain today? If he were having some form of sexual dalliance with the sheriff's wife in *Robin Hood and the Potter*, an audience used to *fabliaux* would not necessarily see it as a moral black mark.[36] Some Robin Hood tales may have been more morally ambiguous than others, but if such stories existed, they have not survived. *Robin Hood and the Potter* seems different from the stories of *Robin Hood and the Monk* or those in the *Lytell Geste*, in that its overtly moralizing content (to our eyes, that is) is not as direct. It may be that this was implied, or was there more than a little truth in the early Protestant reformers' allegations of coarseness, lewdness and riot? On the evidence of Robin Hood's European context, there very well might have been. The surviving medieval Robin Hood 'rimes' have a very moral, even religious, tone, but that tone may not have been shared by all the earlier versions of these stories, which formed part of the stock-in-trade of *trouvères* and minstrels. The minstrel-servants of aristocratic lords had names like Robin and Little John. Two minstrels of Henry VII and Henry VIII were known as Gros and Peti Jean (Big and Little John), while another pair was called 'big' and 'little' Guillaume (William).[37] Minstrels, like heralds, were sometimes known as 'le Roy', or the king, as is Robin Hood. This might be because they had won a prestigious competition such as the annual minstrel contest at Beverley in East Yorkshire, or because their reputation was such that the title was deemed fitting. The late thirteenth-century *trouvère* Adenet was known as Le Roy for similar reasons.[38]

The many talents and the multitasking required of the minstrel can be seen in the story of Fouke FitzWaryn. Fouke has in his service a man called John de Rampaigne. John is a remarkable character, a messenger, a diplomatic speaker, a musician and composer, and an actor who can alter the appearance of his body with special herbs in addition to changing his clothes and his form of speech. A loyal and intimate servant, he carries out all the tasks given to him by his master, but is also able to act on his own initiative:

> *Fouke apela Johan de Raunpaygne. 'Johan,' fet yl, 'vous savez assez de menestralsie e de jogelerye. Estes vous osee d'aler a Blancheville, e juer devant Morys le fitz Roger, e d'enquere lur affere?' 'Oyl,' fet Johan. Yl fist tribler un' herbe, e la mist en sa bouche, e sa face comença d'engroser e emflyr moult gros, e tut devynt si descoloree qe ces compaignons demine a grant peyne le conurent. Johan se vesti asque povrement, e prist sa male ou sa jogelerie, e, un grant bastoun en sa meyn, vynt a Blancheville ...*
>
> Fouke called John of Rampaigne. 'John,' he said, 'you have a good knowledge of minstrelsy and juggling. Do you dare to go to Blancheville, and to play before Morys fitzRoger, and to find out what they are doing?' 'Yes,' said John. He crushed a herb, and put it in his mouth, and his face began to swell up and to become very inflamed, and it became so discoloured that his friends had great trouble in recognizing him. John dressed himself very poorly, and took in his hand his juggling equipment and a big club, and went on his way to Blancheville ...[39]

In the household at Blancheville, John is treated as a fool: he is mocked and has his hair and his feet pulled. In the final scenes, John appears in the lists at a tournament, not as a knight or squire but as a minstrel or a herald, in a ceremonial role. He is Fouke's adviser and his friend, but he is not Fouke's second-in-command. Fouke honours his brothers, but despite his embraces he never treats John with the respect due to a fellow aristocrat. They have a partnership, but it is an unequal one – unlike that of Robin Hood and Little John, but like that of Robin and the Virgin Mary. John of Rampaigne is a servant, a *trouvère* or a minstrel in the medieval sense of the word – a *yeman* – and that makes him a *vilain*. He is not a peasant in the lowest sense of the word, but he is not a *gentilhomme*, a gentleman. He looks a lot like Robin Hood and Little John.

In addition to their real personalities, minstrels had a common cultural persona, which they seem to have adopted and fostered themselves. This is well illustrated in two *fabliaux*: *Boivin de Provins* (Boivin of Provins) and *St Pierre et le jongleur* (St Peter and the Minstrel).[40] Boivin, dressed like a well-to-do peasant, comes into town at fair time and sits down in front of the local whorehouse. He

Medieval performers, in the church of St Margaret of Antioch, Cley next the Sea, Norfolk. One plays a pipe and a tabor (left), and one a *vieille* (centre). The third, dressed as a knight (St George?), appears to be grappling manually with a dragon. St George was very popular as a performance character in Norfolk. The beady-eyed,

begins talking loudly to himself about the large amounts of money he has made by selling his animals. At the same time, he counts and recounts the twelve *deniers* he really has in his (over-large) purse. Again loudly, he regrets to himself that he could not give any of this fortune to his niece Mabile, with whom he lost touch a long time ago. The madame of the establishment, also called Mabile, senses that there is a large profit to be made here. Boivin is invited into the brothel and fed royally, but Mabile refuses to take payment for the meal. She then convinces the visitor that she is his imaginary niece. She also offers him the services of Ysane, one of her girls, which he accepts. While Boivin is taking his pleasure, Ysane gropes furiously but vainly for his purse, which he has already cut off and hidden. Nevertheless, afterwards he goes to Mabile, shows her the cut purse-straps, and complains that he has been robbed. Mabile is secretly delighted, as she wanted the money all along. She now gets rid of the *vilain* by having him thrown out into the street. When

playful-looking lion (holding what may be intended as a human bone) reminds worshippers that the Devil prowls around 'like a roaring lion, seeking who he may devour' (1 Peter 5:8). The figures occur underneath the plinths for what would once have been the images of saints in the nave.

Ysane says she is unable to give her the purse, however, Mabile flies into a temper. She grabs Ysane by the hair, and a catfight ensues. First the pimps, then curious neighbours, are drawn in. Boivin goes to the provost, not to report the theft but to tell the story, 'et li provo l'a escouté / qui molt ama la lecherie' (and the provost gave him a hearing, as he loved dirty stories). The provost enjoys the story so much that he makes Boivin tell it to all his friends and relatives, too. After three days, the provost gives Boivin ten *sous* for his trouble; in another version he gives twenty. So, Boivin leaves having received free meals, free sex, a lot of laughs and ten (or twenty) *sous* profit – and he still has his original twelve *deniers*.

In *St Pierre et le jongleur*, a minstrel, addicted to gambling, dies in abject poverty.[41] His soul goes to hell, where Lucifer – because the minstrel is fit for nothing else – gives him the task of looking after the pot in which the damned souls are boiling. Lucifer and his devils go hunting for more souls, leaving the minstrel to watch the pot while they are away. Along comes St Peter with a gaming board and dice, and he challenges the minstrel to a game of *hasard*, with a few of the souls as a wager. The minstrel cannot resist and loses. Eventually, he has lost all of the souls in hell, and St Peter makes off with his 'winnings'. When the devils return, they are furious, and they round on Lucifer for bringing in the minstrel. Lucifer promises that he will never accept another minstrel in hell. Driven away from hell, the minstrel's soul runs towards Paradise. St Peter accepts him gladly. This should make all minstrels happy, because they will not suffer the pains of hell: 'cil les en a treztoz getez / qui les ames perdi aus dez' (he has saved all of them / the one who lost all the souls at dice).

This is the minstrel of Anglo-French medieval culture; the French composer Colin Muset typifies him:

Ore a Colin Muset muse
Et s'a a devise chanté
Pour la bele au vis coloré
De cuer joli
Maint bon morsel li a done
Et departi
Et de bon vin fort a son gré
. . .
Oncor dognoie
En chantant maine joie
Mult se cointoie

Now Colin Muset has amused [also to sing, play, waste time]
And at her pleasure has sung
For the lovely girl with the pretty face
And joyful heart.
She gave him many a good morsel
And shared it
And good strong wine to his satisfaction
. . .
He still chases women
Enjoys himself singing
Dresses himself elegantly.[42]

This hedonistic lifestyle is backed up by some of the poems in Sloane 2593:

> have a new gardyn
> & newe is be-gunne
> swych an-other gardyn
> know I not under sunne
> In the myddis of my gardyn
> Is a peryr set
> & it wil non per bern
> but a per Jenet [a medieval species of pear].
> The fairest mayde of this toun
> Preyid me
> For to gryffyn her a gryf
> Of myn pery tree.
> Quan I hadde hem gryffyd
> Alle at her wille
> The wyn and the ale
> Che did in fille.
> & I gryffyd her
> ryght up in her home
> & be that day xx wowkes
> it was qwyk in her wombe.
> That day twelfus month
> That mayde I mette
> Che seyd it was a per Robert
> But non per Jonet.
>
> I have a new garden
> and new [it is] begun,
> Such another garden
> I know not under the sun.
> In the middle of my garden
> There is a pear tree set,
> And it will not bear any pear
> But a pear Jonet.
> The fairest maiden of this town,
> Prayed me
> To graft her a graft

From my pear tree.
When I had grafted them
As she so wished,
She filled [me] in
With wine and ale.
And I grafted her
Right up into her house,
And twenty weeks from that day
It enlivened in her womb.
Twelve months after that day
I met that maid.
She said it was a pear Robert
And not a pear Jonet.[43]

The girl had a 'Robert' and not a 'little John': a baby, not a pear. The minstrel has a 'Jack the lad' reputation; he is fond of good food and wine, dressing up and performing, playing tricks, gambling and chatting up pretty girls. He is also attractive and personable (especially to women), no danger to friends or good people, as self-effacing as he is self-promoting. Left to himself, he wishes no one any harm, nor does he do any real harm to anyone. His major concerns are safety on the road, enough money to live on, clothing, food and lodging, and the goodwill of patrons (who will provide most or all of these). Robin Hood, in the early stories, is not noble but a household servant. He fulfils tasks that are military (both defensive and aggressive) and peaceful. He collects and disburses his Lady's revenue, he acts as her messenger and he presides over her hospitality. He is the foremost among her servants, who look up to him and view him as their 'manager'. He is a huntsman and a horn blower, as well as being an actor (sometimes in disguise), musician and dancer. On occasion, he also acts as a fool. He is generally *courtois* in both manner and nature, although he can also be violent and quarrelsome. This multiple functionality is typical of the medieval minstrel.[44] Robin and Little John have peasant, servile, minstrel names; they perform minstrel tasks, and they love to eat well, drink well and gamble. Like the minstrels, they are not good as gold, nor are they necessarily worthy men (although they could be so, especially in the late medieval period), but they can bring delight and even salvation. Even if seen as socially disruptive, disreputable and useless, the minstrel's work has divine approval, and his labour, like Robin Hood's theft, is blessed. Robin Hood sings, dances, seduces, gambles, thieves, plays tricks, challenges and disrupts, but he is Mary's lover, the minstrel 'king' of her household. He may go out on the road, but she is his lord and patron, and the green livery he wears is that of her household. His place in both religious life and festive performance is understandable, natural even, in the light of this. He is both disreputable and 'holy'. Thus this account of Robin Hood's early storyworld ends as it began, with the writing, singing, playing, tale-telling *trouvères*. The character of the outlaw and that of the minstrel are blended together in the greenwood storyworld of Robin Hood, and together they become the hero.

EIGHT

Robin Hood and the Medieval Past

Even in the fifteenth century, the Robin Hood stories were meant to evoke a past time when England was 'mery'. It is difficult to see at what point Robin Hood became representative of a medieval *past*, given that his stories were always nostalgic for a former age. It might seem obvious (from his close association with the Virgin Mary) that the Reformation, beginning circa 1530, would be the end of Robin Hood. Most performance events did end at around that time, but not because Robin Hood was a particularly special case. As a result of a concentrated attack on the infrastructure that had helped to support festive playing in general (the outlawing of non-biblical worship of Mary and the saints, the Dissolution of the Monasteries of 1536–41, and the dissolution of guilds, chantries and fraternities by the Chantries Act of 1547), many of the old performances came to an end. The saint plays, for example, had relied on popular religious beliefs for audiences, impact and income, and much popular religion was non-biblical. Local lords also played a part. In the Thames Valley, Elizabeth I's vice chamberlain Sir Francis Knollys arrived as a new landlord in 1558. Knollys was a reformed, and reforming, Protestant, and the highly popular Robin Hood, king games and other festive performances ended almost immediately. The most stubborn held out only until 1560.[1] Prudent self-censorship also accounted for the curtailment of Robin Hood in performance and in publishing; along with some other profitable subjects such as sermon collections, Robin entered a publication black hole between 1530 and 1560. He never really recovered; apart from the 1560 Copland publication and a London republication by

Edward White when interest revived in the 1590s, the *Lytell Geste* ceased publication until Joseph Ritson's edition of 1795. There was a brief, mostly enthusiastic, revival of festivities during the reign of the Catholic Mary I (1553–8), when Henry Machyn (merchant taylor and parish clerk of Holy Trinity the Less in London) recorded having seen a giant, drums, guns, a pageant with a queen '& divers odur with spechys & then sant gorges & the dragon the mores [morris] dansse & aft- robyn hode & lytyll john & maid marion & frere tuke & thay had specys [speeches] rond a bowt london'.[2]

Several records from the period before 1560 show Robin Hood as synonymous with trivial and anodyne pursuits. When Stephen Gardiner, Bishop of London, told the players of London in the 1540s to stick to performing Robin Hood and Little John as examples of bland popular material that was theologically inoffensive, he was availing himself of an opinion of Robin Hood as trivia that could be seen among the educated classes in the previous century and beyond.[3]

> Robyn hod in scherewod stod, hodud and hathud and
> hosut and schod
> Four and thuynty arowus he bar in hits hondus
>
> Robin Hood in Sherwood stood, with hood and hat and
> hose and shoes
> Four and twenty arrows he carried in his hands[4]

This is, of course, a variation of the phrase 'Robin Hood in Barnsdale stood', from the *Lytell Geste*, which must have been well known. The above lines appear in a Lincoln Cathedral manuscript of grammar texts, doodled in the margin. They seem to be a random attempt at rhyming by a bored student, who then attempted a Latin translation of the lines. An instance from the Court of Common Pleas in 1429 uses the 'Robin Hood in Barnsdale stood' line in a similar 'disposable' way, but in a different context. In the course of an abbot's suit for payment of rent by a parson, the abbot's counsel dismissed the arguments of William Paston, the defendant's lawyer, as equivalent to using this phrase.[5]

This identification of Robin Hood with trivia had some more serious religious applications. In the early fifteenth-century tract *Dives and Pauper*, Robin Hood stories are dismissed as being a trivial alternative to proper religious knowledge, and the author rails against those people who would rather go to the tavern than to church: 'Leuyr to here a songe of Robynhode. Or of some rybaudry . . .'[6] A sermon preached before Henry VI and Parliament by John Stafford, Bishop of Bath and Wells, on 8 July 1433, claimed:

> Many of these ley pepyll dispise presthode, ne they take none hede to the worde of God. They gefe no credens to the Scripture of almyghti God. Thei take more hede to these wanton proficijs, as Thomas of Arsildowne and Robyn Hood, and soch sympyll maters . . .

> Many of these lay people despise priesthood, nor do they pay any heed to the Word of God. They give no credence to the Scripture of almighty God. They pay more heed to these wanton prophets, such as Thomas of Erceldoune and Robin Hood, and such simple matters . . .[7]

In the archives of Worcester Cathedral is a fifteenth-century sermon, in English, for Passion Sunday which berates clergy who lack the learning to preach effectively to their congregations. The preacher says:

> Othur ther ben that for a preui pride in hir herte wil take no scripture but that hem luste [want] for to take . . . for manime seith, spekith of Robyn Hood that schotte neuer in his bowe. Thus they damne & deme othur menis bokis, & al for they drowe neuer the draught of undurstonding in non of hem alle.

> There are others who, because of a private pride in their heart, will accept no learning but what they want to take . . . for many men speak of Robin Hood that never shot his bow. Thus they damn and judge other men's books, in spite of the fact that they never drank the draught of understanding from any of them.[8]

This takes a slightly more serious turn as he continues, 'This pride & this obstinacie makis mani man falle in-to heresie . . .' (This pride and this obstinacy make many men fall into heresy . . .). The earliest reference to Robin Hood stories, by William Langland in *Piers Plowman*, may also be more, or less, than it seems at first glance: 'I can [know] noughte perfitly my pater-noster as the prest it syngeth, but I can rymes of Robyn Hood and Randolf erle of Chestre, Ac neither of owre Lorde ne of owre Lady the leste that euere was made' (I don't know my Paternoster perfectly, as the priest sings it, but I know tales of Robin Hood and of Ranulph earl of Chester, nor [do I know] of Our Lord, or of Our Lady, the least [little bit] that was ever created)[9] definitely refers to Sloth's own idleness and his own lack of basic religious knowledge, but the main emphasis of his assertion (for contemporaries) may lie at the end: 'as the priest teacheth'. If this is the case, Langland is alleging that Sloth's lack of spiritual understanding may also be laid at the door of lazy preachers, who fall back on popular stories and anecdotes as a replacement for true spiritual knowledge, which is biblical and theological – a point that Gardiner was trying to use in a *positive* way. This, the reformers allege, is the root of heresy. Heresy was a major concern in England from the end of the fourteenth century, and both clergy and lay faithful were much occupied with it. This 'unwillingness to distinguish between lay and religious idlers' is evidence of the 'new anticlericalism' in *Piers Plowman*, which was one of the fifteenth century's devotional best-sellers and popular with orthodox and unorthodox Christians alike.[10]

Neither festivities nor plays were outlawed *per se* by religious reformers, with Protestant writers such as John Bale attempting to replace the banned saint plays with anti-papal and pro-reformist versions of their own.[11] Robin Hood activities carried on in some places, in the West Country in particular, well into the reign of Elizabeth I (1558–1603). In Cornwall Robin Hood was still being performed in St Breock (by the players of Mawgan) in 1591–2, in St Columb Major three years later, along with morris dancing. In St Ives Robin played until 1583–4, and after that the summer king and queen and the king of the May game continued into the 1590s.[12] Braunton in Devon provided 'litle Iohns Cote' in 1563–4, and Chagford's Robin is last recorded in that year.[13] Robin's final appearances (apart from an isolated event in Oxfordshire in 1652 as an act of Royalist defiance against the Puritan Commonwealth) were in Westernzoyland, Somerset, in 1607, and at Wells in the same year. The Wells event led to prosecutions; under examination, one Stephen Millard, tailor, aged 43, said that

> the street where they were beeing the markett place was almost full of people with dauncing & with a Robinhood, and that a great number of others at that tyme were assembled togeather, having amongst them a Drumme an ensigne shott & other munition, And that one Robert Prinne of Welles yeoman was the Robinhood, and that this examinat was the sayd Robinhoodes men carrieng [carrying] with him a bowe & arrowes . . .

Millard was answering the (loaded) question:

> were there not dyuers persons lykewyse assembled together, in & vppon the 31th daye of Maye being Trynitye sundaye, with morrice dauncinges & with a Robinhood, what number of persons were assembled at that tyme in armes, with drummes ensignes shott & other munition, whoe was the Robinhood & what office or place had you in the same shewe?

The discourse is one of public order, not particularly of religion, although the religious element is also invoked as support where needed. The 'Robinhood' seems to have been assumed to be a leading role in any disorder, hence the need to establish his identity.[14]

If Robin Hood was already in some trouble with preachers over his ability to distract people from true religious understanding, his association with public order problems was also of long standing. The possibility of disorder and violence was already present in the rural games presented by the *bergeries* and the *pastourelles*.[15] According to the sixteenth-century London antiquary John Stow, Jack Cade wore a yellow straw crown (like that worn by Gautier in *Robin et Marion*) while giving sentence during his rebel occupation of the City of London in 1450. The game was, however, very real: his death sentences were actually carried out.[16] In Sussex and Surrey, one Robert Stafford, the leader of a criminal gang as well as being a priest, went under the alias of 'Frere Tuck'. In Wiltshire, a sheriff's clerk noted in the margins of his official document that a criminal reminded him of a list of fictitious criminals, including Adam Bell,

Robin Hood and Little John, while a group of Derbyshire petitioners in 1439 likened one Piers Venables and his band of criminals to 'Robyn Hode and his meyne'.[17] More threatening still was a gang prosecuted for ambushing and robbing travellers along the road near South Acre in Norfolk. Armed with 'swords, staves and cudgels', they chanted, 'We arn [are] Robynhodesmen, war, war, war.'[18]

These references show that, by the fifteenth century at least, people in all walks of life were accustomed to using Robin Hood, with or without his 'meyne', as a point of reference with which to compare criminals and their deeds. Local Robin Hood revels and games, being boisterous affairs, could turn to violence. They were usually associated with young men (as at Antony in Cornwall, where annual contributions were made by 'Robyn Hodde & the maydyns'), and the young were supposedly liable to hot tempers and 'riot'.[19] A serious incident happened at Walsall, Staffordshire, in 1498, when one Roger Marshall of Wednesbury was accused of causing a riot in Walsall, then:

> Calling himself Robyn Hood, and sir Richard Foxe, priest, with divers other persons to the number of 100 men and above, in harness, came in likewise, and met with the other rioters at the said town of Willenhall, and then and there riotously assembled themselves, commanding openly that if any of the town of Walsall came therefrom, to strike them down . . .

Marshall complained that:

> He did not riotously assemble with any persons in arms . . . hit hath byn of olde tymes used and accustumed on the said fere [fair] day that wyth the inhabitants of the sede townes of Wolverhampton, Wednesbury and Walsall have comyne [come] to the said fere [fair] with the capitanns [captains] called the Abot of Marham or Robyn Hodys to the intent to gether [gather] money whereby great profit hath grown to the said churches in times past.[20]

Popular festivity of all kinds was always potentially a problem for nervous public authorities answerable, ultimately, to the monarch for keeping the peace in their areas. In 1509 the authorities in Exeter (which had provided the first record of a Robin Hood play in 1426) announced a temporary ban: 'that from hensforth ther shall be no riot kept in any parysh by the yong man of the same parish called Robyn hode but oonly the Churche holyday'.[21] And in 1528 the Lord Warden of the Cinque Ports, Sir Edward Guildford, proclaimed to the inhabitants that, by order of the king, they should not

> make or play permytt & suffer to be made or played within eny of your offyces Romes or precynctes of the same noo maner of stage pley Robyn hoodes pley wacches [watches] or wakes reveales [revels] or other such lyke playes wherby that eny grete assemble of the kynges people shuld be made . . .[22]

This combination of public order and religion was most effective in the suppression of popular celebrations, Robin Hood events included. This is evident in events following the performance of a Robin Hood play in Burnley in 1579. The play led to some kind of disorder; this resulted in a group of justices in Manchester threatening the Burnley magistrates with the Privy Council if they did not immediately ban all such performances. In 1587 this ban was extended to the whole of Lancashire, and by 1590 across the Pennine area. The initial pretext was public order, but the language used (and the motivation) was also religious.[23]

In 1575, however, Elizabeth I herself, on a visit to Coventry, was offered entertainment by a group of players including one Captain Cox, of whom it was said that

> greet [great] oversight hath he in matters of storie: for az king Arthurz book, Huon of Burdeaus, the four sons of Aymon, Beuys of Hampton, The squyre of lo degree, The Knight of courtesy, and the Lady Fagnel, Frederik of Gene, Syr Eglamour, Sir Tryamour, Syr Lambwell, Syr Isenbras, Syr Gawyn, Olyuer of the Castl, Lueres and Euricalus, Virgils life, The castl of Ladiez, The wido Edyth, The King & the Tanner, Frier Rous, Howlglas, Gargantua, Robinhood, AdamBel, Clim of the Clough & William of cloudesley, The Churl & the Burd, The seauen [seven] wise Masters, The wife lapt in a Macls skin, The sak full of nuez, The sergeaunt

The iconic meme of Robin Hood as an archer, with deer and tree: Joseph Ritson's edition of Robin Hood ballads (taken from the second edition of 1832) depicts Robin Hood in what would become the standard pose for countless later depictions.

> that became a fryar, Skogan, Collyn Cloout, The Fryar & the boy, Eynar Rumming, and the Nutbroon [Nutbrown] maid, with many moe than I rehearz [rehearse] heere: I beleeue [believe] hee haue tham all at hiz fingers endz.[24]

The grouping of all these subjects together in the repertoire of an ageing 'rustic' reveals something of how Robin Hood, along with other 'old fashioned romances', was coming to be seen by the educated classes of the 1570s. By that time a new generation had grown up whose members generally did not remember the pre-Reformation, pre-Protestant past and had far less interest or investment in it than their parents or grandparents had done. The practices and materials of humanist education, and the interest of exciting new subjects – such as travel stories and accounts of the New World – simply changed the way educated people, in particular, saw the tastes of the past. Romance narratives, bowers and summer kings, and Robin Hood stories were consigned to the nostalgic and the old-fashioned, suitable for the uneducated lower classes and 'old wives'.[25] The vogue for attending the newly established playhouses and the restriction of travelling players to licensed companies only were simply more nails in the coffin. Robin Hood, in the forms in which he had been known and understood in the past, probably just went out of fashion. For the next two hundred years or more Robin Hood stories would be known only in the form of ballads.

'Our' Robin Hoods have a different context: since the period outlined in detail in this book, there have been many additions to Robin Hood's storyworld, while other elements, although present there, have been discarded. Some of the stories we now consider essential to the Robin Hood story arrived later, and many of them first appeared (as far as current research can tell) in the ballads of the seventeenth and eighteenth centuries. Ballads were cheaply printed on one sheet of paper, either broadside (a single printed side) or broadsheet (printed on both sides). These were collected into chapbooks (folded sheets) and garlands: cheap books that contained ballads alongside other items of interest to their audience, such as proverbs, short poems (sometimes to impress lovers, prospective or otherwise) and songs. The contents of the ballad-sheets were intended for performance, and were generally sung to well-known popular tunes in communal gathering places such as taverns or (from the 1650s onwards) coffee houses, at social gatherings or in the home.[26] Sellers would advertise their wares by singing them at stalls or booths at fairs or in the streets.[27] In this respect ballads were somewhat like the *pastourelles* of three hundred years earlier; they bridged the divide between written and oral culture. The rhymed stories they created were open to oral performance, which then fed back into the literature, creating a reciprocal relationship. This made them generally popular, enjoyed by all, whether educated, elite or not. An estimated three to four million broadside ballads alone were published and sold in the second half of the sixteenth century, and even more in the century that followed.[28]

For an understanding of the message received by ballad audiences, the overall context of the form is, as with the early tales, key. It was with the ballads that the ideas of 'tradition' and 'folklore' really took hold, and yet they were largely an urban phenomenon. Throughout the period of the ballads' popularity, a capitalist economy was quickly developing and towns were rapidly expanding. London, in particular, was growing exponentially. The newcomers were mostly young migrants from the British countryside, with the addition of economic migrants and refugees from persecution and wars of religion in continental Europe. The subject matter, format and price of broadsides and broadsheets were tailored to appeal to this audience. Many of these people had been raised in rural cultures – or their parents had – and the ballads reflect this in their complex attitude towards the past, which is presented as rural, centred on the family, with uncomplicated, pre-industrial, pre-capitalist social and economic structures. The idea that a story had been transmitted from these past times was a vital part of its authenticity, along with a presumed (or pretended) provenance that was rural, poor and often aged and/or female. Rural old women, preferably by firesides, were particularly good sources of 'folk' tradition, whether real or imaginary.[29]

The stories spoke of tyrannical lordship, superstition, restriction, injustice and (usually) doomed youth. The subjects of ballads are usually marginal people, often young, both male and female. They may make casual or deliberate choices (especially if they are male) that open them up to dire consequences, of which they may or may not be initially aware. Young men and women as victims are frequent subjects. The victim's fate is taken out of his/her hands – by a seducer/rapist, a persecutor or the legal system – in a society that is presented as seigneurial, brutal and tyrannical, a perversion of a patriarchal ideal that nevertheless addresses the anxieties of being faceless and unprotected in an urban milieu. Sometimes the outcome is fortunate (the seducer is also the husband-to-be or falls in love with, and marries, his victim, or the victim escapes 'justice'), but it can also be very unfortunate (the subject discovers that her seducer/rapist is a close relation and kills herself, the young warrior is killed, or the lawbreaker is hanged). For young men, poaching is an exceptionally risky activity in ballads, as it was in real life; the tightening up of game laws and the introduction of strict laws of trespass in the early eighteenth century led to serious punishments, frequently the death penalty, for poaching offences, and young poachers and encroachers in ballad stories almost always end up dead. Victims usually die alone or are hopelessly afflicted, and often leave behind ageing mothers, despairing lovers or orphaned children. The events are presented in an intensely personal and emotional way, highlighting often gut-wrenching feelings of passion, anger, remorse, powerlessness and pain. Whether acts are criminal or not – and they frequently are – there is a strong emphasis on judgement, whether of God or human law enforcement, and consequences. The criminal confession and recantation, including the 'night before the execution' or the 'speech on the scaffold', were also very popular at this time, as was the criminal memoir.[30] Historical events are usually related, theatrically, in terms of personalities, personal suffering and pathos.

Stories first encountered in ballads include Robin Hood's famous meeting and quarterstaff fight with Little John over the stream (*Robin Hood and Little John*), Robin's playful and unsuccessful attempt to humiliate Friar Tuck by having the friar carry him over the river on his back, ending in a sword fight (*Robin Hood and the Curtal Friar*), and Robin's fight with a cross-dressed Maid Marion (*Robin Hood and Maid Marian*).[31] It is in the ballads that Little John's name is interpreted as a euphemism for a very tall man. Other characters such as Allan a Dale and Guy of Gisborne, as far as we know, are also introduced in ballad stories. There are other characters – tinkers, butchers, beggars, the Pinder of Wakefield, 'Gamwell' – who have not survived.[32] They include some important female characters, such as the Amazon-like forest nymph Clorinda in *Robin Hood's Birth, Breeding, Valour and Marriage* and the queen who outwits her husband in *Robin Hood and Queen Catherine*.[33] The ballads are very self-referential, and characters, names and themes recur regularly.

Robin Hood's death is elaborated (in two versions of a ballad of the same name) from the early story mentioned in the *Lytell Geste*, with added personal trauma and pathos.[34] Ballad writers also liked the idea of mistaken identity and long-lost relatives, a trope which often occurs in ballads of all kinds. Will Scarlet turns out to be a relative named Young Gamwell in *Robin Hood and the Prince of Aragon*, and the pedlar in *The Bold Pedlar and Robin Hood* turns out to be Gamble Gold, another long-lost relation. In one ballad, Robin fights a beautiful youth called Young Gamwell, who has also been outlawed for killing his father's steward. When the young man proves himself by fighting and wounding Robin, he declares that he is the nephew that Robin did not know he had (*Robin Hood Newly Revived*).[35] (This conceit resurfaces in Kevin Reynolds's 1991 film, *Robin Hood, Prince of Thieves*, when Will Scarlet reveals that he is Robin's 'lost' half-brother.)

The ballad writers and audiences also liked the idea of Robin's backstory, which developed rapidly from the later sixteenth century. In ballads, Robin is frequently depicted as a rash but unfortunate young man who is trapped by circumstances into a life of outlawry, often by poaching deer or killing foresters, or both. In *The Bold Pedlar and Robin Hood*, he and Little John are described as 'troublesome blades', and in *Robin Hood and the Curtal Friar* he is 'disposed to play'. This usually leads him into play fights, although in *Robin Hood and the Tinker* he gets the tinker drunk and leaves the inn without paying, in the more disreputable manner of medieval tricksters such as Till Eulenspiegel.[36] Accounts of how and why Robin became an outlaw in the first place begin with Anthony Munday's play (revised by Henry Chettle) of the late 1590s, *The Downfall of Robin Earl of Huntingdon*.[37] Munday's Robert is a young earl outlawed by a jealous and tyrannical Prince John. The main motivators of Munday's characters are love, lust and passion: the story is intensely personalized, as it is in the ballads. Munday's audience would have been familiar with ballad literature (as was Munday himself), and this personalization would have catered for their tastes.

The early tales do not give a backstory for Robin Hood; he just 'is' an outlaw who just 'does' live in the forest or greenwood. There, he is head servant in the household of the Virgin Mary, whose will – and therefore God's – he carries out. She sends his quarry to him, be it deer or people, and because he obeys her will his actions are not entirely his own. When he deviates from this service, as in *Robin Hood and the Monk*, he suffers for falling short. One of the most important consequences of the Reformation for Robin, although not immediately apparent, was his loss of the Virgin Mary. It deprived him not only of his romance love interest, but of his motivation, making him responsible for his own actions. The consequences of this could have been devastating, as Robin's actions consist of theft, grievous wounding and bodily harm, deceit and, on occasion, homicide, not to mention rebellion against the king's authority. He needed a backstory and a good reason for his outlawry to justify his criminal activity. The only modern cinematic retelling which attempts a 'religious' motivation is Richard Carpenter's *Robin of Sherwood* (1984–6), in which the Virgin's vacant space is filled by Herne the Hunter, a nineteenth-century figure who represents the 'religion of nature', a cross between the Green Man and a Wildman, with echoes of the ballad *Robin Hood and Guy of Gisborne* in his garb of a deer's skin (complete with head and antlers – rather than the horse's hide worn by Guy in the ballad).

The·Merry·Friar·carrieth·
Robin·acroſs·the·Water:·

The development of a ballad idea: Ritson's Robin and Tuck wear lavishly plumed helmets, while Howard Pyle's Robin (in the frontispiece to *The Merry Adventures of Robin Hood*) has adopted his familiar hat with its smaller, jaunty feather. *The Adventures of Robin Hood* (dir. Michael Curtiz and William Keighley, 1938) copies Pyle's image, although the facial hair of Pyle's characters (no longer fashionable in the 1930s) is missing from the film version. Robin Hood films and television tend to be self-referential (Errol Flynn's Robin wears a costume based on that worn by Douglas Fairbanks Jr in Allan Dwan's 1922 *Robin Hood*), and this look has persisted, both in film and in the popular imagination. It is not dissimilar to that of the 'Antwerp' edition of the *Lytell Geste*.

A similar 'spirituality of nature' can be found in Alfred Noyes's play *Sherwood* (1911), which is an interesting mix of Munday, *A Midsummer Night's Dream* and *Romeo and Juliet*, with echoes of the ballad of *Robin Hood's Death* and William Copland's *Friar* play.[38] The hero and heroine are star-crossed lovers, the jealous villains are Queen Elinor and Prince, finally King, John. Elinor, disguised as a nun, sets Robin to bleed to death and stabs Marion. Robin rallies to find Marion dead, then submits to death, after shooting an arrow out of the window to mark where he should be buried. Alongside this human story, a group of woodland spirits interact with the human characters, intervening at the end to ensure Robin and Marion will be resurrected as spirits in the 'Shining Glen'. The alternative 'nature religion' allows for the existence of an almighty God, though:

> . . . But I have heard
> There is a great King, out beyond the world,
> Not Richard, who is dead, nor yet King John,
> But a great King who will one day come home
> Clothed with the clouds of heaven from His Crusade.[39]

The difference between *Robin of Sherwood* and Noyes's play is that in the former Robin serves a supernatural ideal, while in *Sherwood* he and Marion are aided by the woodland spirits. The modern television narrative is closer, therefore, to the spirit of the medieval. In *The Adventures of Robin Hood* (dir. Michael Curtiz and William Keighley, 1938) the roles of the Virgin and Robin are reversed. Olivia de Havilland's Marian is a Norman lady who initially despises Robin, but who revises her opinion of him when she sees the poor refugees that he has been helping. On remarking that one of them is a Norman, she also discovers that Robin eschews racism, helping all in need. This leads her to offer her help and eventually her love *to him*, rather than the other way round as in the early tales.

Some modern writers reject the idea of justifying Robin Hood altogether. Novelists Angus Donald and Adam Thorpe present Robin Hood as a form of gangster 'godfather' whose motives are chiefly power and profit.[40] Both Robins are solipsistic and cynically manipulative, but strangely compelling to both followers and onlookers; they are attractive as well as deadly to their victims. Thorpe's Hodd has a strange belief in his own destiny that makes him also unsettling. In a story which is loosely based on *Robin Hood and the Monk*, a former not-so-merry man reflects on how he was first attracted to Hodd, but is now repelled by him and by the act (the killing of the monk's little page) that he made him commit. Donald's narrator, Alan Dale, has a similar love–hate, admiration–revulsion relationship with Robin Hood as he follows Robin to Sherwood, then to the Crusades and back again. In his film *Robin and Marian* (1976), Richard Lester has Robin return not from the Crusades but from Richard I's campaign in France that culminated with the king's death at the siege of Chaluz in 1199.[41] The returning Robin and

Little John's first period of outlawry is unexplained, but they have recently been condemned as a result of Robin's almost casual insults to the dying king.[42] Robin does not have a social conscience or any political beliefs. Rather, his attempts to recover his lost youth and to basically show off dupe the local peasantry into believing that, with his leadership, they can stand up to their aristocratic lords and masters. They do not stand a chance, as the careworn sheriff of Nottingham laconically observes, and end up dead, as do the sheriff, Robin and his lover Marian.

'Maid' Marion is another essential feature of modern Robin Hood stories, although she is not present in the early tales. She is not, and yet she is, in the person of Marion the *pastourelle* shepherdess and her alter ego, the Virgin Mary. She was present in morris dances and possibly in other festive performances of pastoral subjects after the Reformation; it may be that she entered the Robin Hood ballads from performance texts, or perhaps directly from the *pastourelle* tradition, but the modern character dates from the nineteenth century. As a representative of muscular, active Anglo-Saxon manhood in that century, Robin had to meet the right girl, get married and settle down in order to be a respectable, marketable hero. Marian supplied this requirement, and the romantic love interest she provided has remained part of Robin Hood's storyworld from popular theatre to Disney. In the early nineteenth century there were many very popular stage Marians, in the metropolis and in regional repertory theatres, where the part offered female actors a chance to escape, however temporarily and partially, from the restrictions of female costume and passive, subordinate roles.[43] When Alfred Lord Tennyson wrote his Robin Hood play, *The Foresters*, in the 1890s, the part of Marian was originally envisaged for Ellen Terry, one of the most famous – if not the most famous – female actors of her day.[44]

In film, Olivia de Havilland was a major figure in promoting Marian to a powerful character with agency of her own. A major star at MGM studios, de Havilland was able to influence the nature of her character, and had to be given a fair amount of screen time in relation to the male stars with whom she worked. Her Marian is a woman of high standing and intelligence, treated respectfully by Prince John and Sir Guy: she cannot be forced to marry Sir Guy against her will, and she answers back in front of the whole company when Robin addresses her in a patronizing way. She makes the decision to help him, plays a major part in his escape from the gallows, and is herself tried for treason when she tries to reveal John and Guy's plot to kill King Richard. In the end, the king asks her if she wishes to marry Robin, now restored to his earldom, and she replies that she does.

Audrey Hepburn's Marian in *Robin and Marian* (1976) has equal billing – and an equally important part – with Sean Connery's Robin, although she does not don male clothing or take on a masculine persona. Uma Thurman's Marian in John Irvin's *Robin Hood* (1991) does cross-dress; she hunts, she fights, chops wood and even does her own rope-swing. Like de Havilland, she accepts Robin as a partner only on her own terms. Cate Blanchett, in Ridley Scott's *Robin Hood* (2010), protects her aged father, their land and their property, helps in the deception with Robin to this end, dons armour and rides to the aid of Robin and the kingdom against an invading force. She then makes her own decision to join Robin and his merry men in Sherwood Forest. A similarly strong character is Lucy Griffiths's Marian in the Minghella/Allan *Robin Hood* television series (2006–9). Her own 'social bandit' figure is operative before Robin Hood arrives back from the Crusades to take over. Although she loves Robin, she retains her own independence of thought and action. She, too, protects an ageing father (a former sheriff of Nottingham) and helps Robin because she believes his causes to be right. She tells him when she disagrees, and will not always support his actions or act on his ideas. She lives, and eventually dies, on her own terms.

Tony Robinson's television series *Maid Marian and her Merry Men* (1989–94) is an interesting example of 'world upside down' parody that carries echoes of the medieval *pastourelles*, Adam de la Halle and the *fabliaux*. The reversals of *fabliau* frequently place the women on top, and here Robin is conceived as an ineffective, immature, gullible, 'southern softie', while Marian runs the gang of outlaws. The brilliant schemes are hers, she is the bold leader, and it is she who effectively combats the dastardly sheriff and Prince John. Little John has become Little Ron, who is genuinely small, and the other outlaw characters, such as the Rastafarian Barrington and the aptly named Rabies, have evocative names reminiscent of *fabliau* churls, and of Robert of Normandy's outlaw band in the medieval *Robert le Dyable*. As in Adam's *Jeu*, it is Marian who gets herself out of difficult situations and who rescues Robin from danger. Like Adam's Marian, she still loves him, because despite his deficiencies, he has a good heart. Mel Brooks's *Robin Hood: Men in Tights* (1993) is a more modern parody; it sends up the legend, principally Reynolds's *Prince of Thieves*, by injecting it with absurdities and modern incongruities, such as Robin's bow, which has become a multi-arrow-propelling weapon of mass destruction, and 'Maid' Marian's chastity belt. There are some *fabliau*-esque moments, such as when Cary Elwes's Robin enters the hall carrying a pig across his shoulders in a comic inversion of Errol Flynn's entrance with a deer corpse in *The Adventures of Robin Hood* (1938), or when he serenades Marian in silhouette, with the shadow of his sword rising from his crotch. The reduction of love to the physical and the sexual, and the coarse connotations of the pig (grunting, wallowing, eating rubbish) as opposed to the noble deer, are – intentionally or not – very much in tune with medieval comic inversion.

To speak of Robin Hood in the modern world is to speak of England or Scotland or the United States: which nation he actually represents is the choice of the writer, or of the audience, or both. He can do this because he is not a historical character, bound to one time or place. From the end of the eighteenth century, at least, his stories began to spread outwards from the British Isles. In some cases, they influenced the perception of national heroes and freedom fighters, and in North America they became associated with the legendary outlaws of the western frontier.[45] The idea of Robin as somehow representing the nation (whichever nation that may be) owes much to the ballads. For all the writers' invocation of 'merry England' and the appearances of the king, there is no connection with nationalism *per se* in the early stories; even if chroniclers like Bower wanted to make such connections in relation to Scotland, this was their own agenda rather than that of the people who were celebrating the outlaw in their country. In the later ballads Robin represents a 'world we have lost' spirit of Englishness (or Scottishness, as ballads often have Scottish versions or survive in Scottish collections). It was in this nostalgic spirit that Joseph Ritson published his Robin Hood collection in 1795. In an age of revolutions, Ritson's sympathies were not entirely with the political status quo; his attitude to Robin's anti-authoritarian stance is stated in his own introduction:

> In these forests, and with this company, he for many years reigned like an independent sovereign; at perpetual war,

Robin Hood in the romantic imagination: the Great Tor, Matlock Spa, Derbyshire, in sunny and 'moody' mode. According to Francis Child, writing in 1857/8, this was also called 'Robin Hood's Tor'. Features of interest in the landscape, sometimes previously attributed to Woden or to the Devil, were reattributed to Robin Hood or Little John in order to attract tourist interest from the 17th century onwards.

> indeed, with the king of England . . . It is not, at the same time, to be concluded that he must, in this opposition, have been guilty of manifest treason or rebellion; as he most certainly can be justly charged with neither.[46]

Ritson's work influenced Thomas Love Peacock's *Maid Marian*, written in 1818.[47] In 1819 Sir Walter Scott's novel *Ivanhoe* appeared. For Scott, Robin Hood (who appears under the pseudonym of Locksley for most of *Ivanhoe*) aligns himself with the interests of the Saxon nation (now described in terms of nation and of race) against their Norman overlords. In the guise of the woodsman Locksley, Robin tells Ivanhoe, 'But for my purpose . . . thou shouldst be as well a good Englishman as a good knight; for that which I have to speak of concerns, indeed, the duty of every honest man, but is more especially that of a true-born native of England.'[48] Scott's novel is set against the background of the Third Crusade, in which Richard I took part, with both Sir Wilfrid of Ivanhoe and his nemesis Sir Brian de Bois Guilbert being returned Crusaders. The action takes place in South Yorkshire – a nod to the early tales – but the presence of the Jewish characters, Rebecca and her father, and the Templars lends exoticism to the landscape. The Crusade was a feature of British and American Robin Hood and Maid Marian stage plays in the nineteenth century that spilled over into film in the 1922 movie, and has been recently repeated in *Robin Hood, Prince of Thieves*, in the Minghella/Allan television series and in the latest *Robin Hood* film (Otto Bathurst, 2018), where it takes on connotations of the conflict in Afghanistan.

Robin Hood was popular in the United States in the form of stage plays, literature (cheap 'dime' novels and less cheap works such as those of Howard Pyle), nickelodeon 'shorts' and eventually feature films. It may be his association with the heroes of the Wild West that was partly responsible for this, as these were also the media in which Western fiction was circulated. Robin Hood was a popular subject on the American stage as well as the British. Traffic was two-way, as American productions crossed the Atlantic to play in London. Reginald de Koven's opera *Maid Marian*, which opened under the title *Robin Hood* in Chicago in 1890, opened in London in the following year.[49] The story was largely based on the influential retelling of the Robin Hood legend (*The Merry Adventures of Robin*

The statue of Robin Hood outside Nottingham Castle was given to the city (by Philip E. Clay) in 1949, to celebrate the city's quincentennial celebrations, and to commemorate a visit by the then Princess Elizabeth and the Duke of Edinburgh in that year.

Hood) for younger audiences by Howard Pyle. No individual contributor can be credited with the invention of the modern image of Robin Hood, but Pyle, who was a talented artist and admirer of the Arts and Crafts movement in Britain, created his own influential illustrations – of a man in a tunic, hose and boots, and a pointed (version of the bycocket) hat with a feather.[50] Pyle's influence can be seen in the enduring modern perception that Robin Hood is family entertainment, although this and later retellings of the story for children, by writers such as Henry Treece and Roger Lancelyn Green, do reflect the socio-political contexts in which they were written.[51]

Plaques on the wall behind the statue illustrate iconic episodes in the life of Robin: fighting over the stream with Little John (right), being united with Maid Marion by Richard the Lionheart, shooting Guy of Gisborne accompanied by Marion and Tuck, and firing his last arrow from the window of Kirklees priory (left). Although these episodes are an indelible part of the legend now, not one of them appears in any of the manuscript or early print versions of Robin Hood stories.

Some versions of the Robin Hood stories, such as those by children's writer and illustrator Marcia Williams, tell and illustrate the older material in new, and very interesting, ways for a young audience.[52]

Robin Hood is still with us in more ways than this, as regionally he forms part of a lucrative heritage tourist industry. Although increasing in economic value and in regional marketing, this is not a new phenomenon, but dates from as far back as the seventeenth century, at least. The early modern period saw a proliferation of inns named Robin Hood in Yorkshire, and by the eighteenth century there was a group of tourist 'objects' locally in the area of Kirklees, including Robin Hood's grave on the priory site and Robin Hood's well on the Great North Road (now the A1) at Barnsdale Bar. The Armitage family sponsored brewing in the area, which benefited also from the development of the springs at Harrogate and the Dropping Well at Knaresborough as destinations for what we would call 'health tourism'.[53] There were other places; in the Peak District (the land of Gilbert Pilkington's manuscript and one of the earliest major tourist destinations), Hathersage became associated, and still is, with Little John's grave. Francis Child notes that the Great Tor outside Matlock – another popular health spa – was also known as Robin Hood's Tor.[54]

The area most frequently represented, however, was in and around Nottingham, and here there is a concentration of Robin Hood sites and features, including hills, wells, caves, the Major Oak in Sherwood Forest and the church at Edwinstowe nearby, where Robin Hood is said to have married Maid Marian.[55] Robin Hood games had concentrated, fostered and projected local community identity in the early period, and this can be seen again in events such as the presentation of the play *Robin Hood and his Crew of Souldiers* to the newly restored Charles II in Nottingham in 1660. As might be expected from the occasion, the short performance delivers expressions of loyalty to the king – although perhaps with an underlying warning about good kingship, not stated but implicit in the subject matter.[56] The idea of Robin as 'the spirit of Nottingham' can be seen not only in the local tourist industry today, but in marketing for organizations such as the local building society (whose logo is a 'Robin Hood' head) and the local county cricket club (Nottingham CCC, 'the Outlaws', with a deer as a shirt logo). Heritage tourism generally sees the romanticized Robin Hood (from the eighteenth century onwards) who is associated with folklore, and who represents the soul of a nation no longer apparent in a capitalist, post-industrial, increasingly urbanized world. It is the Robin Hood of the ballads, of Walter Scott, of Howard Pyle and of Alfred Noyes, rather than the Robin of the early stories, of the pre-Reformation period. In one of the final scenes from John Irvin's *Robin Hood*, Will Scarlet confronts his defeated and embattled Norman overlord on the castle stairs. On being asked by his adversary what he wants, Will demands that the Baron – who represents to him everyone of Norman extraction – give him back his country. 'It's my country, too,' the Baron replies. This moment of epiphany leads to mutual understanding and accord; they agree to share 'their' England. It is a very medieval moment, entirely in the spirit of the early Robin Hood tales, whose cultural heritage was built upon inputs from British, German/Flemish, Scandinavian and French culture, and whose tellers expressed themselves in at least two, or more, languages current in Britain at the time. Their Robin Hood was, in other words, very English indeed, in that he was made out of elements that had come from many other places. The early Robin Hood was outward-facing, community-based and fun (while also being spiritually and morally beneficial) for people of all classes, genders and ages. As the servant of the Virgin Mary, he represented the popular religious beliefs of people who felt a sense of belonging to a universal, Western, Latin Church – no matter what they might think about its popes and its higher clergy, or how 'secularized' or proto-capitalist their moral values might be. Above all, although he was English, he was European, and part of a bilingual or trilingual culture that was shared by people across the Continent. English culture, like the English themselves, was always hybrid, and so was he. It is some sense of that faith, morality, fun and European-ness that this book (although far from comprehensive) has sought to convey in the hope that it will open up new ways of 'seeing' Robin Hood.

Appendix: The Texts in Modern English Translation

These are translated into modern English: lines numbered to enable comparison with 'original' sources. The texts are arranged in assumed chronological order of the surviving sources, as their exact times of origin are unknown. The manuscript transcriptions of Thomas H. Ohlgren, in Thomas H. Ohlgren, ed., and Lister M. Matheson, *Early Rymes of Robyn Hood: An Edition of the Texts ca. 1425 to ca. 1600* (Tempe, AZ, 2013) are recommended. A good, accessible, earlier edition is *Robin Hood and Other Outlaw Tales*, edited by Stephen Knight and Thomas H. Ohlgren (Kalamazoo, MI, 2000). Incunabula versions of the *Lytell Geste* are available online at *Early English Books Online* (https://eebo.chadwyck.com) and a digitized version of the Antwerp *Geste* is available on the National Library of Scotland website: https://digital.nls.uk.

For the translation, early versions in manuscript and in print have been consulted, and compared with the Ohlgren/Matheson and the Knight/Ohlgren printed editions. The partial text of the Antwerp *Lytell Geste*, the earliest surviving text of any length, has been interpolated with lines from the Wynkyn de Worde edition of circa 1506. Notes in the text show where this has taken place.

In some cases, the 'old' familiar form 'thee' (that is, 'you') has been retained, in order to preserve the original rhyme. This is particularly true in the *Lytell Geste*.

ROBYN AND GANDELEYN

Robyn lies in the green wood, bound.

I heard the singing of a clerk at yonder wood's end, of good Robyn and Gandeleyn; there was no other company. These young men were not strong thieves at all but bowmen, good and respectable; they went to the woods to get some meat if God would send it.

All day those young men went about it, and they found no meat until it was almost evening and the youths would go home. They came upon half a hundred fat fallow deer; and all were very fair and fat enough, and none of them were marked.

'By dear God,' said good Robyn, 'we shall have one of these.'

Robyn got out his fine bow and in it he set an arrow. When the fattest deer was not half flayed out of its hide, there came a crafty arrow out of the west that felled Robert's pride. Gandeleyn looked him east and looked west, on every side.

'Who has killed my master? Who has done this deed? I shall not go out of the greenwood until I see their sides bleed.'

Gandeleyn looked him east and looked west, and sought under the sun. He saw a little boy he called Wrennok of Donne, a good bow in his hand, a broad arrow therein and four and twenty good arrows trussed up in a lace.

'Beware thee, ware thee, Gandeleyn, hereof you'll get plenty.'

'Every one for its other,' said Gandeleyn, 'bad luck to him who flees.' 'Whereat shall our mark be?' said Gandeleyn.

'Each at the other's heart,' said Wrennok again.

'Who shall give the first shot?' said Gandeleyn.

'And I shall give the one before [the first],' said Wrennok again. Wrennok shot a really good shot and he didn't shoot too high. Through the thick part of his breeches it hit his nether thigh.

'Now have you given me one before,' thus to Wrennok said he, 'and through the might of Our Lady a better I shall give thee.' Gandeleyn bent his good bow and set therein an arrow. He shot through his green kirtle [tunic]; his heart he cut in two.

'Now you shall never boast, Wrennok, at ale or at wine, that you have killed good Robyn and his knave Gandeleyn.'

Robin lies in the green wood, bound.

ROBIN HOOD AND THE MONK

In summer, when the woods are bright,
And leaves are broad and long,
It is very merry in the fair forest
To hear the birds' song.
To see the deer draw to the dale,

And leave the hills high,
And take shadow in the leaves green,
Under the greenwood tree.
It befell on Whitsuntide,
Early on a May morning,
The risen sun was shining fair
And birds were merrily singing.
'This is a merry morning,' said Little John,
'By him that died on the Tree [Cross];
A merrier man than I am
Lives not in Christendom.'
'Pluck up your spirits, my dear master,'
Little John said,
'And think that it is a very good time
On a morning in May.'
'Yea, one thing grieves me,' said Robin,
'And causes my heart much woe,
That I may not on a day of Solemnity [a 'special' day in the Church calendar]
To Mass or Matins go.'
'It is a fortnight and more,' said he,
'Since I saw my Saviour;
Today I will go to Nottingham,' said Robin,
'By the might of mild Mary.'
Then up spoke Much, the miller's son,
May he always have good fortune!
'Take twelve of your fit yeomen,
Well weaponed, by your side.
Anyone who would kill you alone,
Would not take on the twelve.'
'Of all my merry men,' said Robin,
'By my faith, I will have none,
But Little John shall bear my bow,
Until I want to draw it.'
'You'll carry your own,' said Little John,
'Master, and I will carry mine,
And we'll shoot for a penny,' said Little John,
'Under the greenwood canopy.'
'I'll not shoot for a penny,' said Robin Hood,
'In faith, Little John, with thee,
But for every one that you wager,' said Robin,
In faith I'll wager three.'
Thus they shot forth, these two yeomen,
Both at bushes and shrubs,
Until Little John won from his master
Five shillings, for hose and shoes.
A mighty strife began between them,
As they went on their way,
Little John said he'd won five shillings,

And Robin said, curtly, 'nay'.
With that Robin Hood said Little John lied,
And hit him with his hand,
Little John grew angry with that,
And pulled out his bright brand [sword or dagger].
'Were you not my master,' said Little John,
'You would be badly hit,
Get a man wherever you can,
For you won't have me any more.'
Then Robin goes to Nottingham
That morning, all by himself alone,
And Little John back to merry Sherwood,
The paths he knew, each one.
When Robin came to Nottingham,
Truly, not in disguise,
He prayed to God and mild Mary
To bring him safely out again.
He goes into St Mary's church,
And knelt before the Rood [crucifix],
All who were then in the church
Had a good look at Robin Hood.
Beside him stood a large-headed monk,
I pray to God he comes to no good!
He quickly recognized good Robin,
As soon as he saw him.
Out of the door he ran,
As quickly as he could,
All the gates of Nottingham
He caused to be barred, each one.
'Rise up,' he said, 'you proud sheriff,
Ready yourself and get prepared,
I have seen the king's felon
Truly, he's in this town.
I have seen the false felon,
As he stands at Mass,
It will be your fault,
If he gets away from us.
This traitor's name is Robin Hood,
Under the greenwood canopy;
He robbed me once of a hundred pounds,
It will never go out of my mind.'
Up then rose this proud sheriff,
And quickly readied himself,
Many was the mother's son,
That went with him to the church.
In at the doors they forcibly pushed,
With plenty of sturdy staves,
'Alas, alas!' said Robin Hood,
'Now I miss Little John.'

But Robin took out a two-handed sword,
That was hanging down by his knee,
Where the sheriff and his men were most crowded,
Thitherward went he.
Three times through them he ran,
As truly to you I say,
And wounded many a mother's son,
And twelve he killed that day.
His sword upon the sheriff's head
He definitely broke in two
'The smith that made you,' said Robin,
'I pray God give him ill!
For now I am weaponless,' said Robin,
'Alas! Against my will,
Unless I can flee from these traitors,
I know they will kill me.'
Robin . . . the church . . . ran,
Among them every one . . .
[two lines and part lines are missing here]
[there is a gap here; when the story begins again, we are in the woods with the outlaws]
Some fell swooning, as if they were dead,
And lay as still as any stone,
None of them were in their right mind
Except for Little John.
'Let be your moaning,' said Little John,
'For the love of him who died on the Tree –
You who should be doughty men –
it is a great shame to see.
Our master has been hard beset
And yet escaped away
Pluck up your spirits, and leave this moaning,
And listen to what I shall say.
He has served Our Lady many a day
And still will, for sure,
Therefore I trust in Her especially
No wicked death shall he die.
Therefore be glad,' said Little John,
'And let this mourning be;
And I shall be the monk's guide
With the might of mild Mary.'
Then up spoke Much, the miller's son,
'We will go, just we two,'
'And when I meet him,' said Little John,
'I trust to do him harm.
Take care that you guard our trysting tree,
Under the leaves small,
And spare none of the venison,
That goes in this vale.'

Forth then went these yeomen two,
Little John and Much, together,
And looked out from Much's uncle's house;
The highway was very near.
Little John stood at a window in the morning,
And looked out from upstairs,
He was aware that the monk came riding,
And with him a little page.
'By my faith,' said Little John to Much,
'I can give you good news;
I see where the monk comes riding,
I know him by his wide hood.'
They went out on the road, these yeomen both,
Like courteous and gracious men;
They asked for news from the monk,
As if they were his friends.
'From whence come ye?' said Little John,
'Tell us some news, I ask you,
Of a false outlaw called Robin Hood,
Who was taken yesterday.
He robbed me, and my companions both,
Of twenty marks for sure,
If that false outlaw is taken,
It would make me really glad.'
'So did he me,' said the monk,
'of a hundred pounds and more;
I laid the first hand on him,
You may thank me for it.'
'I pray God thanks you,' said Little John,
'And we will when we may;
We will go with you, by your leave,
And bring you on your way.
For Robin Hood has many a wild fellow,
I tell you this for sure,
If they knew you rode this way,
In faith, you would be slain.'
As they went talking by the way,
The monk and Little John,
John took the monk's horse by the head,
Quickly, and immediately.
John took the monk's horse by the head,
Truly, as I tell you,
So did Much the little page,
So that he shouldn't get away.
By the neck of the hood
John pulled the monk down;
John was not afraid of him at all,
He let him fall on his crown.
Little John was really aggrieved,

And drew out his sword on high;
The monk saw that he would be dead,
Loudly, 'Mercy', he began to cry.
'He was my master,' said Little John,
'That you have brought to harm;
You will never come to our king,
In order to tell him the tale.'
John cut off the monk's head,
No longer would he wait,
And so did Much to the little page,
For fear that he would tell.
They buried them both there,
In neither bog nor heath,
And Little John and Much together
Carried the letters to our king.
[*one line is missing here, counted in the line numbering*]
He kneeled down on his knee;
'God save you, my liege lord,
Jesus save and look out for you!'
'God save you, my lord king!'
John was very bold to speak:
He gave the letters into his hand,
The king unfolded them.
The king read the letters straight away,
And said, 'May I thrive,
There never was a yeoman in merry England,
I longed so much to see.
Where is the monk who should have brought these?'
Our king said,
'By my troth,' said Little John,
'He died along the way.'
The king gave Much and Little John
Twenty pounds for sure,
And made them yeomen of the Crown,
And told them to go again.
He gave John the seal in his hand
To carry to the sheriff,
To bring Robin Hood to him,
And no man do him harm.
John took his leave from our king,
I'm telling you the truth:
The nearest road to Nottingham
To take, he went on the way.
When John came to Nottingham
The gates were barred, every one;
John called out the porter,
He answered him right away.
'What is the cause,' said Little John,
'that you bar the gates so fast?'

'Because Robin Hood,' said the porter,
'is thrown into the deep prison.
John and Much and Will Scarlett,
Truly I tell you,
They killed our men upon our walls,
And assaulted us every day.'
John hurried after the sheriff,
And soon he found him;
He opened the king's privy seal
And gave it into his hand.
When the sheriff saw the king's seal
He took off his hood straight away,
'Where is the monk that carried the letters?'
He said to Little John.
'He is so happy with him,' said Little John,
'Truly I tell you –
He has made him abbot of Westminster,
A lord of that abbey.'
The sheriff made John good cheer,
And gave him wine of the best;
At night they went to bed,
And every man to his rest.
When the sheriff was asleep,
Drunk with wine and ale,
Little John and Much, forsooth,
Made their way to the jail.
Little John called up the jailer,
And bade him rise immediately;
He said Robin Hood had broken jail,
And out of it was gone.
The porter rose right away, for sure,
As soon as he heard John call;
Little John was ready with a sword,
And pinned him to the wall.
'Now I will be porter,' said Little John,
'And take the keys in hand.'
He went on the way to Robin Hood,
And soon he unbound him.
He gave him a good sword in his hand,
To guard his head therewith,
And where the wall was lowest
They leapt down right away.
By the time the cock began to crow,
The day began to break:
The sheriff found the jailer dead,
The common bell [to summon the people] he began to ring.
He made a hue and cry throughout the town,
Whether a yeoman or a knave,
Whoever could bring him Robin Hood,

His reward he should have.
'For I never dare,' said the sheriff,
'Come before our king;
For if I do, I know for certain,
Truly, he will hang me.'
The sheriff made a search of Nottingham,
Both by street and alleyway,
And Robin was in merry Sherwood,
As happy as a leaf on a tree.
Then spoke good Little John,
To Robin Hood he said,
'I have done you a good turn for an evil,
Pay back when you can.
I have done you a good turn,' said Little John,
'Truly, I say to you;
I have brought you back to the greenwood trees;
Farewell, and have good day.'
'Nay, by my troth,' said Robin Hood,
'So shall it never be,
I make you master,' said Robin Hood,
'Of all my men and me.'
'No, by my troth,' said Little John,
'So shall it never be;
But let me be one of the men,' said Little John,
'Nothing else do I care to be.'
Thus John got Robin Hood out of prison,
Truly, without any fakery,
When his men saw him fit and unharmed,
Truly, they were really glad.
They took lots of wine, and made themselves glad,
Under the leaves small,
And ate venison pasties,
That went down well with ale.
Then word came to our king
How Robin Hood was gone,
And how the sheriff of Nottingham
Durst never him look upon.
Then said our comely king,
In a great anger;
'Little John has beguiled the sheriff,
In faith, so he has me.
Little John has beguiled us both,
And I can that full well see:
Or else the sheriff of Nottingham,
Hanged high, should he be.
I made them yeomen of the Crown,
And gave them fee with my hand;
I gave them a pardon,' said our king,
'Throughout all merry England.

I gave them pardon,' then said our king,
'I say, as I may thrive,
Truly such a yeoman as he is one,
In all England there are not three.
He is true to his master,' said our king,
'I say, by sweet Saint John,
He loves better Robin Hood
Than anyone does me.
Robin Hood is ever bound to him,
Both on the road and at home;
Speak no more of this matter,' said our king,
'But John has beguiled us all.'
Thus ends the talking of the monk
And Robin Hood, indeed;
God, who is always a crowned king,
Bring us all to his bliss!

A ROBIN HOOD PERFORMANCE SCRIPT [FRAGMENT?]

'Sir sheriff, for thy sake Robin Hood will I take.'
'I will give thee gold and fee. To this promise you may hold me.'
'Robin Hood, fair and free; under this [woodland] canopy shoot we.'
'I will shoot with thee, to fulfil all your desires.'
'Have at the target.'
'And I cleave the wand.'
'Let us cast the stone.'
'I grant well, by Saint John.'
'Let us cast the axle-tree.'
'Have a foot in front of thee.'
'Sir Knight, you have a fall [wrestling?].'
'And Robin, I shall match thee.'
'Out on thee, I blow my horn. It was better not to have been born.'
'Let us fight to the death. He who flees, God give him misfortune.'
'Now I have the mastery here. Off I smite this sorry head.
This Knight's clothes I will wear, and in my hood his head will bear.'

'Well met, my fellow, what have you heard about good Robin?'
'Robin Hood and his followers have been taken by the sheriff.'
'Let's go on foot, with good will, and the sheriff we will kill.
Behold well Friar Tuck, how he does his bow pluck.'

'Yield you, sirs, to the sheriff, or else your bows will be broken.'
'Now all of us are bound . . . Friar Tuck, this is no game.'
'Come forth, you false outlaw; you shall be hanged and drawn!'
'Now, alas! What shall we do?'
'We must to the prison go.'
'Open the gates – fast, now! And let these thieves go in.'

[There are various ways of arranging punctuation of this piece, all of which imply different speakers and staging. This is just my own interpretation.]

ROBIN HOOD AND THE POTTER

In summer, when the leaves spring,
The blossoms on every bough,
So merry do the birds sing,
In woods that are merry now.
Hearken, good yeomen,
Comely, courteous and good,
One of the best that ever carried a bow,
His name was Robin Hood.
Robin Hood was the yeoman's name,
That was both courteous and free [generous and noble]:
For the love of Our Lady,
All women worshipped he.
But as the good yeoman stood one day,
Among his merry men,
He was aware of a proud potter,
Who came driving over the lea [meadow].
'Yonder comes a proud potter,' said Robin,
'That has long travelled this way;
He was never so courteous a man
One penny of *pavage* [road tax] to pay.'
'I met them both at Wentbridge,' said Little John,
'And for that evilly may he thrive!
Three such strokes he gave me,
That my sides are still hurting.
I lay forty shillings,' said Little John,
'To pay it this same day,
That there isn't a man among us all
That a fine can make him pay.'
'Here is forty shillings,' said Robin,
'More, than you have said,
That I shall make that proud potter,
Pay a fine to me.'
There they wagered the money,
And gave it to a yeoman to keep;
Robin rushed out in front of the potter,
And told him to stand still.
He laid hands upon his horse,
And told the potter to stand very still:
The potter curtly said to him,
'Fellow, what is your will?'
'All these three years, and more, potter,' he said,

'You have been coming this way,
Yet were you never so courteous a man
One penny of *pavage* to pay.'
'What is your name?' said the potter,
'That you ask *pavage* of me?'
'Robin Hood is my name,
A fine you will leave me.'
'I will not leave a fine,' said the potter,
'Nor any *pavage* will I pay;
Take away your hand from my horse!
I'll do you some harm, otherwise, by my faith!'
The potter went to his cart,
He didn't have to search:
A good two-handed staff he pulled from it,
Before Robin he leapt.
Robin pulled out a curved sword,
A buckler in his hand;
The potter went to Robin,
And said, 'Fellow, let my horse go.'
They fought together then, these two yeomen;
It was a good sight to see:
Robin's men laughed at it,
Where they stood, under a tree.
Little John to his fellows said,
'Yonder potter will sturdily stand.'
The potter, with a crafty stroke,
Smote the bucker out of his hand.
And before Robin could take it again,
His buckler at his feet,
The potter took him in the neck,
And knocked him to the ground.
Robin's men saw that,
As they stood under a bough;
'Let us help our master,' said Little John,
'Or yonder potter will kill him.'
These yeomen went quickly:
To their master they came.
Little John said to his master,
'Who has won the wager?'
'Shall I have your forty shillings?' said Little John,
'Or you, master, shall have mine?'
'If they were a hundred,' said Robin,
'In faith, they are all thine.'
'It is not at all courteous,' said the potter,
'As I have heard wise men say,
If a poor yeoman is going on his way,
To hinder him on his journey.'
'By my troth, you tell the truth,' said Robin,
'You speak like a good yeoman;

If you drive forth every day,
You will never be stopped by me.
I pray you well, good potter,
Will you have fellowship [with me]?'
Give me your clothing, and you shall have mine,
I will go to Nottingham.'
'I agree to that,' said the potter,
'You will find me a good fellow;
If you can sell my pots well,
Come again, as you went.'
'No, by my troth,' said Robin
'And then beshrew my head,
I'll not bring any pots back again,
If any woman will buy them.'
Then spoke Little John,
And all his fellows with him,
'Master, beware of the sheriff of Nottingham,
For he is not at all our friend.'
'Through the help of Our Lady,
Fellows, leave me alone:
Ho, walk on!' said Robin,
'To Nottingham will I go.'
Robin went to Nottingham
The pots for to sell;
The potter stayed with Robin's men,
There he feared no evil.
Then Robin drove on his way,
So merry, over land;
There is more, and I can say,
The best is still to come.
When Robin came to Nottingham,
Truth is to tell,
He stabled his horses right away,
And gave them oats and hay.
In the middle of the town,
There he showed his wares:
'Pots, pots!' he soon began to call,
'A free gift if you buy more!'
Right up against the sheriff's gate
He showed off all his wares:
Wives and widows gathered around them,
And eagerly bought his wares.
Yet, 'Pots, great bargains!' cried Robin,
'I hate having to stand here':
And all that saw him sell
Said he'd not been a potter long.
The pots that were worth five pence,
He sold them for three pence;
In private, men and women said,

'Yonder potter will never thrive.'
Robin sold them very quickly,
Till he had only five pots left;
He took them out of his cart,
And sent them to the sheriff's wife.
She was really glad about that,
'Thank you very much,' said she then:
'When you come to this region again,
I will buy some of your pots, so may I thrive.'
'You shall have of the best,' said Robin,
And swore by the Trinity;
Very courteously she began to call him,
'Come and dine with the sheriff and me.'
'Thank you very much,' said Robin,
'Your will shall be done';
A maid carried the pots inside,
Robin and the sheriff's wife followed immediately.
When Robin came into the hall,
He soon met the sheriff:
The potter knew how to be courteous,
And he soon greeted the sheriff.
'See, sir, what this potter has given you and me;
Five pots, small and large!'
'He is very welcome,' said the sheriff,
'Let us wash, and go and eat.'
As they sat at their meal,
With a noble cheer;
Two of the sheriff's men began to speak
Of a great wager;
Of a shooting match, that was good and fine,
That was arranged the other day,
Of forty shillings, truth to tell,
Whoever this wager should win.
This proud potter then sat still,
Thus then thought he:
'As I am a true Christian man,
This shooting match will I see.'
When they had had the best,
Of bread and ale and wine,
To the butts they made their way
With bows and arrows, very fine.
The sheriff's men shot very fast,
Like archers that were good:
There came no one near the mark
By half a good archer's bow.
Still then stood the proud potter,
Thus then said he,
'If I had a bow, by the Rood,
One shot should you see.'

'You shall have a bow,' said the sheriff,
'The best that you will choose of three;
You seem a stalwart and strong man,
Tried you will be.'
The sheriff commanded a yeoman that stood by them
To go fetch the bows;
The best bow that the yeoman brought
Robin set on a string.
'Now shall I know if you're any good!
And pull up to your ear';
'So help me God,' said the proud potter,
'This is only very poor gear.'
To a quiver Robin went,
A good arrow from it he took:
So near unto the mark he went,
That he missed by less than a foot.
All of them shot again,
The sheriff's men and he;
He did not fail to hit the mark,
He split the prick [stick or wand] in three.
The sheriff's men thought it great shame
That the potter was the winner;
The sheriff laughed and made game of it,
And said, 'Potter, you are a man;
[*two lines are missing here, counted in the line numbering*]
You are worthy to bear a bow
In whatever place you go.'
'In my cart I have a bow,
'Forsooth,' he said, 'and that a good one;
In my cart is the bow
That Robin Hood gave me.'
'Do you know Robin Hood?' said the sheriff,
'Potter, I pray you, tell me':
'A hundred bouts I have shot with him,
Under his trysting tree.'
'Rather than a hundred pounds I'd have it,' said the sheriff,
'I swear by the Trinity,
[*one line missing, counted in the line numbering*]
That the false outlaw stood by me.'
'If you will follow my advice,' said the potter,
'And boldly go with me,
Tomorrow, before we eat bread,
Robin Hood will we see.'
'I will reward you,' said the sheriff,
'And swear by the God of might.'
The shooting they left, and home they went,
Their supper was already laid out.
In the morning, when it was day,
They got ready to ride out:

The potter began to get his cart ready,
And would not leave it behind.
He took leave of the sheriff's wife,
And thanked her for everything;
'Dame, for my love and if you will wear this,
I give you here a gold ring.'
'Thank you very much,' said the wife,
'Sir, God reward you for it.'
The sheriff's heart was never so light,
The fair forest to see.
And when he came into the forest,
Under the leaves green,
Birds sang freely on the boughs,
It was great joy to see.
'It is a mercy to be here,' said Robin,
'For a man that had anything to spend;
By my horn he shall find out
If Robin Hood is here.'
Robin set his horn to his mouth,
And blew a blast that was very good;
His men heard it that stood there,
Far down in the wood.
'I hear my master blow,' said Little John
[*two lines are missing here, counted in the line numbering*]
They ran as if they were mad.
When they to the master came,
Little John would not wait:
'Master, how have you fared in Nottingham?
How have you sold your wares?'
'Yes, by my troth, ay, Little John,
Do not be full of care:
I have brought the sheriff of Nottingham,
As goods for us all.'
'Had I known that before,
When we were at Nottingham,
You would not have come into the fair forest,
For all these thousand years.'
'That I know well,' said Robin,
'I thank God that you are here;
Therefore you will leave your horse with us,
And all your other gear.'
'That I defy and God forbid,' said the sheriff,
'In such a way to lose my goods;
[*two lines are missing here, counted in the line numbering*]
'Hither you came on a very high horse,
And home you shall go on foot:
And greet well your wife at home,
The woman is really good.
I shall send her a white palfrey,

It ambles, by my faith,
[*two lines are missing here, counted in the line numbering*]
I shall send her a white palfrey,
It ambles as you go:
If it were not for the love of your wife
For more sorrow should you sing.'
Thus parted Robin Hood and the sheriff:
To Nottingham he took the way.
His fair wife welcomed him home,
And to him did she say:
'Sir, how have you fared in the green forest?
Have you brought Robin home?'
'Dame, the devil speed him, both body and bone,
I have had a very great scorn.
Of all the goods that I have taken to the greenwood,
He has taken them from me:
All but this fair palfrey,
That he has sent to thee.'
With that she started to laugh loudly,
And swore by Him that died on the Tree,
'Now have you paid for all the pots
That Robin gave to me.
Now you are come home to Nottingham,
You will have goods enough.'
Now speak we of Robin Hood,
And of the potter under the green boughs.
'Potter, what were your pots worth
That I took to Nottingham with me?'
'They were worth two nobles,' said he,
'So may I thrive, or thee.
As much could I have got for them,
And had I been there.'
'You shall have ten pounds,' said Robin,
'Of money fair and free;
And ever when you come to the greenwood
You are welcome, Potter, to me.'
Thus parted Robin, the sheriff, and the potter,
Underneath the greenwood tree:
God have mercy on Robin Hood's soul,
And save all good yeomanry.

THE LITTLE GEST (LITTLE [BOOK OF] DEEDS) OF ROBIN HOOD

Fytte One

Pay attention and listen, gentlemen,
That be of freeborn blood;
I shall tell you of a good yeoman,
His name was Robin Hood.
Robin was a proud outlaw,
Whilst he walked on the ground;
So courteous an outlaw as he was one
Was there never found.
Robin stood in Barnsdale,
And leaned against a tree;
And beside him stood Little John,
A good yeoman was he.
And also did good Scarlet,
And Much, the miller's son;
There was not an inch of his body
But it was worth a man's.
Then up spoke Little John
Unto Robin Hood;
'Master, if you would eat now
It would do you much good.'
Then to him said good Robin,
'To dine I have no desire;
Until I have some bold baron,
Or some exotic guest.
Till I have some bold baron,
That may pay for the best;
Or some knight or some squire,
That dwells here in the West.'
A good custom then had Robin,
In whatever land he were,
Every day before he would dine,
Three masses would he hear.
The one in worship of the Father,
And another of the Holy Ghost;
The third of Our dear Lady,
That he loved altogether most.
Robin loved Our dear Lady;
For fear of deadly sin,
Would he never do a gathering harm
That any woman was in.
'Master,' then said Little John,
'Before we our table shall spread
Tell us whither we shall go
And what life we shall lead –

Where we shall take, where we shall leave,
Where we shall wait behind,
Where we shall rob, where we shall take [abduct],
Where we shall beat and bind.'
[*Antwerp version is in prose to here*]
'Don't worry about that,' then said Robin,
'We shall do well enough;
But look you do no husbandman harm
That tills with his plough.
No more shall you no good yeoman
That walks by the wood's green canopy;
Nor no knight nor no squire
That will be a good fellow.
These bishops and these archbishops,
You shall them beat and bind;
The high sheriff of Nottingham,
Him hold in your mind.'
'This word shall be heeded,' said Little John,
'And this lesson shall we learn;
It is far gone in the day, God send us a guest,
So that we can have our dinner.'
'Take thy good bow in your hand,' said Robin,
'Let Much go with thee;
And so shall William Scarlet
And no man stay with me.
And walk up to the Sayles,
And so to Watling Street;
And await some exotic guest,
On the chance you may them meet.
Be he an earl, or any baron,
Abbot, or any knight;
Bring him to my lodging to me,
His dinner shall be prepared.'
They went up to the Sayles,
These yeoman all three;
They looked east, they looked west:
They might no man see.
But as they looked into Barnsdale,
By a secret track;
Then came a knight riding –
Very soon they did him meet.
Miserable was his appearance,
And little was his pride;
His one foot in the stirrup set,
And the other hung beside.
His hood hung in his eyes two,
He rode in simple array [clothing];
A sorrier man than he was one,
Rode never in a summer's day.

Little John was very courteous,
And went down on his knee;
'Welcome be ye, gentle knight,
Welcome you are to me.
Welcome be ye to the greenwood,
Gracious knight and free [noble, generous];
My master has awaited you fasting
Sir, all these hours three.'
'Who is your master?' said the knight.
John said, 'Robin Hood.'
'He is a good yeoman,' said the knight,
'Of him I have heard much good.
I grant', he said, 'with you to wend [go]
My brothers, all together;
My purpose was to have dined today
At Blyth or Doncaster.'
Forth then went this gentle knight,
With a troubled cheer [countenance];
The tears out of his eyes ran,
And fell down his face.
They brought him to the lodge door,
When Robin did him see,
Most courteously he took of his hood,
And went down on his knee.
'Welcome, sir knight,' said Robin,
'Welcome you are to me,
I have awaited you fasting, sir,
All these hours three.'
Then answered the gentle knight,
With words fair and free [noble, gracious];
'God thee save, good Robin,
And all your fair company.'
They washed together and both wiped [their hands],
And sat down to their dinner;
Bread and wine they had right enough,
And mumbles [entrails] of the deer.
Swans and pheasants they enjoyed,
And birds of the river;
And not even the smallest bird was missing,
That ever bred on a briar.
'Enjoy your food,' said Robin,
'Many thanks, sir,' said he;
'Such a dinner I have not had
In all these weeks three.
If I come again, good Robin,
Here by this country,
As good a dinner I shall you make
As you have made for me.'
'Many thanks, sir knight,' said Robin;

'My dinner, when I it have,
I was never so greedy, by the great dear God,
My dinner for to crave.
But pay before you go,' said Robin,
'I think that it is right;
It was never the custom, by the great good God,
A yeoman to pay for a knight.'
'I have nothing in my coffers,'
said the knight,
'That I may offer, for shame.'
'Little John, go look,' said Robin,
'Do not be made to delay.
Tell me the truth,' then said Robin,
'As God is witness to thee;'
'I have no more than ten shillings,' said the knight,
'As God is witness to me.'
'If you have no more,' said Robin,
'I will not have one penny;
And if you have need of any more,
More shall I lend thee.
Go now, Little John,
The truth tell to me;
I there be no more than ten shillings,
No penny that I may see.'
Little John took off his cloak
And spread it on the ground,
And there he found in the knight's coffer [travelling box]
Only half a pound.
Little John let it lie undisturbed,
And went to his master, bowing low;
'What tidings, John?' said Robin,
'Sir, the knight says true enough.'
'Fill a cup of the best wine,' said Robin,
'The knight to talk shall begin;
It is a great wonder, thinketh me,
Your clothing is so thin.
Tell me one word,' said Robin,
'And secret it shall be;
I guess you were made a knight by force,
Or else are of yeomanry.
Or else you have been a bad husband,
And lived in stroke and strife;
A usurer, or else a lecher,' said Robin,
'With wrong hast led thy life.'
'I am none of those,' said the knight,
'By God that made me;
A hundred winters here before
My ancestors knights have been.
But often it has happened, Robin,

That a man has been downgraded;
But God that sits in heaven above,
May put right his state.
Within these two years, Robin,' he said,
'My neighbours know it well,
Four hundred pounds of good money
I might very well spend.
Now I have no possessions,' said the knight,
'God has shaped such an end,
My wife and children suffer
Till God it may amend.'
'In what manner,' then said Robin,
'Have you lost your riches?'
'By my great folly,' he said,
'And by my kindness.
I had a son, in truth, Robin
Who should have been my heir;
When he was twenty winters old
In the field he wanted to joust full fair.
He killed a knight of Lancaster,
And a squire bold;
In order to save him in his rights
My goods I pledged and sold.
My lands are put in pledge, Robin,
Against a certain day,
To a rich abbot here beside
Of Saint Mary's Abbey.'
'What is the sum?' said Robin,
'The truth tell to me;'
'Sir,' he said, 'four hundred pounds;
The abbot told it to me.'
'Now if you lose your land,' said Robin,
'What will happen to thee?'
'Hastily I will take myself off,' said the knight,
'Over the salt sea,
And see where Christ was alive and dead,
On the mount of Calvary;
Farewell, friend, and have good day;
It may no better be.'
Tears fell out of his two eyes;
He would have gone on his way;
'Farewell, friend, and have good day;
I have no more to pay.'
'Where are your friends?' said Robin;
'Sir, no one me will know;
Whilst I was rich enough at home
Great boasts would they make,
And now they run away from me
Like beasts in a row;

They take no more heed of me
Than if they had never seen me.'
For pity then wept Little John,
Scarlet and Much together;
'Fill up with the best wine,' said Robin,
'For here is simple fare.
Have you any friend?' said Robin,
'Your pledge who would be?'
'I have none,' then said the knight,
'But God, who died on the Tree.'
'Away with your tricks,' then said Robin Hood,
'Thereof I will right none;
Do you think I would have God as a pledge,
Peter, Paul, or John?
No, by him who made me,
And shaped both sun and moon,
Find me a better pledge,' said Robin,
Or money you'll get none.'
'I have no other,' said the knight,
'The truth for to say,
Unless it be Our dear Lady;
She failed me never before this day.'
'By the great good God,' said Robin,
'I searched throughout all England,
Yet I never found, to my liking,
A much better pledge.
Come forth now, Little John,
And go to my treasure,
And bring me four hundred pounds,
And look it be counted well.'
Forth then went Little John,
And Scarlet went before;
He counted out four hundred pounds,
By eight and twenty score [560].
'Is this well counted?' said little Much,
John said, 'What grieveth thee?
It is alms to help a gentle knight
That is fallen in poverty.
Master,' then said Little John,
'His clothing is very thin;
You must give the knight a livery
To help his body therein.
For you have scarlet and green, master,
And many a rich array;
There is no merchant in merry England,
So rich, I dare well say.'
'Take him three yards of every colour,
And look well measured it be.'
Little John took no other measure

But his bow-shaft.
At every handful that he measured
He leapt three feet –
'What devil's draper,' said little Much
'Do you think for to be?'
Scarlet stood very still and laughed,
And said, 'By God Almighty,
John may give him good measure,
Because it's costing him very little!'
'Master,' then said Little John,
To gentle Robin Hood;
'You must give the knight a horse
To carry home these goods.'
'Take him a grey courser,' said Robin,
'And a saddle new;
He is Our Lady's messenger –
God grant that he be true.'
'And a good palfrey,' said little Much,
'To maintain him in his right.'
'And a pair of boots,' said Scarlet,
'For he is a gentle knight.'
'What will you give him, Little John?'
Said Robin.
'Sir a pair of gilt spurs shining,
To pray for all this company;
God bring him out of trouble.'
'When shall my day be?' [to pay back], said the knight,
'Sir, according to your will?'
'Twelve months from today,' said Robin,
'Under this greenwood tree.
It would be a great shame,' said Robin,
'A knight alone to ride,
Without a squire, yeoman or page,
To walk by his side.
I shall lend you Little John, my man,
For he shall be your knave [servant],
In a yeoman's stead he may you stand,
If you great need have.'

Fytte Two

Now has the knight gone on his way,
The game he thought very good;
When he looked on Barnsdale,
He blessed Robin Hood.
And when he thought of Barnsdale,
Of Scarlet, Much and John;
He blessed them for the best company . . .
[*missing lines from here in Antwerp, supplied from de Worde*]

That ever he was come in.
Then spoke that gentle knight,
To Little John he did say:
'Tomorrow I must to York town,
To Saint Mary's Abbey.
And to the abbot of that place
Four hundred pounds I must pay;
And unless I'm there upon this night,
My land is lost for ever.'
The abbot said to his convent,
Where he stood on the ground,
'This day twelve months ago there came a knight,
Who borrowed four hundred pounds.
He borrowed four hundred pounds
Upon all his land free;
Unless he comes this very day
Disinherited shall he be.'
'It is very early,' said the prior,
'The day is not yet far gone;
I had rather pay a hundred pound,
And lay [it?] down now.
The knight is far beyond the sea.'
'In England he is alright,
He suffers hunger and cold,
And many a miserable night.'
'It would be a great pity,' said the prior,
'In this way to have his land;
If you be so light in your conscience,
You do to him much wrong.'
'You're always in my beard,' said the abbot,
'By God and Saint Richard!'
With that came in a fat-headed monk,
The high cellarer.
'He is dead or hanged,' said the monk,
'By God that bought me dear,
And we shall have to spend, in this place,
Four hundred pounds a year.'
The abbot and the high cellarer
Leapt forth right bold,
The justice of England
The abbot there did hold.
The high justice and many more
Had taken into their hand
Wholly, all the knight's debt,
To do that knight wrong.
They judged the knight very wrongly
The abbot and his followers;
'Unless he comes this very day,
Disinherited shall he be.'

'He will not come yet,' said the justice,
I dare well undertake.'
But in a sorrowful time for them all
The knight came to the gate.
Then up spoke that gentle knight
To his company;
'Now put on your simple clothes
That you brought from the sea.'
They came at once to the gates:
The porter was ready himself,
And welcomed them every one.
'Welcome, Sir Knight,' said the porter,
'My lord at dinner is he,
And so is many a gentle man
For the love of thee.'
The porter swore a great big oath:
'By God that made me,
Here is the best-built horse
That ever yet I saw.
Lead them into the stable,' he said,
'That rested might they be;'
'They shall not come therein,' said the knight,
'By God that died on a Tree.'
Lords were sitting at their meal
In that abbot's hall;
The knight went forth and knelt down
And saluted them great and small.
'Good day, sir abbot,' said the knight,
'I have come to keep my day.'
The first word the abbot spoke [was],
'Have you brought my pay?'
'Not one penny,' said the knight,
'By God that made me.'
'You are a wicked debtor,' said the abbot,
'Sir justice, drink to me.
What are you doing here,' said the abbot,
'If you have not brought your pay?'
'For God,' then said the knight
'To pray for a longer day [extension of the loan].'
'Your day is broken,' said the justice,
'Land you will get none.'
'Now, good Sir Justice, be my friend,
And defend me from my foes.'
'I take sides with the abbot,' said the justice,
'Both with cloth and fee.'
'Now, good sir sheriff, be my friend.'
'Nay, for God,' said he.
'Now, good sir abbot, be my friend,
For your courtesy,

And hold my lands in your hand,
Till I have given you satisfaction.
And I will be your true servant,
And truly serve thee,
Until you have four hundred pounds
Of money good and free.'
The abbot swore a great big oath,
'By God that died on a Tree,
Get the land how you may,
For you will get none from me.'
'By the dear worthy God,' then said the knight,
'That all this world made,
Unless I have my land again
Very dearly it shall be bought.
God, who was of a virgin born,
Grant us well to speed.
Because it is good to try a friend
When a man has need.'
The abbot hatefully on him looked,
And evilly began to call;
'Out,' he said, 'you false knight,
Hurry up out of my hall!'
'Thou liest,' then said the gentle knight,
'Abbot, in thy hall;
False knight was I never,
By God that made us all.'
Then up stood that gentle knight,
To the abbot said he,
'To suffer a knight to kneel so long,
Thou knowest no courtesy.
In jousts and in tournaments
A very long way have I been,
And put myself as far in the melee
As any that ever I have seen.'
'What will you give more?' said the justice,
'And the knight shall make his release?
And unless you do I dare safely swear
You'll never hold your land in peace.'
'A hundred pounds,' said the abbot,
The justice said, 'Give him two;'
'Nay, by God,' said the knight,
[*Antwerp picks up the story again here*]
'You will not get it like that.
Though you would give a thousand more,
Yet it wouldn't benefit you –
There shall never be my heir
Abbot, justice, nor friar.'
He leapt up towards a cupboard at once
To a table round;

And there he shook out of a bag
Exactly four hundred pounds.
'Have here your gold, Sir Abbot,' said the knight,
'Which you lent to me;
If you had been courteous at my coming
Rewarded you would have been.'
The abbot sat still, and ate no more,
For all his royal fare;
He laid his head upon his shoulder
And immediately began to stare.
'Give me back my gold,' said the abbot,
'Sir Justice, that I gave thee.'
'Not a penny,' said the justice,
'By God that died on the Tree.'
'Sir Abbot, and you men of law
[*Antwerp has next lines missing, supplied from de Worde*]
Now have I kept my day;
Now shall I have my land again
For ought that you can say.'
The knight went out of the door,
Away was all his care;
And on he put his good clothing,
The other he left there.
He went out singing merrily,
As men have told in the tale;
His lady met him at the gate
At home in Verysdale.
'Welcome, my lord,' said his lady,
'Sir, are all your possessions lost?'
'Be merry, wife,' said the knight,
[*Antwerp picks up again here*]
'And pray for Robin Hood,
That his soul shall ever be in bliss,
He helped me out of trouble;
If it had not been for his kindness,
Beggars would we have been.
The abbot and I are accorded,
He has been given his pay;
The good yeoman lent it to me,
As I came by the way.'
The knight then lived well at home,
The truth for to say,
Till he had got four hundred pounds,
All ready for to pay.
He got himself a hundred bows,
The strings well maintained,
A hundred sheaves of good arrows,
The heads burnished very bright.
And every arrow an ell long,

With peacock feathers well dressed;
Worked all over with white silver:
It was a seemly sight.
He got himself a hundred men
[*lines missing in Antwerp, supplied from de Worde*]
Well harnessed in that place;
And himself among them sat,
Clothed in white and red.
He carried a gay lance in his hand,
And a man led his trunk [on a pack horse or mule?],
And they rode with a merry song
Towards Barnsdale.
But as he went over a bridge there was a wrestling match,
And there delayed was he;
And there were all the best yeomen
Of all the west country.
A very fair contest was set up there,
A white bull was set up,
A great courser, with saddle and bridle,
[*Antwerp picks up again here*]
With gold burnished very bright.
A pair of gloves, a red gold ring,
A pipe of wine, in truth;
'The man that does the best, I understand,
The prize shall bear away.'
There was a yeoman in that place,
And most worthy was he,
But because he was a stranger and disadvantaged by this,
Slayn he was likely to be.
The knight had pity on this yeoman
In the place where he stood,
He said that yeoman should not be harmed,
For love of Robin Hood.
The knight pushed into the place,
A hundred followed him freely,
With bows bent and arrows sharp,
To attack that company.
They shouldered their arms and made him room,
To see what he would say;
He took the yeoman by the hand,
And gave him all the prize.
He gave him five marks for his wine,
Where it lay on the earth,
And ordered it should be broached,
So all who would could drink.
Thus long tarried this gentle knight,
Until that play was done,
So long waited Robin fasting
Three hours after noon.

Fytte Three

Pay attention and listen, gentle men,
All who are now here;
Of Little John, who was the knight's man,
Good mirth ye shall hear.
It was upon a merry day
That young men would go shoot;
Little John fetched his bow at once,
And said he would them meet.
Three times Little John joined the shooting,
And always he slit the wand [split the arrow];
The proud sheriff of Nottingham
Will have to pay up.
The sheriff swore a great big oath,
'By him that died on the Tree,
This man is the best archer
That ever yet saw we.
Tell me now, brave young man,
Now, what is your name?
In what country [region] were you born,
And where is your dwelling place?'
'In Holderness, sir, I was born
I knew this from my dame [mother];
Men call me Reynold Greenleaf
When I am at home.'
'Tell me, Reynold Greenleaf,
Do you want to live with me?
And every year I will give you
Twenty marks as your fee.'
'I have a master,' said Little John,
'A courteous knight is he;
If you may get permission from him,
The better it may be.'
The sheriff got Little John
Twelve months from the knight;
Therefore he gave him right then and there
A good horse and a wight [manservant].
Now is Little John the sheriff's man,
God let us all well speed!
But Little John was always thinking
How to pay him back his deserts [as he deserved].
'Now so help me God,' said Little John,
'And by my true loyalty,
I shall be the worst servant to him
That ever yet had he.'
It fell upon a Wednesday,
The sheriff hunting was gone;
And Little John lay in his bed,

And was forgotten, at home.
Therefore he was fasting,
Till it was past noon.
'Good sir steward, I pray thee,
Give me my dinner,' said Little John.
'It is a long time for Greenleaf
Fasting for to be;
Therefore I pray you, sir steward,
My dinner give to me.'
'You shall never eat nor drink,' said the steward,
Till my lord is come to town.'
'I make my vow to God,' said Little John,
'I'd rather crack your crown!'
The butler was very discourteous,
Where he stood on the floor,
He leapt up to the buttery
And shut fast the door.
Little John gave the butler such a tap
His back went nearly in two;
Though he was to live a hundred years, he wouldn't know worse.
He pushed the door with his foot,
It opened well and fine
And he was able to take a large allowance
Both of ale and of wine.
'Since you will not dine,' said Little John,
'I shall give you drink,
And if you live a hundred winters
On Little John you will think.'
Little John ate, and Little John drank,
As long as he liked.
The sheriff had in his kitchen a cook,
A stout man and a bold.
'I make my vow to God,' said the cook,
'You are an evil servant
In any house for to dwell,
To ask in this way to dine.'
And then he gave Little John
Good strokes three;
'I make my vow to God,' said Little John,
'These strokes well liked me.
You are a bold man and a hardy,
And so thinketh me;
And before I pass from this place,
Better tried shall you be.'
Little John drew a very good sword
The cook took another in his hand:
They had no thought to flee,
But unyielding to stand.
There they fought bitterly together,

Across two miles and more,
Neither might do the other harm,
Though they fought for an hour.
'I make my vow to God,' said Little John,
'And by my true loyalty,
You are one of the best swordsmen
That ever yet saw we.
If you could shoot as well with a bow
Into the greenwood you should come with me,
And two times a year your clothing
Changed should be.
And every year from Robin Hood
Twenty marks for your fee.'
'Put up your sword,' said the cook,
'And fellows [brothers] will we be.'
Then he fetched to Little John
The mumbles of a doe;
Good bread, and very good wine,
They ate and drank thereto.
And when they had drunk well,
Their word to each other they plight [swore]
That they would be with Robin
That very same night.
Then they went to the treasure house,
As fast as they could go;
The locks, that were of very good steel,
They broke them every one.
They took away the silver vessels
And all that they might get,
Pieces, goblets, nor spoons,
Would they not forget.
Also they took good money,
Three hundred pounds and more;
And went straight with them to Robin Hood,
Under the misty greenwood.
'God save you, my dear master,
And Christ protect and save you!'
And then said Robin to Little John,
'Welcome may you be.
Also be that fair yeoman,
That you bring there with you;
What tidings from Nottingham?
Little John, tell you me.'
'The proud sheriff greets you well,
And sends you here by me
His cook and his silver vessels,
And three hundred pounds and three.'
'I make my vow to God,' said Robin,
'And to the Trinity;

It was never by his goodwill
These goods have come to me.'
Little John then thought
Of a crafty trick;
Five miles through the forest he ran –
And it happened as he devised.
Then he met the proud sheriff,
Hunting with hounds and horn,
Little John knew his courtesy,
And knelt him down before.
'God save you, my dear master,
And Christ save and protect you!'
'Reynold Greenleaf,' said the sheriff,
'Where have you just been?'
'I have been in this forest,
A fair sight I did see;
It was one of the fairest sights
That ever yet I saw me.
Yonder I saw a right fair hart
His colour is of green;
Seven score of deer in a herd
Are with him all together.
Their tines [antlers] are so sharp, master,
Of sixty and even more;
That I dared not shoot for dread
In case they would me kill.'
'I make my vow to God,' said the sheriff,
'That sight I'd like to see!'
'Hurry this way, my dear master,
At once, and go with me.'
The sheriff rode, and Little John
He was very swift of foot.
And when they came before Robin
'Lo, sir, here is the master hart!'
Still stood the proud sheriff,
A sorry man was he;
'A plague on you, Reynold Greenleaf,
Now you have betrayed me.'
'I make my vow to God,' said Little John,
'Master, you are to blame,
I was not served well of my dinner,
When I was with you at home.'
Soon he was sitting at supper,
And served well with silver white,
And when the sheriff saw his vessels,
For sorrow he might not eat.
'Cheer up,' said Robin Hood,
'Sheriff, for charity!
And for the love of Little John

Thy life I grant to thee!'
When they had eaten well,
The day was all gone;
Robin commanded Little John
To take off his hose and his shoes.
His robe and his short jacket,
That was well furred and fine;
And took him a green cloak
To wrap his body therein.
Robin commanded his bold young men,
Under the greenwood tree,
They should lie down in that same way,
So the sheriff might them see.
All night lay the proud sheriff
In his breeches and his shirt;
No wonder it was, in the greenwood,
That his sides began to smart.
'Cheer up,' said Robin Hood,
'Sheriff, for charity!
For this is the way we do things, I tell you,
Under the greenwood tree.'
'This is a harder way,' said the sheriff,
'Than any anchorite or friar;
For all the gold in merry England
I wouldn't stay longer here.'
'All these twelve months,' said Robin,
'You shall dwell with me;
I will teach you, proud sheriff,
An outlaw for to be.'
'Before I stay here another night,' said the sheriff,
'Robin, I pray you
Cut off my head rather, tomorrow
And I'll forgive you for it.
Let me go,' then said the sheriff,
'For Saint Charity!
And I will be the best friend
That ever yet had ye.'
'You shall swear me an oath,' said Robin,
'On my bright brand [sword],
That you will never do me harm,
By water nor by land.
And if you find any of my men
By night or day,
Upon your oath you shall swear,
To help them all you may.'
Now has the sheriff sworn his oath,
And home began to go;
He was as full of the greenwood
As ever was a heap of stone.

Fytte Four

The sheriff dwelt in Nottingham,
He was glad he had gone;
And Robin and his merry men
Went to the wood at once.
'Go we to dinner,' said Little John,
Robin Hood said, 'Nay,'
For I fear Our Lady is angry with me –
For she sent me not my pay.'
'Have no doubt, master,' said Little John,
'The sun is not yet at rest;
For I dare say, and confidently swear,
The knight is true and trustworthy.'
'Take your bow in your hand,' said Robin,
'Let Much go with you,
And so shall Will Scarlet,
[*Antwerp has lines missing here, supplied from de Worde*]
And no one stay with me.
And walk up under the Sayles
And to Watling Street,
And look out for some exotic guest,
On the chance you may them meet.
Whether he is a messenger,
Or a man who can entertain,
Or if he is a poor man
Of my goods he shall have some.'
Forth then went Little John,
Half in anger and annoyance,
And girded him with a very good sword,
Under a cloak of green.
They went up to the Sayles,
These yeomen all three;
They looked east, they looked west:
They might no man see.
But as they looked into Barnsdale,
By the highway,
Then they were aware of two black monks,
Each on a good palfrey.
Then up spoke Little John,
To Much he did say,
'I dare lay my life in pledge,
That these monks have brought our pay.'
'Be of good cheer,' said Little John,
'And [make] ready our bows of yew,
And look your hearts be strong and sober,
Your strings trusty and true.
The monk has two and fifty men,
And seven packhorses strong;

There rides no bishop in this land
So royally, as I reckon.
Brothers,' said Little John,
'Here are no more than we three;
Unless we bring them to dinner,
Our master we may not see.
Bend your bows,' said Little John,
'Together you must stand;
The monk at the front, his life and his death,
Are held in my hand.
Stop, churl monk,' said Little John,
'Do not go any further;
If you do, by dear worthy God,
Your death is in my hand.
Bad luck on your head,' said Little John,
'Right under your hatband!
For you have made our master angry,
He has fasted so long.'
'Who is your master?' said the monk.
Little John said, 'Robin Hood.'
'He is a strong thief,' said the monk,
'Of him heard I never good.'
'You lie,' said then Little John,
'And you shall sorry be;
He is a yeoman of the forest,
And he's invited you to dinner.'
Much was ready with a bolt
Quickly and at once,
He aimed at the monk's breast
So he got down on the ground.
Of two and fifty bold young men
There remained not one,
Except a little page and a groom,
To lead the revels with Little John.
They brought the monk to the lodge door,
Whether he wanted to or not;
To speak with Robin Hood,
Despite their resistance.
Robin took off his hood,
When he monk did see;
The monk was not so courteous,
He let his hood be.
'He is a churl, master, by dear worthy God,'
Said then Little John,
'No matter,' said Robin,
'Because courtesy he knows none.
How many men,' said Robin,
'Had this monk, John?'
'Fifty and two when we met,

But many of them have gone.'
'Have a horn blown,' said Robin,
'That the fellowship may us know.'
Seven score of bold yeomen
Came riding in a row.
And each of them a good cloak
Of scarlet and of stripes;
They all came to Robin,
To know what he had to say.
They made the monk to wash and wipe,
And sit down to his dinner;
Robin Hood and Little John,
They served him both together.
'Eat up, monk,' said Robin,
'Many thanks, sir,' said he,
'Where is your abbey, when you are at home,
And who is your patron?'
'Saint Mary's Abbey,' said the monk,
'Though I appear humble here.'
'In what office?' said Robin.
'Sir, the high cellarer.'
'You are the more welcome,' said Robin,
'As I may prosper me;
Fill up with the best wine,' said Robin,
'This monk shall drink to me.
But I wonder greatly,' said Robin,
'All through this long day
I fear Our Lady is angry with me,
She sent me not my pay.'
'Have no doubt, master,' said Little John,
'You have no need, I say
This monk has brought it, I dare well swear,
For he is from her abbey.'
'And she was a pledge,' said Robin,
'Between a knight and me,
For a little money that I lent him,
Under the greenwood tree.
And if you have that silver brought,
I pray you, let me see.
And I shall help you soon enough,
If you have need of me.'
The monk swore a great big oath,
With very little cheer;
'Of the borrowing of what you speak to me,
Have I never heard before.'
'I make my vow to God,' said Robin,
'Monk, you are to blame;
For God is considered a righteous man;
And so is his dame [mother].

You said to me with your own tongue,
You may not say nay,
How you are her servant,
And serve her every day.
And you are made her messenger,
My money for to pay,
Therefore I owe you the more thanks
That you are come my way.
What is in your coffers?' said Robin,
'Truly, then, tell to me.'
'Sir,' he said, 'twenty marks,
As I hope to thrive.'
'If there be no more,' said Robin,
'I do no want a penny;
If you have need of any more,
Sir, more I will lend to you.
I judge you shall go without it,
For of your spending silver, monk,
I do not want any.
Now go, Little John,
And the truth tell to me –
If there be no more than twenty marks,
I do not want a penny.'
Little John spread his cloak out,
As he had done before,
And he counted out of the monk's purse
Eight hundred pounds and more.
Little John let it lie undisturbed,
And went to his master in haste;
'Sir,' he said, 'the monk is true enough –
Our Lady has doubled your cast [bet].'
'I make my vow to God,' said Robin,
'Monk, what did I tell you?
Our Lady is the truest woman
That ever yet I found.
By dear worthy God,' said Robin,
'If I seek all England through,
Yet I've never found for all my pay
A much better pledge.
Fill up with the best wine, and give him a drink,' said Robin,
'And greet well your gracious lady.
If she has need of Robin Hood
She will find him a friend.
And if she needs any more silver,
Come again to me:
And, by this token she has sent me
She shall have of such tokens three.'
The monk was going to London-ward,
There to hold a great assembly,

The knight that rode so high on his horse,
To bring him under his foot [to get him under control].
'Where are you going,' said Robin,
'Sir, to manors in this land.
To reckon with our reeves
That have done much wrong.'
'Come forth, now, Little John,
And listen to my tale
A better yeoman I know none,
To search a monk's bag.
How much is in yonder other courser?
The truth we must see.'
'By Our Lady,' then said the monk,
'That would not be courtesy,
To ask a man to dinner,
And then beat and bind him.'
'It is our ancient custom,' said Robin,
'To leave but little behind.'
The monk spurred on his horse,
He would no longer abide,
'Come and drink,' then said Robin,
'Before you further ride.'
'Nay, for God,' then said the monk,
'I'm sorry I came so near;
For better value I might have dined
In Blyth or Doncaster.'
'Greet well your abbot,' said Robin,
'And your prior, I you pray,
And bid him send me such a monk
To dinner every day.'
Now we'll leave that monk alone,
And speak we of the knight:
Yet he came to keep his day,
Whilst it was still light.
He went straight to Barnsdale,
Under the greenwood tree,
And he found there Robin Hood,
And all his merry men.
The knight got down off his good palfrey,
When Robin he did see;
So courteously he doffed his hood,
And got down on his knee.
'God save you, Robin Hood,
And all this company.'
'You are welcome, gentle knight,
And right welcome to me.'
Then Robin Hood spoke to him,
To that knight so free;
'What need drives you to the greenwood,

I pray you, Sir Knight, tell me.
And you are welcome, gentle knight,
Why did you take so long?'
'Because the abbot and the justice
Would have had my land.'
'Have you got your land again?' said Robin,
'Truth then tell to me.'
'Yes, for God,' said the knight,
'And for that I thank God and thee.
But take not offence,' said the knight,
'That I have been so long;
I came by a wrestling match,
And there I helped a poor yeoman,
Who was beset by wrong.'
'Nay, for God,' said Robin,
'Sir knight, for that I thank you,
Whatever man helps a good yeoman,
His friend then will I be.'
'Have here four hundred pounds,' then said the knight,
'The which you lent to me;
And here are also twenty marks
For your courtesy.'
'Nay, for God,' then said Robin,
'You enjoy it well for ever;
For Our Lady, by her high cellarer,
Has sent to me my pay.
And if I took it twice,
It would be shame to me.
But truly, gentle knight,
Welcome you are to me.'
When Robin had told his tale,
He laughed and had good cheer.
'By my troth,' then said the knight,
'Your money is ready here.'
'Enjoy it well,' said Robin,
'You gentle knight so free [generous];
And welcome are you, gentle knight,
Under my trysting tree.
But what shall these bowmen do,' said Robin,
And these arrows feathered free?'
'By God,' then said the knight,
'A poor present to you.'
'Come forth now, Little John,
And go to my treasure,
And bring me there four hundred pounds,
The monk over-paid me.
Have here four hundred pounds,
You gentle knight and true,
And buy a good horse and harness,

And gild your spurs anew.
And if you lack any spending money,
Come to Robin Hood,
And by my troth you shall not be without,
Whilst I have any possessions.
And use well your four hundred pound
Which I lent to thee;
And make yourself no more so bare,
By counsel of me.'
Thus then helped him good Robin,
The knight out of his care;
God, that sits in heaven high,
Grant us well to fare.

Fytte Five

Now has the knight taken his leave
And gone on his way;
Robin Hood and his merry men
Did nothing special for many a day.
Listen well, gentlemen,
And listen to what I say:
How the proud sheriff of Nottingham
Announced a noble game.
That all the best archers of the North
Should come together one day,
And they that shot the best of all
Should carry the prize away.
He that shoots best of all
The furthest, clean and low,
At a pair of godly targets
Under the greenwood leaves,
A very good arrow he shall have,
The shaft of white silver,
The head and the feathers of rich red gold;
In England is not its like.
This then heard good Robin,
Under his trysting tree;
'Make you ready, you goodly young men,
That shooting will I see.
Make ready, my merry young men,
You shall go with me:
And I will know the sheriff's worth,
Whether true he be.'
When they had bent their bows
And feathered their arrows,
Seven score of Robin's young men
Stood by Robin's knee.
When they came to Nottingham

The courses were good and long,
Many was the bold archer
That shot with bows strong.
'There shall but six shoot with me,
The others shall keep lookout;
And stand with good bows bent,
That I be not deceived.'
The fourth outlaw began to bend his bow,
And that was Robin Hood,
And that beheld the good sheriff
He stood right by the target.
Three times Robin shot about,
And always they [*sic*] slit the shaft,
And so did good Gilbert
With the white hand.
Little John and good Scarlett
Were good archers, and noble,
Little Much and good Reynold,
The worst they would not be.
When they had shot about,
These archers handsome and good,
Always the best was,
Truly, Robin Hood.
He was awarded the goodly arrow,
For the most worthy was he:
He took the gift so courteously
And would return to the greenwood.
They raised a hue and cry for Robin Hood,
And began to blow great horns:
'Woe to you, treason!' said Robin,
'You are right evil to know.
And woe to you, proud sheriff,
Making so light of your word;
You promised otherwise to me
In yonder wild forest.
If I but had you in the greenwood,
Under my trysting tree,
You should give me a better pledge,
Than your true obedience.'
Many bows there were bent,
And arrows they set off,
Many a garment there was rent,
And hurt was many a side.
The outlaws shot so strongly
That no man could drive them away;
And the proud sheriff's men
They fled quickly away.
Robin saw the ambush was broken
In the greenwood he would be:

Many an arrow there was shot
Among that company.
Little John was hurt very badly,
With an arrow in his knee;
So that he could neither run nor ride
It was a great pity.
'Master,' then said Little John,
'If ever you love me,
And for that same Lord's love
That died upon a Tree,
And for the rewards of my service,
That I have served thee;
Never let the proud sheriff
Alive now find me.
But take out thy brown sword
And completely cut off my head
And give me wounds deep and wide
Leave no life in me.'
'I don't want that,' said Robin,
'John, for you to be killed,
For all the gold in Merry England,
Though it lay here in a row.'
'God forbid,' said little Much,
'That died on a Tree,
That you should, Little John,
Leave our company.'
He took him up on his back
And carried him a good mile
Many a time he laid him down,
And shot a little while.
Then was there a fair castle,
A little way into the wood,
Double-ditched around it was,
And walled, by the Rood!
And there lived that noble knight
Sir Richard atte Lee,
To whom Robin had lent his goods
Under the greenwood tree
He took in good Robin
And all his company;
'Welcome are you, Robin Hood,
Welcome you are to me!
And I thank you very much for your help,
And for your courtesy,
And for your great kindness,
Under the greenwood tree.
I love no man more in all this world
As much as I do thee;
Despite the great sheriff of Nottingham,

Here you'll be alright.
Shut the gates, draw up the bridge,
[*Antwerp picks up again here*]
And let no man come in,
And arm you well, and make you ready,
And take your places on the walls.
For one thing, Robin, I ask thee,
I swear by St Quentin;
These forty days you'll stay with me,
To sup, eat and dine.'
Tables were laid, and clothes spread out,
Quickly and right away;
Robin Hood and his merry men
Went to eat their meal.

Fytte Six

Listen and pay attention, gentlemen,
And listen to our song:
How the proud sheriff of Nottingham
And well-armed soldiers
Came very quickly to the high sheriff,
To stir up the country,
And they besieged the knight's castle,
All around the walls.
The proud sheriff began to cry out,
And said, 'You traitor knight,
You are keeping here the king's enemies,
Against the law and right.'
'Sir, I will pledge to what I have done,
The deeds that here are done,
With all the lands that I have,
As I am a true knight.
Go forth, sirs, on your way,
And do no more to me
Until you know our king's will,
What he will say to thee.'
The sheriff thus had his answer,
Without any lying;
Forth he went to London town,
In order to tell the king.
There he told him of that knight
And also of Robin Hood,
And also of the bold archers
That were so noble and good.
'He will answer for what he has done
To protect the outlaws strong,
He will be the lord, and set you at nought,
In all the North land.'

'I will be at Nottingham,' said our king,
'Within these fourteen nights,
And I will take Robin Hood,
And so I will that knight.
Go home now, sheriff,' said our king,
'And do as I tell thee,
And get ready good archers enough
From all the wild country.'
The sheriff had taken his leave,
And went on his way,
And Robin Hood to the greenwood
Went on a certain day.
And Little John was healed of the arrow
That was shot into his knee,
And he went straight to Robin Hood
Under the greenwood tree.
Robin Hood walked in the forest
Under the leaves green
The proud sheriff of Nottingham
Was really brassed off by this.
The sheriff couldn't find Robin Hood
He might not have his prey;
Then he waited in ambush for this noble knight,
Both by night and day.
Ever he waited for the noble knight,
With well-armed men,
And took him towards Nottingham
Bound hand and foot.
The sheriff swore a great big oath,
By Him that died on the Rood,
That rather than have a hundred pounds,
He would have Robin Hood.
This heard the good knight's wife,
A fair and a noble lady;
She sat upon a good horse,
And to the greenwood she rode
When she arrived in the forest
Under the greenwood tree,
She found there Robin Hood
And all his fair company.
'God save you, good Robin,
And all thy company;
For Our dear Lady's sake,
A favour grant to me.
Do not allow my wedded lord
Shamefully slain to be;
He is taken bound towards Nottingham
For the love of thee.'
Immediately then said good Robin

To that noble lady,
'What man has taken your lord?'
For truly as I you say,
He has not yet gone
Three miles on his way.
Up then jumped good Robin
Like a man who had gone mad;
'Get ready, my merry men,
For Him that died on the Rood.
And he who will not take this challenge,
By Him that died on the Tree,
He shall never live in the greenwood
Any longer live with me.'
Soon there were good bows bent,
More than seven score;
They spared neither hedge nor ditch
That was them before.
'I make my vow to God,' said Robin,
'The sheriff I will see,
And if I may him take,
Avenged it shall be.'
And when they came to Nottingham
They walked in the street;
And with the proud sheriff
Soon did they meet.
'Wait, you proud sheriff,' he said,
'Wait, and speak with me;
Some news about our king
I want to hear from thee.
These seven years, dear worthy God,
I never went on foot so fast,
I make my vow to God, you proud sheriff,
It won't be good for you.'
Robin bent a really good bow,
An arrow he let fly at will,
He so hit the proud sheriff
Upon the ground he lay really still.
And before he might get up
On his feet to stand
He cut off the sheriff's head
With his bright brand.
'Lie there, you proud sheriff,
May evil become you;
There might no man trust you
[*Antwerp text finishes here – completed from de Worde*]
Whilst you were alive.'
His men drew out their bright swords
That were so sharp and keen,
And set upon the sheriff's men

And bore them down forthwith.
Robin went up to the knight
And cut in two his hood;
And took in his hand a bow,
And asked him to stand beside him.
'Leave your horse behind you,
And learn to run;
You shall go with me to the greenwood,
Through mire, and moss and fen.
You shall with me to the greenwood,
I do not lie;
Until I have gained us a pardon
From Edward, our comely king.'

Fytte Seven

The king came to Nottingham,
With knights in regal array,
In order to take that noble knight
And Robin Hood, if he may.
He asked the men of that country
After Robin Hood,
And after that noble knight,
That was so bold and good.
When they told him the story,
Our king understood their tale;
And took into his own hand
The knight's lands all.
The length and breadth of Lancashire
He went, both far and near,
Until he came to Plumpton Park –
He missed many of his deer.
There was our king accustomed to see
Many herds, not one;
He could hardly find one deer
That bore any good horns.
The was very angry at this,
And swore by the Trinity;
'I wish I had Robin Hood
With my own eyes I would him see.
And he that would cut off the knight's head,
And bring it to me,
He shall have the knight's lands,
Sir Richard atte Lee.
I give it to him with my charter,
And seal it with my hand,
To have and evermore to hold,
In all Merry England.'
Then spoke up a noble old knight,

That was trusted in his word;
'Ah, my liege lord the king,
One word I'll to you say.
There is no man in this country
May have the knight's lands,
Whilst Robin Hood may ride or go,
And carry a bow in his hands,
That he shall not lose his head,
That is the best ball in his hood,
Give it to no man, my lord the king,
That you wish any good.'
Half a year stayed our comely king
In Nottingham, and well more;
He could not hear about Robin Hood
In what region that he was.
But always went good Robin
By hiding places and by the hills,
And always killed the king's deer,
And did with them what he would.
Then up spoke a proud forester
That walked by the king's knee;
'If you will see good Robin,
You must obey me.
Take five of the best knights
That are in your company;
And walk down beside yonder abbey
And get yourself monk's clothing.
And I will be your companion,
And show you the way,
And before you come to Nottingham
My head as a bet I'll lay,
That you shall meet with good Robin,
Alive if he be;
Before you come to Nottingham
With your own eyes you'll him see.'
With great haste our king got ready
And so did his knights five;
Each of them in monk's clothing,
And went their way quickly.
Our king was well-built above his cowl,
A broad hat on his crown,
As if he were abbot-like,
They rode into the town.
Strong boots our king had on,
Truly, as I you say;
He rode singing to the greenwood,
The convent was clothed in grey.
His packhorse and his great baggage-train
Followed our king behind,

Until they came to the greenwood,
A mile inward under the trees.
There they met with good Robin,
Standing in their way,
And so did many a bold archer,
Truly, as I you say.
Robin took the king's horse,
Quickly in that place,
And said, 'Sir Abbot, by your leave,
Awhile you must abide.
We are yeomen of this forest,
Under the greenwood tree;
We live by the king's deer,
Other means we have not any.
And you have churches and rents both,
And gold in great plenty;
Give us some of your liquid assets
For Holy Charity.'
Then up spoke our comely king,
Immediately said he,
'I brought no more to the greenwood,
Than forty pounds with me.
I have stayed at Nottingham
These fourteen nights with our king,
And I have spend a lot of money
On many a great lord.
And I have but forty pounds,
No more than that have I with me;
But if I had a hundred pounds,
I would give it in pledge to thee.'
Robin took the forty pounds,
And divided it in two parts;
Half he gave to his merry men,
And told them to be merry.
Very courteously Robin then said,
'Sir, have this for your ready cash;
We shall meet another day.'
'Thank you very much,' said our king.
'But Edward greets you well, our king,
And sends to you his seal,
And bids you come to Nottingham,
Both to eat and dine.'
He took out the broad seal,
So that Robin could see;
Robin knew his courtesy,
And went down on his knee.
'I love no man in all the world
As well as I do my king
Welcome is my lord's seal,

And, monk, for your tiding.
Sir abbot, because of your tidings,
Today you shall dine with me,
For the love of my king,
Under my trysting tree.'
He led forth our comely king,
Leading him by the hand;
Many a deer there was slain,
And quickly made ready.
Robin took a great big horn,
And loudly he began to blow;
Seven score of fit young men,
Came, ready, all in a row.
They all kneeled down on their knee
Fittingly, before Robin;
The king noted this himself,
And swore by Saint Austin,
'Here is a wondrous, goodly sight
I think, by God's agony,
His men are more at his bidding
Than my men are at mine.'
Very quickly was their dinner prepared,
And in to eat they went;
They served our king with all their might,
Both Robin and Little John.
Right in front of our king was set
The fat venison;
The good white bread, the good red wine,
And also fine ale, and brown.
'Make good cheer,' said Robin,
'Abbot, for charity,
And because of this same tiding,
Blessed may you be.
Now you shall see what life we lead,
Before you go from here;
Then you may inform our king,
When you stay together.'
Up they jumped hastily,
Their bows were smartly bent;
Our king was so horrified,
He thought he was lost.
Two stakes there were set up,
Up to these they went
By fifty paces, our king said,
The courses were too long.
On each side a rose garland
They shot inside this barrier;
'Whoever misses the rose garland,' said Robin,
'His tackle he shall forfeit.

And give it to the victor,
Be it never so fine,
For no man will I spare,
As I drink ale or wine.
And receive a blow on his head,
Which shall be all bare.'
And all that fell in Robin's way
He hit them really well.
Twice Robin shot about,
And twice he split the shaft,
And so did good Gilbert
With the White Hand.
Little John and good Scarlett,
For nothing would they spare;
When they missed the garland,
Robin hit them well.
At the last shot that Robin shot,
For all his friends fair,
Yet he missed the garland
By three fingers and more.
Then up spoke good Gilbert,
And thus he did say;
'Master,' he said, 'your tackle is lost,
Step forward and take your pay.'
'If that is so,' said Robin,
'It may no better be;
Sir Abbot, I give you my arrow,
I pray you, Sir, be my guest.'
'It does not fit with my orders,' said our king,
'Robin, by your leave,
Thus to smite a good yeoman,
Doubtless I should him grieve.'
'Smite on boldly,' said Robin,
'I give you generous leave.'
Then our king, with that word,
He folded up his sleeve,
And such a thump he gave Robin,
He nearly fell to the ground;
'I make my vow to God,' said Robin,
'You are a doughty friar.
There is strength in your arm,' said Robin,
'I'll bet you can shoot well.'
Thus our king and Robin Hood
Together they were met.
Robin looked at our comely king
Intently, at his face;
So did Sir Richard atte Lee,
And knelt down in that place.
And so did all the wild outlaws,

When they saw them kneel;
'My Lord the king of England,
Now I know you well.'
'Mercy, then, Robin,' said our king,
'Under your trysting tree,
For your goodness and your grace,
For my men and me.'
'Yes, for God,' said Robin,
'And also, God me save,
I ask mercy, my Lord the king,
And for my men, I crave.'
'Yes, for God,' said our king,
'And for that I came to you
Will you leave the greenwood,
And all your company:
And come home, sir, to my court,
And there dwell with me?'
'I make my vow to God,' said Robin,
'And right so shall it be.
I will come to your court,
Your service for to see,
And bring with me of my men,
Seven score and three.
If I don't like your service,
I will come back very soon,
And shoot at the brown deer,
As I am used to doing.'

Fytte Eight

'Have you any green cloth,' said our king,
'That you will now sell to me?'
'Yes, for God's sake,' said Robin,
'Thirty yards and three.'
'Robin,' said our king,
'Now I pray you,
Sell me some of that cloth,
To me and my company.'
'Yes, for God's sake,' said Robin
'If not I'd be a fool;
Another day you will clothe me
I believe, for Yule.'
The king put off his cowl, then,
A green garment he put on,
And every knight in turn,
Had another very soon.
When they were clothed in Lincoln green,
They cast away their grey;
'Now we shall go to Nottingham,'

Thus our king did say.
Their bows bent, forth they went,
Shooting all together,
Towards the town of Nottingham,
Outlaws as they were.
Our king and Robin rode together,
Truly, I you say,
And they shot in competition,
As they went on their way.
And many a thump our king won,
From Robin Hood that day;
And Robin didn't hold back
From giving the king his 'pay'.
'God help me,' said our king,
'Your skill is hard to learn.
I would not win a shot from thee
If I should shoot all year.'
All the people of Nottingham
They stood and beheld;
They saw nothing but coats of green
That covered all the field.
Then every man to the other said,
'I fear our king is slain;
Robin Hood is come to the town, you see,
He left not one alive.'
Very hastily they began to flee,
Both yeomen and knaves;
And old women who could hardly walk,
They hopped on their crutches.
The king laughed very loudly,
And commanded them again;
When they saw our comely king,
I tell you, they were really glad.
They ate and drank, and were very glad,
And sang with notes high;
Then up spoke our comely king,
To Sir Richard atte Lee.
He gave him there his land again,
A good man he bade him be.
Robin thanked our comely king,
And went down on his knee.
When Robin had lived in the king's court
But twelve months and three,
He had spent a hundred pounds,
And all his men's fee.
In every place where Robin went,
He had only two men;
Little John and good Scarlett,
Along with him to go.

Robin saw the young men shoot
On one fine day;
'Alas!' then said good Robin,
'My wealth has gone away!
Once I was an archer good
An upright and a strong,
I was considered the best archer
That was in Merry England.
Alas!' then said good Robin,
'Alas and weilaway!
If I live any longer with the king,
Sorrow will me slay.'
Forth then went Robin Hood
Until he came to our king;
'My Lord the king of England,
Grant me what I ask.
I made a chapel in Barnsdale,
That lovely is to see;
It is of [dedicated to] Mary Magdalene,
And that's where I would be.
I might never these seven nights
Sleep a single wink,
Nor in all these seven days
Either eat or drink.
I long to be in Barnsdale,
I can't be kept therefrom:
Clothed in a penitent's hair shirt
I am bound to go.'
'If it be so,' then said our king,
'It may no better be;
I give you leave for seven nights,
No longer, to part from me.'
'Many thanks, Lord,' then said Robin,
And went down on his knee,
He took his leave most courteously,
To the greenwood then went he.
When he came to the greenwood,
On a merry morning,
There he heard the chirping call
Of merry birds singing.
'It is so long,' said Robin,
'Since I was last here;
I'd like to have a little shot
At the brown deer.'
Robin killed a great big hart:
His horn then he began to blow,
So all the outlaws of the forest
That horn they would know.
And they all gathered together

In a little while.
Seven score of fit young men
Were ready, all in a row.
And they graciously doffed their hoods,
And went down on their knee,
'Welcome,' they said, 'our master,
Under this greenwood tree.'
Robin lived in the greenwood
Twenty years and two;
For all the fear of Edward our king,
Away he would not go.
Yet he was tricked, you see
By means of a wicked woman,
The prioress of Kirklees,
That was his close kin.
For the love of a knight,
Sir Roger of Doncaster,
Who was her lover –
May evil befall them both.
They conspired together
Robin Hood to slay,
And how they might best do that deed,
His murderers to be.
Then up spoke good Robin,
In the place where he stood;
'Tomorrow I must go to Kirklees,
To be skilfully let blood.'
Sir Roger of Doncaster,
By the prioress he lay,
And there they betrayed good Robin Hood,
Through their false play.
Christ have mercy on his soul,
Who died on the Rood.
For he was a good outlaw,
And did poor men much good.

References

INTRODUCTION: WHO WAS ROBIN HOOD?

1 Maurice Keen, *The Outlaws of Medieval Legend* (London, 1961), p. 1; compare with the legend/mythos ideas of Stephen Knight, *Robin Hood: A Mythic Biography* (Ithaca, NY, and London, 2003). Keen proposed that 'the matter of the greenwood' should be considered on a par with 'the matter of Britain' (that is, Arthurian legend) and 'the matter of Rome'.

2 For the idea of the storyworld, see T. P. Wiseman, *The Myths of Rome* (Liverpool, 2004).

3 Like the storyworld of Robin Hood, that of King Arthur has survived and retained some relevance today, unlike some others (romances of Rome and of Troy, miracles of the Virgin Mary and the saints) that were far more popular in medieval England than they are now.

4 These processes are documented in Ronald Hutton, *The Rise and Fall of Merry England: The Ritual Year, 1400–1700* (Oxford and New York, 1994), pp. 111–226, and in Eamon Duffy, *The Stripping of the Altars: Traditional Religion in England, 1400–1580* (New Haven, CT, and London, 1992), pp. 379–523, 565–93.

5 In film: Kevin Reynolds, *Robin Hood, Prince of Thieves* (1991); John Irvin, *Robin Hood* (1991); Ridley Scott, *Robin Hood* (2010). On television: Greg Berlanti, Marc Guggenheim, Andrew Kreisberg, *Arrow* (2012–18); Dominic Minghella, Foz Allan, *Robin Hood* (2006–9).

6 Ohlgren gives the date of publication as *c.* 1495: Thomas H. Ohlgren, *Robin Hood: The Early Poems, 1465–1560: Texts, Contexts, and Ideology* (Newark, NJ, 2007), pp. 99–109; also John Marshall, 'Picturing Robin Hood in Early Print and Performance: 1500–1590', in *Images of Robin Hood: Medieval to Modern*, ed. Lois Potter and Joshua Calhoun (Newark, NJ, 2008), pp. 60–81.

7 Geoffrey Chaucer, *The Canterbury Tales*, 'General Prologue', ll. 103–8: Larry D. Benson, ed., *The Riverside Chaucer*, 3rd edn (Oxford, 1988), p. 25.

8 A facsimile is available: Wilhelm Schlag, ed., *The Hunting Book of Gaston Phébus: Manuscrit Français 616, Paris, Bibliothèque Nationale* (London, 1998). The book was written between 1387 and 1389, but most illustrated versions date from the early fifteenth century, as does this one. For the idea of Robin Hood as a forester, see A. J. Pollard, *Imagining*

Robin Hood: The Late-Medieval Stories in Historical Context (London and New York, 2004), pp. 49–56.

9 Ohlgren, *Early Poems*, pp. 112–20, and Marshall, 'Picturing Robin', pp. 66–72. Marshall suggests that de Worde got the factotum images from Caxton's workshop by the agency of Robert Copland, Caxton's assistant and then de Worde's. Ohlgren believes that Copland assisted in the creation of de Worde's edition, and left his 'mark' upon it.

10 Douglas Fairbanks Junior wore a brown leather tunic and green hose, and the pointed hat was red, in publicity posters for Allan Dwan's film *Robin Hood* (1922), although because the film was in black-and-white, the colour was not apparent to audiences. The 'look' – also worn by Richard Greene in the long-running television series *Adventures of Robin Hood* (1955–60) – was satirized by Mel Brooks in his film, *Robin Hood: Men in Tights* (1993), along with many other Robin Hood stereotypes.

11 Thomas H. Ohlgren and Lister M. Matheson, eds, *Early Rymes of Robyn Hood: An Edition of the Texts, ca. 1425 to ca. 1600* (Tempe, AZ, 2013), p. 70. This is a comprehensive edition of all the surviving early Robin Hood texts from manuscript and early print sources.

12 The thirteenth-century chronicler Ralph of Coggeshall, however, says that *plurimi* (many people) detested John in his own lifetime: J. Stevenson, ed., *Ralph of Coggeshall: Chronicon Anglicanum*, Rolls Series 66 (London, 1875), p. 106.

13 Leopold of Austria, who had taken Richard captive in 1192 on his return from the Crusade, handed him over to the Holy Roman Emperor Henry VI, who demanded the ransom. Richard's brother John was offering money for his brother to remain in prison. In other films, such as John Irvin's *Robin Hood* (1991) and Richard Lester's *Robin and Marian* (1976), John imposes unfair taxation because he is greedy, arrogant and out of touch with his people.

14 Sir Walter Scott, *Ivanhoe: A Romance*, 3 vols (Edinburgh, 1820), has been published in many subsequent modern editions. One of the most accessible, with a very good introduction, is A. N. Wilson, ed., *Ivanhoe*, Penguin Classics (London, 1982).

15 R. Freebairn, ed., *John Major: Historia Majoris Britanniae* (Edinburgh, 1740), p. 128. Also in Richard B. Dobson and John Taylor, eds, *Rymes of Robyn Hood: An Introduction to the English Outlaw* (Stroud, 1977), p. 5, and Stephen Knight and Thomas H. Ohlgren, eds, *Robin Hood and Other Outlaw Tales* (Kalamazoo, MI, 2000), p. 26. It is discussed by Stephen Knight in *Robin Hood: A Complete Study of the English Outlaw* (Oxford, 1994), p. 37.

16 Simon Taylor and D.E.R. Watt, eds, *Scotichronicon by Walter Bower in Latin and English*, 8 vols (St Andrews, 1987–94), vol. V, pp. 354–5, 35–7, and Knight and Ohlgren, *Robin Hood*, p. 25. This goes some way towards exonerating the Scots' liking for these characters in the fifteenth century, while berating the uneducated for celebrating a couple of 'robbers'. This was not entirely the case, as the celebrants could be anything but 'common' in many cases: see Chapters Two and Three for more about performances.

17 Ohlgren and Matheson, *Early Rymes*, p. 138.

18 A contemporary chronicler complained that all Edward II had managed to do in the first seven years of his reign was have handsome children: N. Denholm-Young, ed., *Vita Edwardi Secundi: The Life of Edward the Second by the so-called Monk of Malmesbury* (London, 1957), pp. 39–40. Edward V was twelve years old when he became king; a month after this he entered the Tower of London, never to be seen again. See also Thomas H. Ohlgren, 'Edwardus Redivivus in *A Gest of Robyn Hode*', *Journal of English and Germanic Philology*, XCIX/1 (2000), pp. 1–29.

19 Knight and Ohlgren, *Robin Hood*, p. 24.

20 Passus V, ll. 395–7: George Kane and E. Talbot Donaldson, eds, *Will's Visions of Piers Plowman, Do-Well, Do-Better and Do-Best* (London, 1975), p. 331; also A.V.C. Schmidt, ed., *William Langland: The Vision of Piers Plowman, a Complete Edition of the B-text* (London, 1978), p. 56. The line is not in the earlier A-text.

21 As it was for *pastourelles*: see Chapter Two below.

22 In 1412 Dame Alice de Bryene entertained an ever-increasing number of guests over the Christmas holiday, culminating in a New Year celebration for 36 guests, three hundred tenants 'and other strangers': John Southworth, *The English Medieval Minstrel* (Woodbridge, 1989), p. 100.

23 Ibid., pp. 72, 73, 79.

24 Ibid., p. 110.

25 That is, they spoke and understood French even if they did not like the French themselves: England and France were continually, if intermittently, at war from the late thirteenth to the mid-fifteenth centuries.

26 Plays on the lives of the saints and the Virgin Mary, for example. See Chapter Four for more on these.

ONE: ROBIN HOOD AND THE WRITTEN WORD

1 Edward issued a declaration alleging that the French wanted to destroy the English language, a reference to English perceptions of the Norman Conquest: for the text see William Stubbs, ed., *Select Charters and Other Illustrations of English Constitutional History from the Earliest Times to the Reign of Edward I*, 9th edn (Oxford, 1913), pp. 412–16.

2 F. J. Furnivall, ed., *Adam Davy's Dreams about Edward the Second*, Early English Text Society Original Series 69 (London, 1878), gives the text. Edward is depicted prophetically, as the future Holy Roman Emperor and successful crusader.

3 In art, he promoted the so-called International Court Style popular in the courts of Europe, and of France in particular.

4 Thomas H. Ohlgren and Lister M. Matheson, eds, *Early Rymes of Robyn Hood: An Edition of the Texts, ca. 1425 to ca. 1600* (Tempe, AZ, 2013), p. 7, ll. 25–6.

5 Ibid., p. 8, ll. 41–2; 45-6.

6 Ibid., p. 11, ll. 133-6; 138–40.

7 Ibid., p. 16, ll. 304–5.

8 Ibid., p. 16, ll. 312–16.

9 It does not mean that Robin Hood's rulership is elective. This point is

also established by Langland in the episode of 'belling the cat', where a company of rats reject the idea of protecting themselves by putting a bell on the local cat. They decide that they are better off with 'the devil they know', and none of them dare to do the deed, anyway, for fear of being killed. *Piers Plowman*, 'Prologue', ll. 146–210, in George Kane and E. Talbot Donaldson, eds, *Piers Plowman: The B Version*, 2nd edn (London and Berkeley, CA, 1988), pp. 235–9.

10 Ohlgren and Matheson, *Early Rymes*, p. 17, ll. 332–41.

11 Ibid., p. 17, ll. 354–7.

12 Thomas H. Ohlgren, *Robin Hood: The Early Poems, 1465–1560: Texts, Contexts and Ideology* (Newark, NJ, 2007), pp. 29–31, accepts the idea of two scribes. The manuscript has, however, become disordered, so there is actually no clear section attributable to this second scribe, although this appears to be the case from the way in which the manuscript is now arranged.

13 This is the scribe, not necessarily the author either of the manuscript texts or of the northern Passion, which it follows. One editor has expressed some doubts about Pilkington as scribe, but – given that the 'naming' of books by scribes and owners is a feature of this period – there seems little mileage in such arguments, and even a cursory glance at the writing in this part of the book shows that this is the same hand as the Gilbert Pilkington colophon.

14 Ohlgren, *Early Poems*, pp. 33–5; the shelf mark is Cambridge, University Library, MS ff.5.48, fols 128v–135v.

15 Ibid., pp. 35–9; David Hepworth, 'A Grave Tale', in *Robin Hood: Medieval and Post-medieval,* ed. Helen Phillips (Dublin, 2005), pp. 91–112.

16 This work was done by Lister Matheson.

17 The handwriting differs slightly in a few sections of the manuscript, but not sufficiently to draw the conclusion that this is a different scribe.

18 Ohlgren notes that the texts in the early part of the manuscript, including the *Instructions for the Parish Priest* and the *Passio Domini*, seem to have been copied 'in one long stint'. Ohlgren, *Early Poems*, p. 67.

19 The 'basyn' story is similar (interesting given the dialect and origin of the book) to an episode in the Third Branch of the Old Welsh *Mabinogion*, where Rhiannon and Pryderi find themselves stuck by an enchantment to a cauldron. This could, therefore, be a *fabliau*, or comic parody, of a courtly tale from the Welsh border.

20 Ohlgren, *Early Poems*, pp. 31–2 and endnotes, produces a similar argument. Ohlgren has done much detailed work on the ordering of the folios in the manuscript.

21 Alfred B. Emden, *A Biographical Register of the University of Cambridge to 1500* (Cambridge, 1963), p. 454.

22 Richard J. Bennett, *Community, Class and Careerism: Cheshire and Lancashire Society in the Age of Sir Gawain and the Green Knight* (Cambridge, 1983), p. 168.

23 The main dialect is that of south Norfolk, which Lister Matheson, in his study of the dialect, favours over north Suffolk, although the forms displayed are frequently found in both areas. The fact that there

are no 'chi' symbols (X) for 'sch', nor is there any use of 'qw' for 'wh', strengthens the idea that the scribe came from the south of the county, too. The speech of the area running roughly from north of Norwich through Broadland and the Waveney Valley was (and still is) distinct from that of north and west Norfolk and the Orwell Valley in the south.

24 Ohlgren, *Early Poems*, p. 69.

25 This does not mean that such works were exclusively the property of middle-class individuals; good reading could reinforce good breeding, too.

26 James H. Morey, ed., *Prik of Conscience* (Kalamazoo, MI, 2012).

27 Their letters show that younger members of the Paston family, contrary to their mother's wishes, kept in touch with Calle and Margery, and supported Calle's business.

28 Ohlgren, *Early Poems*, pp. 74–5. The first Richard Calle had a son, also named Richard, and he – given the date – would seem to be the most likely person to have marked his ownership in this way when he came into possession of the book. The nature of the contents reflects what the urban and rural elites were interested in, and collecting, at the time. There is no particular association with the life history of the ex-steward Richard Calle or anyone else. They are simply the type of texts which late fifteenth-century people valued.

29 British Library, London, Additional MS 42130, fol. 49r. Available at www.bl.uk/manuscripts, accessed 23 September 2018.

30 Ohlgren and Matheson, *Early Rymes*, p. 30, ll. 83–4.

31 Ibid., pp. 31–2, ll. 135–6, 139–40.

32 Ohlgren, *Early Poems*, p. 35, ll. 218–19.

33 See Gervase Rosser, 'Roles in Life: The Drama of the Medieval Guilds', in *REED in Review: Essays in Celebration of the First Twenty-five Years*, ed. Audrey Douglas and Sally-Beth MacLean (Toronto, Buffalo and London, 2006), pp. 140–56.

34 Cameron Louis, ed., *Records of Early English Drama: Sussex* (Turnhout and Toronto, 2000), pp. 80–81; James Stokes, ed., *Records of Early English Drama: Somerset*, 2 vols (Toronto, Buffalo and London, 1996), vol. I, pp. 23–78, 967–72.

35 Records from towns in Somerset show members of the same families being both churchwardens and 'Robin Hoods' over much of the sixteenth century: see Stokes, *Records*, for examples.

36 Ronald Hutton, *The Stations of the Sun: A History of the Ritual Year in Britain* (Oxford, 1996), pp. 273–4. Stephen Knight discusses Robin Hood in Scotland in *Reading Robin Hood: Content, Form and Reception in the Outlaw Myth* (Manchester, 2015), pp. 36–54.

37 Wiles called this 'a scenario or mnemonic providing a framework for improvisation', and Ohlgren restates this. David Wiles, *The Early Plays of Robin Hood* (Woodbridge, 1981), p. 37; Ohlgren, *Early Poems*, p. 92.

38 Norman Davis, ed., *Paston Letters and Papers of the Fifteenth Century*, 2 vols (Oxford, 1971), vol. I, p. 461.

39 Elements of this story are very similar to the ballad, which survives only in an eighteenth-century version. It does not necessarily mean that

the later version was derived from a surviving medieval tradition: it could have been made up from existing literature by the ballad writers themselves.

40 John Marshall, '. . . goon in-to Bernysdale: The Trail of the Paston Robin Hood Play', *Leeds Studies in English*, n.s. XXXII (2001), pp. 345–68.

41 David Galloway, ed., *Records of Early English Drama: Norwich, 1540–1642* (Toronto and London, 1984), p. xxvi.

42 Hutton, *Seasons of the Sun*, pp. 262–76.

43 Richard B. Dobson and John Taylor, eds, *Rymes of Robyn Hood: An Introduction to the English Outlaw* (Stroud, 1977), pp. 140–45.

44 John Marshall, 'Gathering in the Name of the Outlaw: REED and Robin Hood', in *REED in Review*, ed. Douglas and MacLean, pp. 72–3; David N. Klausner, ed., *Records of Early English Drama: Herefordshire and Worcestershire* (Toronto, Buffalo and London, 1990), pp. 461–529.

45 Klausner, *Records*, pp. 461–2.

46 C. M. Woolgar, *The Great Household in Late Medieval England* (New Haven, CT, and London, 1999), pp. 25–9.

47 In 1384–5 the mayor of Lynn rewarded visiting players for their Corpus Christi play and for another play on St Thomas, martyr (probably Becket): John Southworth, *The English Medieval Minstrel* (Woodbridge, 1989), p. 147.

48 Ibid., pp. 142–52.

49 Ibid., p. 94. There were also many unlicensed minstrels, but they were generally paid less.

50 Ibid., pp. 123–6, 128–9; John Wasson, ed., *Records of Plays and Players in Norfolk and Suffolk, 1330–1642*, Malone Society Collections XI (Oxford, 1981), pp. 104–8.

51 A number of folios are missing from the beginning of the manuscript, creating a space that might have featured more songs and lyrics, but could also have contained a longer work, such as a devotional or liturgical piece.

52 Rossell Hope Robbins, *Secular Lyrics of the XIVth and XVth Centuries*, 2nd edn (Oxford, 1955), pp. i–lv, calls it a minstrel's songbook.

53 For example, Stephen Knight and Thomas H. Ohlgren, eds, *Robin Hood and Other Outlaw Tales* (Kalamazoo, MI, 2000), pp. 227–32.

54 British Library, London, MS Sloane 2593, fols 14v–15v.

55 He was also patron of the parish church at Great Yarmouth, on the southeastern Norfolk coast, from his association with seafarers.

56 It now marks the beginning of a coastal 'wolf trail' based on the saint's legend.

57 Wasson, *Plays and Players in Norfolk and Suffolk*, pp. 85–95.

58 Ibid., p. 38.

59 Richard Leighton Greene, ed., *The Early English Carols* (Oxford, 1935), p. 330, links the name with the Bardwell family from Suffolk, and identifies the Sloane compiler as a monk of this name from Bury St Edmunds, giving the material on Edmund as a link. Greene cites a note on fol. 19r, 'Eadmundo sancto pertinet iste liber' / 'this book pertains/

belongs to St Edmund' as evidence for Bury ownership, but he appears unaware of the north Norfolk tradition.

60 This last is now in the care of English Heritage. A third church, dedicated to the Virgin Mary, is situated at Wiveton on the other side of the harbour inlet, and is visible from what was once the quayside at Cley.

61 G. R. Proudfoot, ed., *Records of Plays and Players in Lincolnshire, 1300–1585*, Malone Society Collections VIII (Oxford, 1974), p. xiii.

62 Ibid.

63 John Wasson prints the records from the Lestrange household accounts for the years 1519–1639; these record continuous payments, some on a regular basis, to minstrels, waits and other performers: Wasson, *Plays and Players in Norfolk and Suffolk*, pp. 20–30.

64 The contents include verses for performance at all of the times of the ritual year (St Nicholas, Nativity, Holy Innocents, Epiphany, Candlemas, Passion, Corpus Christi, Annunciation and Trinity), as well as songs of praise for the Virgin Mary and some less spiritual verses. Many are published in Greene's *Early English Carols*.

65 This is what happened to the Virgin's *Miracles* as featured in Chapter Five.

66 Cited in B. E. Harris, *The Victoria County History of Cheshire*, vol. II (Oxford, 1979), p. 176.

67 Ibid., p. 172. The forest contained a mixture of red and fallow deer.

68 See Victoria Flood, *Prophecy, Politics and Place in Medieval England* (Cambridge, 2016), pp. 149–54.

69 Given the European connections of some of these places, west and east, it is also worthy of note that mention of Robin Hood (with that name) has not been found in any country outside England and Scotland in the Middle Ages.

TWO: ROBIN HOOD AND THE PRINTED WORD

1 Ronald Hutton, *The Stations of the Sun: A History of the Ritual Year in Britain* (Oxford, 1996), p. 273; John Marshall, 'Revisiting and Revising Robin Hood in Sixteenth-century London', in *Robin Hood in Outlaw/ed Spaces: Media, Performance and Other New Directions*, ed. Lesley Coote and Valerie B. Johnson (London, 2017), pp. 111–31.

2 These are listed in A. W. Pollard and G. R. Redgrave, eds, *A Short Title Catalogue of Books Printed in England, Scotland and Ireland and of English Books Printed Abroad, 1475–1640* (London, 1950), p. 304.

3 Thomas H. Ohlgren and Lister M. Matheson, eds, *Early Rymes of Robyn Hood: An Edition of the Texts ca. 1425 to ca. 1600* (Tempe, AZ, 2013), p. 32, ll. 154–9. The books are also available through Early English Books Online: www.eebo.chadwyck.com, last accessed 3 October 2018.

4 Ohlgren and Matheson, *Early Rymes*, p. 36, ll. 248–59.

5 Ibid., p. 107, ll. 473–7.

6 Ibid., pp. 109–10, ll. 553–64.

7 Ibid., p. 111, ll. 593–6.

8 Ibid., p. 126, ll. 1112–3.

9 Ibid., pp. 127–8, ll. 1149–60 for the archery contest.
10 Ibid., p. 86, l. 673.
11 Ibid., p. 88, ll. 725–31: Robin disables the sheriff with an arrow, rendering him helpless on the ground, before cutting off his head.
12 Ibid., p. 147, ll. 1799–1803.
13 Since Francis Child decided to place the Lettersnijder edition first, this was the accepted norm, but Ohlgren has now made a virtually unassailable case for this being a copy of the Richard Pynson edition, which he has placed earlier than previously thought – not the 1510–15 given in the *Short Title Catalogue* of early printed books, but somewhere around 1495. This is due to Pynson's reuse of the woodcut illustration he had previously used in his earlier edition of Chaucer's *Canterbury Tales*. Thomas H. Ohlgren, *Robin Hood: The Early Poems, 1465–1560: Texts, Contexts and Ideology* (Newark, NJ, 2007), pp. 109–12.
14 Interestingly, neither was as wealthy or successful as the bookbinder and seller John Taverner, who was worth £307 in the same roll. C. Paul Christiansen, 'The Rise of London's Book Trade', in *Cambridge History of the Book, 1400–1557*, ed. Lotte Hillinga and Joseph B. Trapp (Cambridge, 1999), pp. 128–47.
15 Ohlgren, *Early Poems*, pp. 120–24.
16 Christiansen, 'London's Book Trade', p. 129.
17 Norman F. Blake, ed., *The History of Reynard the Fox* (Oxford, 1970), pp. 3–5.
18 André Bouwman and Bart Besamusca, eds, Thea Summerfield trans., with Matthias Hüning and Ulrika Vogl, *Of Reynaert the Fox: Text and Facing Translation of the Middle Dutch Epic Van den Vos Reynaerde* (Amsterdam, 2009), gives the text of the Flemish version.
19 Ohlgren, *Early Poems*, pp. 102–8.
20 Pollard and Redgrave, *Short Title Catalogue*, pp. 230, 482; later Reynard work is covered in Charles C. Mish, 'Reynard the Fox in the Seventeenth Century', *Huntington Library Quarterly*, XVII (1954), pp. 327–44, but this is largely superseded by the later chapters of Kenneth Varty, *Renard, Renart, Reinaert and Other Foxes in Medieval England: The Iconographic Evidence* (Amsterdam, 1999).
21 Rudolf Hirsch, *Printing, Selling and Reading, 1450–1550* (Wiesbaden, 1974), pp. 127–48.
22 Blake, *Reynard the Fox*, p. 6.
23 Hirsch, *Printing, Selling and Reading*, p. 148; also Margaret Lane Ford, 'The Private Ownership of Printed Books', in *Cambridge History of the Book*, ed. Hillinga and Trapp, pp. 205–28.
24 Ibid.
25 Ohlgren, *Early Rymes*, p. 233, ll. 113–18.
26 Ohlgren and Matheson, *Early Rymes*, p. 233, ll. 114–18.
27 Hutton, *Stations of the Sun*, pp. 274–5.
28 Alan J. Somerset, ed., *Records of Early English Drama: Shropshire*, 2 vols (Toronto, Buffalo and London, 1994), vol. I, p. 203, records the purchase of clothing for the abbot in 1551–2.
29 Sandra Billington, *Mock Kings in Medieval Society and Renaissance Drama* (Oxford, 1991), pp. 1–117, and the same author's *Midsummer:*

A Cultural Sub-text from Chrétien de Troyes to Jean Michel (Turnhout, 2000), pp. 19–37.

30 Rosalind Couklin Hays and C. E. McGee, eds, *Records of Early English Drama: Dorset and Cornwall* (Toronto, Buffalo and London, 1999), p. 522.

31 Ibid., p. 32.

32 John M. Wasson, ed., *Records of Early English Drama: Devon* (Toronto, Buffalo and London, 1986), p. 285.

33 David George, ed., *Records of Early English Drama: Lancashire* (Toronto, Buffalo and London, 1991), pp. 283–5. Kingston and Thames Valley 'king games' and 'Robin Hood games' feature in records from the end of the fifteenth century (1499) to the 1520s; David Wiles, *The Early Plays of Robin Hood* (Woodbridge, 1981), pp. 7–8; also Alexandra F. Johnston and Sally-Beth MacLean, 'Reformation and Resistance in Thames/Severn Parishes: The Dramatic Voice', in *The Parish in English Life*, ed. Katherine L. French, Gary C. Gibbs and Beat A Kümin (Manchester and New York, 1997), pp. 178–202.

34 Johnston and MacLean, 'Reformation and Resistance', pp. 182–3.

35 The Chagford records are late, however, beginning in the 1560s. There is no record of how long this contest had already been running, but an annual Robin Hood event appears to have been well established by the time records begin: Wasson, *Records of Early English Drama: Devon*, pp. 53–6, 118.

36 For more on archery contests, see John Block Friedman, 'Robin Hood and the Social Context of Late Medieval Archery', in *Robin Hood in Greenwood Stood: Alterity and Context in the English Outlaw Tradition*, ed. Stephen Knight (Turnhout, 2011), pp. 67–85.

37 John Wasson, ed., *Records of Plays and Players in Norfolk and Suffolk, 1330–1642*, Malone Society Collections XI (London, 1980), shows a wide variety of plays, ales and processions in large and small towns, and in rural parishes, throughout both counties for the fifteenth through the sixteenth centuries.

38 An interesting viewpoint on this is Douglas Gray, 'Everybody's Robin Hood', in *Robin Hood: Medieval and Post-Medieval*, ed. Helen Phillips (Dublin, 2005), pp. 21–41.

39 Clive Burgess, 'Time and Place: The Late Medieval English Parish in Perspective', in *The Parish in Late Medieval England*, ed. Clive Burgess and Eamon Duffy (Donington, 2006), pp. 1–28.

40 Wasson, *Records of Early English Drama: Devon*, p. 57.

41 Ibid., pp. 52–3.

42 John Marshall, 'Gathering in the Name of the Outlaw: REED and Robin Hood', in *REED in Review: Essays in Celebration of the First Twenty-five Years*, ed. Audrey Douglas and Sally-Beth MacLean (Toronto, Buffalo and London, 2006), pp. 65–80.

43 Katherine French, 'Parochial Fund-raising in Late Medieval Somerset', in *The Parish in English Life*, ed. French, Gibbs and Kümin, pp. 115–32.

44 On quality and the price of costume, see Diane Murphy, *Medieval Mystery Plays as Popular Culture: Performing the Lives of Saints* (Lewiston, Queenston and Lampeter, 2006), pp. 130–31; also Clifford

Davidson, 'The Middle English Saint Play', in *The Saint Play in Medieval Europe*, ed. Clifford Davidson (Kalamazoo, MI, 1986), pp. 31–122.

45 Ronald Hutton, *The Stations of the Sun: A History of the Ritual Year in Britain* (Oxford, 1996), p. 273.

46 Jelle Koopmans, *Le Théâtre des exclus au moyen âge: Hérétiques, sorcières et marginaux* (Paris, 1997), pp. 98–100.

47 Mary C. Erler, ed., *Records of Early English Drama: Ecclesiastical London* (Toronto, Buffalo and London, 2008), p. 123. Marshall, 'Revising and Revisiting Robin Hood in Sixteenth-century London', pp. 111–31, suggests that Henry Machyn himself may have helped out this poor parish by making the coats for them; see pp. 124–6. Machyn was both a merchant tailor and the parish clerk of Holy Trinity church.

48 Anthime Fourrier, ed., *Jean Froissart, 'dits' et 'debats'* (Geneva, 1979), pp. 12–18. In the *Joli Buisson de Jonesce* (*Pretty Bush of Youth*), Jean Froissart uses the term *dit* to designate *pastourelles* (ibid., p. 443).

49 It may be that they were extracted from longer romance material, but we have no real evidence for this, apart from the fact that Earl Ranulf may have been the subject of a longer romance narrative, roughly contemporary with the early versions of *Fouke le FitzWaryn* and *Robert le Dyable*. It could have been a *chanson de geste*, but nothing now remains, apart from what appears to be a short extract from a story about the earl.

THREE: ROBIN HOOD AND 'MAID' MARION

1 For the spread of *pastourelles*, see William Paden, ed. and trans., *The Medieval Pastourelle*, 2 vols (New York and London, 1987): I have used Paden's editions of Old French poems, but the translations are my own. The classical background and nature of the medieval form are covered in Helen Cooper, *The Pastoral: Medieval into Renaissance* (Ipswich and Totowa, NJ, 1977), and Michel Zink, *La Pastourelle: Poésie et folklore au moyen âge* (Paris, 1972); content is discussed in Geri L. Smith, *The Medieval French Pastourelle Tradition* (Gainesville, FL, 2009).

2 Paden includes some English and Welsh poetry written under *pastourelle* influence, but form and content (the encounter between knight/cleric and shepherdess) are different from the European tradition. These forms do survive in some English poetry on the Virgin Mary.

3 Paden, *Pastourelle*, vol. I, no. 111, pp. 286–7 (anon., 13th-century French).

4 Ibid., no. 113, pp. 290–91 (anon., 13th-century French). *Amorete* (little love) conveys the idea of fleeting, or perhaps fragile or passing, love, unlike *fin amour*, true love.

5 One girl is clearly just under age: 'Treze anz a que je fui nee / par mien escient' (It is thirteen years since I was born / to my knowledge): ibid., no. 115, pp. 294–5 (anon., 13th century).

6 Ibid., no. 34, pp. 110–11 (anon., early 13th century).

7 Ibid., no. 115, pp. 294–5 (anon., 13th century).

8 Ibid., no. 80, pp. 224–5 (anon. 13th century).

9 Ibid., no. 74, pp. 208–9 (anon., 13th century).

10 James Holt, *Robin Hood*, rev. edn (London, 1989), p. 49, gives the variants Scarlett, Scathelocke and Shacklock.
11 Paden, *Pastourelle*, vol. I, no. 118, pp. 304–5 (anon., 13th century).
12 Ibid., no. 21, pp. 72–3 (Jean Bodel, *c.* 1200).
13 Ibid., no. 77, pp. 216–17 (Ernoul de Gastinois, 13th century).
14 Ibid., no. 62, pp. 172–3 (Jean Erart, *c.* 1250).
15 Ibid., no. 43, pp. 134–5 (Thibaut, 1201–1253, comte de Champagne, King of Navarre).
16 Ibid., no. 81, pp. 224–5 (anon., 13th century).
17 Ibid., no. 37, p. 119 (anon., 13th century).
18 Ibid., no. 86, pp. 238–9 (anon., 13th century).
19 Ibid., no. 66, pp. 183–5 (Perrin d'Angicourt, fl. 1245–1250).
20 This (to us) harsh judgement is also apparent in the morality of comic tales: see also Chapter Seven, for similar observations on the *fabliau* story *La Pucelle qui volait voler* (The Girl who Wanted to Fly).
21 Paden, *Pastourelle*, vol. I, no. 87, pp. 238–9 (anon., 13th century).
22 Thomas Ohlgren and Lister M. Matheson, eds, *Early Rymes of Robyn Hood: An Edition of the Texts ca. 1425 to ca. 1600* (Tempe, AZ, 2013), pp. 7, 27: *Robin Hood and the Monk*, ll. 1–8; *Robin Hood and the Potter*, ll. 1–4.
23 Paden, *Pastourelle*, vol. I, no. 62, pp. 170–71 (Jean Erart, fl. 1240–1254). Sometimes a place is named.
24 Ohlgren and Matheson, *Early Rymes*, pp. 228–33, give the text of the play.
25 Paden, *Pastourelle*, vol. I, no. 21, pp. 72–3 (Jean Bodel, *c.* 1200).
26 Ibid., no. 81, pp. 226–7 (anon., 13th century): there is also an Occitan version by Gautier de Murs (second half of 13th century): ibid., vol. II, no. 148, pp. 390–91:

G'ay ami, fetes amia,
Je ne seron d'un acort;
A Robin du boy m'acort,
A qui y ay m'amor plevia

27 Ibid., vol. I, no. 44, pp. 134–5 (Thibaut, King of Navarre).
28 The complete works of Adam de la Halle, including the *Chanson du Roi de Sicile*, are currently available for free download from Google Books: http://books.google.co.uk, accessed 23 September 2018.
29 There is an edition with translation: Shira I. Schwam-Baird and Milton G. Scheuermann, eds and trans., *Le Jeu de Robin et de Marion* (New York, 1994); other editions are Kenneth Varty, ed., *Le Jeu de Robin et de Marion, précédé du jeu du pèlerin* (London, 1960), and Jean Dufournet, ed., *Le Jeu de Robin et de Marion* (Paris, 1989). I have used Varty's excellent text; the translations are my own.
30 Paden, *Pastourelle*, vol. I, no. 89, pp. 242–3 (anon., 13th century).
31 Ibid., no. 89, pp. 244–5.
32 Varty, *Robin et Marion*, p. 74, ll. 40–44.
33 Dufournet, *Robin et Marion*, pp. 25–30, gives several examples.
34 Varty, *Robin et Marion*, p. 76, ll. 75–6.
35 For possible carnivalesque elements in the story, see Kenneth Varty,

'Le Mariage, la courtoisie et l'ironie comique dans le Jeu de Robin et de Marion', *Marche Romaine*, xxx (1980), pp. 287–92.

36 There is further material on this in Stephanie Thompson Lundeen, 'Dressing Down: Aristocratic Identity in *Le Jeu de Robin et Marion*', *Essays in Medieval Studies*, XXII (2005), pp. 67–74.

37 At one point in the encounter with Robin, the knight resorts to violence, knocking him down, as in this anonymous thirteenth-century French *pastourelle* (Paden, *Pastourelle*, vol. 1, no. 95, pp. 254–5):

> *Je boutai Robin arriere*
> *Per maniere*
> *Si que point ne lou blesai.*
>
> I knocked Robin backwards
> In such a way
> That I didn't wound him at all.

38 When Robin looks at the knight, he sees a *chevalier* (knight, a man of class status), whereas Marion sees *un homme à cheval* (a man on a horse, a physical situation without any class implications): Dufournet, *Robin et Marion*, p. 11.

39 Varty, *Robin et Marion*, p. 93, ll. 367–70. Also Cooper, *Pastoral*, p. 56.

40 On the Edenic 'eternal life' of pastoral literature, see Cooper, *Pastoral*, pp. 82–97.

41 Varty, *Robin et Marion*, p. 111, ll. 622–4.

42 Ibid., p. 101, ll. 471–3.

43 Ibid., p. 120, ll. 756–9, 762–3.

44 Kevin Brownlee, 'Transformations of the Couple: Genre and Language in the *Jeu de Robin et de Marion*', *French Forum*, XIV, supplement 1 (December 1989), pp. 419–43.

45 See Gary Waller, *The Virgin Mary in Late Medieval and Early Modern English Literature and Popular Culture* (Cambridge and New York, 2011), especially pp. 31–54, and Miri Rubin, *Mother of God: A History of the Virgin Mary* (London and New York, 2009), pp. 191–211.

46 On the specific case of the *Jeu de Robin et de Marion*, there is also Mark Cruse, Gabriella Parussa and Isabelle Ragnard, 'The Aix "Jeu de Robin et Marion": Image, Text, Music', *Studies in Iconography*, xxv (2004), pp. 1–46.

47 This can be seen in psalters (books of psalms) from the later thirteenth and fourteenth centuries: Michael Camille, *Image on the Edge: The Margins of Medieval Art* (London, 1992), pp. 11–55. A very common image warning against the danger of sin featured an archer shooting his arrow at the bare anus of another character. An early example can be seen on the west door of Lincoln Cathedral, and there are many examples in English manuscripts of the later Middle Ages.

48 Paden, *Pastourelle*, vol. 1, no. 41, pp. 125–7 (Gautier de Coinci, first half of 13th century). Robert L. A. Clark, 'Gautier's Wordplay as Devotional Ecstasy', in *Gautier de Coinci: Miracles, Music and Manuscripts*, ed. Kathy M. Krause and Alison Stones (Turnhout, 2006), pp. 113–26, discusses this link between the secular and the spiritual in the worship of Mary.

49 Richard Leighton Green, *The Early English Carols*, 2nd edn (Oxford, 1977), pp. cxlii–cxlviii, describes the link between clergy and popular song in medieval Europe.

50 Sin as consumption was biblical: in his first epistle, Peter says, 'Be sober, be vigilant; because your adversary the devil, as a roaring lion, walketh about, seeking whom he may devour' (1 Peter 5:8).

51 Dives was a very rich man, and Lazarus the poor beggar who begged at his door. Both of the men die; Dives goes to hell and Lazarus goes to Paradise. Dives is told that this is because, in his own lifetime, he had much of the world's good things and Lazarus had none – now he must pay, while Lazarus can have all he wants (Luke 16:19–30).

52 Dufournet says that Marion is a peasant with the knight, but 'un peu la dame avec Robin' (a little of the lady with Robin): Dufournet, *Robin et Marion*, p. 21. I would say that she is truly a lady all the time, but the knight does not see it, being blinded by aristocratic prejudice. Also Brownlee, 'Transformations', pp. 422–5.

53 On devotion to Mary, see Eamon Duffy, *The Stripping of the Altars: Traditional Religion in England, 1400–1580* (New Haven, CT, and London, 1992), pp. 256–65.

54 There is also an element of human love: Adam de la Halle's wife was called Marie.

55 John Southworth, *The English Medieval Minstrel* (Woodbridge, 1989), p. 72. Southworth, too, believes that this was *the* Adam le Bossu: Adam de la Halle.

FOUR: ROBIN HOOD AND THE VIRGIN MARY

1 A similar point is made by Gary Waller, *The Virgin Mary in Late Medieval and Early Modern English Literature and Popular Culture* (Cambridge and New York, 2011), p. 83.

2 Eamon Duffy, *Marking the Hours: English People and their Prayers, 1240–1570* (New Haven, CT, and London, 2006), gives examples; see pages 104–5 for 'good prayer'. Also see *The Stripping of the Altars: Traditional Religion in England, 1400–1580* (New Haven, CT, and London, 1992), pp. 211–65, 266–98, by the same author.

3 Diane Murphy, *Medieval Mystery Plays as Popular Culture: Performing the Lives of Saints* (Lewiston, Queenston and Lampeter, 2006), pp. 60–62. Today, most film and TV writers are middle-class and university-educated, although their product may be directed towards a lower-class audience: for example, the BBC's *Eastenders* and Granada's *Coronation Street*. The former is a very good example of popular fiction in the medieval sense, as the Queen is said to watch it, too.

4 If Robin Hood became associated with Pentecost, then Gamelyn, or some part of his 'tales', may have been considered suitable for use at Shrovetide. Shrovetide, the short period from Sunday to Shrove Tuesday, before Ash Wednesday began the Lenten fast, was a violent time associated with excesses of consumption and festive beatings. Food to be forbidden during the Lenten fast had to be eaten. Cock-fighting was a traditional Shrovetide sport, and so was the beating or

'threshing' of cocks and chickens, during which a group of people, sometimes blindfolded, attempted to kill a cock or chicken by beating it with sticks or throwing missiles at it. Football, which was a very violent game with few or no rules at that time, was also traditionally played at Shrovetide. The violence in the Gamelyn story often consists of extremely serious beatings handed out by the hero and his sidekick to priests. There is a moral and confessional element to this that corresponds to the moral violence meted out by Robin and his men, and to Robin's 'truth tests'. The priests in the Gamelyn story – like the abbot of St Mary's and his monks – have the opportunity to behave conscientiously towards a vulnerable young adult, but they do the opposite, abusing him in *vilain* language. All their bones are broken as a result. The twin elements of excessive consumption (by the hero and his friends) and violent beatings (of the clergy at his brother's feast) would have made some parts at least of the Gamelyn story suitable for Shrovetide. Thus Gamelyn could have had his religious uses, too; he and Robin Hood might have bookended the two important liturgical celebrations of late spring and early summer.

5 David Galloway, ed., *Records of Early English Drama: Norwich, 1540–1642* (Toronto and London, 1984).

6 Sally Badham, *Seeking Salvation: Commemorating the Dead in the Late-Medieval English Parish* (Donington, 2015), pp. 163–78; K. Farnhill, *Guilds and the Parish Community in Late Medieval East Anglia, c. 1470–1550* (York, 2001), is a study of a particular area, but one in which there was considerable economic growth during the period. This would not apply to some areas in the East of England, where Robin Hood was traditionally celebrated, although it was where the Pastons and Calles lived. Paul Whitfield White, 'Holy Robin Hood! Carnival, Parish Guilds and the Outlaw Tradition', in *Tudor Drama before Shakespeare, 1485–1590: New Directions for Research, Criticism and Pedagogy*, ed. Lloyd Edward Kermode, Jason Scott-Warren and Martine van Elk (New York, 2004), pp. 67–89, gives some information on parish guilds and performances, but not that much on Marian worship specifically. A survey of Robin Hood performance is given by Alice Blackwood, 'By Words and By Deeds: The Role of Performance in Shaping the "Canon" of Robin Hood', in *Robin Hood and the Outlaw/ed Literary Canon*, ed. Lesley Coote and Alexander L. Kaufman (London and New York, 2018), pp. 51–68.

7 Donald Maddox and Sara Sturm-Maddox, eds, *Parisian Confraternity Drama of the Fourteenth Century: The Miracles de Nostre Dame par personnages* (Turnhout, 2008), Introduction, pp. 17–25.

8 Ibid., pp. 21–2.

9 Caroline Barron, 'The Parish Fraternities of Medieval London', in *The Church in Pre-Reformation Society: Essays in Honour of F.R.H. du Boulay*, ed. Caroline Barron and Christopher Harper-Bill (Woodbridge, 1985), pp. 13–37; also Peter Happé, *English Drama before Shakespeare* (London and New York, 1999), pp. 162–3.

10 Maddox and Sturm-Maddox, *Confraternity Drama*, p. 1.

11 Graham Runnalls, 'Medieval Trade Guilds and the *Miracles de Nostre Dame par personnages*', ibid., pp. 29–65, dating on p. 31.

12 Ther was also a Nonne, a Prioresse,
That of her smylyng was ful symple and coy;
Hir grettest ooth was but by Seinte Loy
There was also a Nun, a Prioresse,
Who smiled in a really simple and coy way;
Her greatest oath was, 'By St Loy'

Geoffrey Chaucer, *The Canterbury Tales*, 'General Prologue', ll. 118–20: Larry D. Benson and F. N. Robinson, eds, *The Riverside Chaucer*, 3rd edn (Oxford, 1988), p. 25.

13 *Le Miracle de . . . un enfant que Nostre Dame resuscita* (The Miracle of a Child which Our Lady Resurrected): Gaston Paris and Ulysse Robert, eds, *Miracles de Nostre Dame par personnages*, 7 vols (Paris, 1876–83), vol. II, p. 283.

14 Here the writer is probably referring to the gold coin minted in Byzantium, rather than the silver coins of the same name minted in Western Europe . . . in either case, a substantial amount of money.

15 *Le Miracle de . . . un marchand et un juif* (The Miracle of a Merchant and a Jew), ibid., vol. VI, pp. 169–223.

16 *Le Miracle . . . de un marchand et un larron* (The Miracle . . . of a Merchant and a Thief): ibid., vol. II, pp. 89–119. It may be through the *pastourelle* or the Marian link that a rose garland made its way into the *Lytell Geste*.

17 Thomas H. Ohlgren and Lister M. Matheson, eds, *Early Rymes of Robyn Hood: An Edition of the Texts ca. 1425 to ca. 1600* (Tempe, AZ, 2013), p. 144, *Lytell Geste*, ll. 1711–18.

18 *Le Miracle de . . . Pierre le changeur* (*The Miracle of . . . Peter the Money-Changer*): Paris and Robert, *Miracles*, vol. VI, pp. 225–300.

19 *Le Miracle de . . . la femme du Roy de Portugal* (The Miracle of the Wife of the King of Portugal): ibid., vol. I, pp. 147–202, quote on p. 175, ll. 713–15.

20 M. D. Anderson, *Drama and Imagery in English Medieval Churches* (Cambridge, 1963), pp. 188–192; Emily Howe et al., *Wall Paintings of Eton* (London, 2011); Roger Rosewell, *The Eton College Chapel Wall Paintings: England's Forgotten Masterpieces* (Woodbridge, 2014).

21 Ohlgren and Matheson, *Early Rymes*, p. 67, *Lytell Geste*, ll. 180–87.

22 *Le Miracle de . . . Roi Thierry* (The Miracle of King Thierry): Paris and Robert, *Miracles*, vol. V, pp. 257–338.

23 *Le Miracle de . . . la fille du Roy de Hongrie* (The Miracle of the Daughter of the King of Hungary): ibid., vol. V, pp. 1–88.

24 *Le Miracle de . . . Amis et Amille*: ibid., vol. IV, pp. 1–67.

25 *Le Miracle de . . . saint Jehan le Paulu hermite* (The Miracle of Saint John the Paulu [Hairy] Hermit): ibid., vol. V, pp. 89–151.

26 Ibid., vol. II, pp. 281–346.

27 *L'Advocacie de Nostre Dame* (The Advocacy of Our Lady): Gérard Gros, ed., Judith M. Davis and F.R.P. Akehurst, trans., *Our Lady's Lawsuits in L'Advocacie de Nostre Dame and La Chapelerie Nostre Dame de Baiex* (Tempe, AZ, 2011), pp. 32–3, ll. 665–8; also Judith M. Davis, 'Giving the Devil his Due: Justice and Equity in *L'Advocacie Nostre Dame*', in *Courtly Arts and the Art of Courtliness: Selected Papers from the Eleventh Triennial*

Congress of the International Courtly Literature Society, University of Wisconsin, Madison, 29 July–4 August 2004, ed. Keith Busby and Christopher Kleinhenz (Cambridge, 2006), pp. 373–84.

28 *La Miracle de . . . l'Abbesse Grosse*: Paris and Robert, *Miracles*, vol. I, pp. 57–100; *Le Miracle de . . . un prevost que Nostre Dame delivra* (The Miracle of a Provost whom Our Lady Rescued): ibid., vol. II, pp. 227–80.

29 The archdeacon feels that the bishop is not of good enough birth and upbringing to be elected to such a high office; it should have been him instead. *Le Miracle de l'evesque que l'arcediacre murtrit* (The Miracle of the Bishop whom the Archdeacon Murdered): ibid., vol. I, pp. 101–46.

30 See Chapter One for more on this manuscript. For example, on fol. 10v., 'I synge of a myden [maiden] that is makeles [either 'matchless', or 'without a mate']' is followed by the much more *risque* 'I have a gentil cook [cock]'.

31 Pierre Kunstmann, ed., *Miracles de Nostre Dame: Tirés du Rosarius* (Ottawa and Paris, 1991).

32 An edited, printed version can be found in Achille Jubinal, ed., *Nouveau Recueil de contes, dits, fabliaux et autres pieces inedits des XIIIe, XIVe et XVe siècles*, 2 vols (Paris, 1839), vol. I, pp. 89–95, quote p. 95.

33 Printed, edited version in Anatole de Montaiglon and Gaston Raynaud, eds, *Recueil generale et complet des fabliaux des xiiie et xive siècles imprimés et inédits: Publiés avec notes et variants d'après les manuscrits*, 6 vols (Paris, 1872–90), vol. II, pp. 24–30.

34 See Chapter Seven for this story.

35 Mary Jane Evans, *Amis et Amille and Robert le Dyable: A Contextual Appreciation of Two of the Miracles de Nostre Dame par personnages*, PhD Thesis, Duke University, 1981.

36 The idea is expounded and developed in Mike Rodman Jones, *Radical Pastoral, 1381–1594: Appropriation and the Writing of Religious Controversy* (Farnham, 2011).

37 Runnalls, 'Medieval Trade Guilds', pp. 56–7.

38 See Eric Hobsbawm, *Bandits* (London, 1969), especially pp. 19–33 (on social banditry) and pp. 46–62 (on 'noble robbers').

39 Here I am following the arguments of Elliot Kendall, *Lordship and Literature: John Gower and the Politics of the Great Household* (Oxford and New York, 2008). Kendall explores Gower's use of the great household as a model for political structure, for confessional discourse and retainership, and for the political implications of styles of rulership demonstrated by Venus and Cupid.

40 For confession and self-determination, see Katherine C. Little, *Confession and Resistance: Defining the Self in Late Medieval England* (Notre Dame, IN, 2006), especially pp. 50–58.

41 Matthew 6:24; Luke 16:13.

FIVE: ROBIN HOOD AND ROMANCE NARRATIVES

1 Jennifer Brewer, 'Let Her Be Waived: Outlawing Women in Yorkshire, 1293–1294', in *British Outlaws of Literature and History: Essays on Medieval and Early Modern Figures from Robin Hood to Twm Shon Catty,*

ed. Alexander L. Kaufman (Jefferson, NC, 2011), pp. 28–44, has some interesting cases of 'female outlawry', and for outlaws in general see Barbara H. Hanawalt, 'Portraits of Outlaws, Rebels and Felons in Late Medieval England', ibid., pp. 45–64.

2 Antha Cotten-Spreckelmeyer, 'Robin Hood, Outlaw or Exile', ibid., pp. 133–45.

3 Elaine Treharne, *Old and Middle English, c. 890–c .1450: An Anthology*, 3rd edn (Oxford, 2010), pp. 76–7, has a parallel translation (not quite the same).

4 Hermann Pàlsson and Magnus Magnusson, eds and trans., *King Harald's Saga: Hardradi of Norway* (Harmondsworth, 1966), and Rita Hamilton and Janet Perry, eds and trans., *The Poem of the Cid: A Bilingual Edition with Parallel Text*, 2nd edn (London, 1984), have good English translations. English translations of *Fouke le Fitz Waryn* can be found in Glyn S. Burgess, ed. and trans., *Two Medieval Outlaws: Eustace the Monk and Fouke Fitz Waryn* (Woodbridge, 1997), pp. 132–83, and in Thomas H. Ohlgren, ed., *Medieval Outlaws: Ten Tales in Modern English* (Stroud, 1998), pp. 106–67. I have used the easiest-access Old French version: E. J. Hathaway et al., eds, *Fouke le Fitz Waryn,* Anglo-Norman Texts 26–28 (Oxford, 1975): translations are my own.

5 Hathaway et al., *Fouke,* pp. 22–3.

6 Maldwyn Mills, ed., 'Sir Gowther', in *Six Middle English Romances* (London, 1973), pp. 143–68.

7 Élisabeth Gaucher, *Robert le Diable: Histoire d'une légende* (Paris, 2003), pp. 21, 101–11.

8 Ibid., pp. 131–4. Kari Sajavaara, 'The Sixteenth-century Editions of Robert the Devil', *Neuphilologische Mitteilungen*, LXXX (1979), pp. 335–47. De Worde's version differs from the surviving Old French versions.

9 Gaucher, *Robert le Diable*, pp. 64–9, believes this may be so.

10 E. Löseth, ed., *Robert le Diable: Roman d'aventures*, Société des Anciens Textes Français (Paris, 1903), p. 8, B. ll. 98, 101–3. This is the most readily available edition, although the edition by Élisabeth Gaucher (Paris, 2003) is more recent. There is a recent translation by Samuel L. Rosenberg (Philadelphia, PA, 2018). 'A' and 'B' designate the two surviving manuscript copies, of which 'A' dates from the early thirteenth century, and 'B' from the end of the fourteenth century, or the beginning of the fifteenth. Both manuscripts originated in northern France (Picardy and Hainault respectively) and the story was included in the *Grande Chronique de Normandie*, *c.* 1350.

11 This is a trope found also in the *Miracles de Nostre Dame par personnages*, where it forms the basis for the first recorded play, *Le Miracle de Nostre Dame de l'enfant donné au Diable* (*The Miracle of Our Lady of the Child given to the Devil*). Gaston Paris and Ulysse Robert, eds, *Miracles de Nostre Dame par personnages*, 8 vols (Paris, 1881), vol. I, pp. 5–9.

12 Löseth, *Robert le Diable*, pp. 24–5, A. ll. 341–5, 348–50.

13 They are Lambin ('Little Lambert', the most important), Rigolet (either after the name of a dance or 'little purse'), Brise Godet ('glass breaker'), and Boute en Couroie ('cut purse').

14 Paris and Robert, *Miracles,* vol. VI, p. 23, ll. 596–9.

15 Ibid., p. 31, ll. 864–8.

16 William J. Thoms, ed., *Robert the Deyull, Emprynted in Flete-strete at the sygne of the sonne by Wynkyn de Worde* (Edinburgh, 1904), p. 16. Available at Early English Books Online, www.eebo.chadwyck.com, accessed 3 October 2018.

17 Thomas H. Ohlgren, *Robin Hood: The Early Poems, 1465–1560: Texts, Contexts and Ideology* (Newark, NJ, 2007), pp. 63, 64.

18 Löseth, *Robert le Diable*, p. 197, A. ll. 5047–8. In the *Miracles*, Robert is told that God wants him to return, marry the princess, and found a dynasty to his (God's) glory.

19 Thomas H. Ohlgren and Lister M. Matheson, eds, *Early Rymes of Robyn Hood: An Edition of the Texts, ca. 1425 to ca. 1600* (Tempe, AZ, 2013), p. 146, *Lytell Geste*, ll. 1771–3. These must be 'new' people, as Robin has been at court for over twenty years.

20 A. J. Pollard, *Imagining Robin Hood: The Late-Medieval Stories in Historical Context* (London and New York, 2004), pp. 57–81.

21 Angus J. L. Winchester, 'Baronial and Manorial Parks in Medieval Cumbria', in *The Medieval Park: New Perspectives*, ed. Robert Liddiard (Macclesfield, 2007), pp. 165–84; N. J. Higham, *A Frontier Landscape: The North West in the Middle Ages* (Macclesfield, 2004), pp. 99–125.

22 There are many editions of *Sir Orfeo*; a very good one can be found in Treharne, *Old and Middle English*, pp. 550–62. Andrew Joynes, ed. and trans., *Medieval Ghost Stories: An Anthology of Miracles, Marvels and Prodigies* (Woodbridge, 2001), pp. 183–8, gives a good translation among other woodland-based 'supernatural' tales. Nigel Bryant, ed. and trans., *Perceval: The Story of the Grail* (Cambridge, 1982), gives an English translation of Chretién de Troyes' *Conte du Graal*, and 'The Wife of Bath's Prologue and Tale' can be found in Larry D. Benson and F. N. Robinson, eds, *The Riverside Chaucer*, 3rd edn (Oxford, 1988), pp. 105–22.

23 J.A.H. Murray, ed., *The Romance and Prophecies of Thomas of Erceldoune*, Early English Text Society Original Series 61 (London, 1875). St Eustace, the hunter-saint, saw his vision of a divine stag with the cross between its antlers while out hunting. An alternative perspective on this topic is provided in Amy Lambert, 'Morgan Le Fay and Other Women: A Study of the Female Phantasm in Medieval Literature', PhD thesis, University of Hull, 2015.

24 Paris and Robert, *Miracles*, vol. v, pp. 101–3.

25 Mary Carruthers, *The Book of Memory: A Study of Memory in Medieval Culture*, 2nd edn (Cambridge, 2008), p. 38.

26 'Sir Orfeo', in J. A. Burrow and Thorlac Turville-Petre, eds, *A Book of Middle English*, 2nd edn (Oxford, 1997), p. 121; References for the *Morte Darthur* in Helen Cooper, ed., *Sir Thomas Malory Le Morte Darthur: The Winchester Manuscript* (Oxford, 1998), p. 214 (Tristram) and pp. 288, 292–7 (Lancelot). At the end of his period in the wilderness, Lancelot is taken in and attired as a 'fool' by Sir Castor, the nephew of King Pelles.

27 This is explained by Gerald of Wales in the *Itinerarium Kambrie*, in J. S. Brewer, J. F. Dimock and G. F. Warner, eds, *Giraldi Cambrensis opera*, 8 vols, Rolls Series 21 (London, 1861–91), vol. VI, p. 133, where he notes that there were two Merlins, one of whom (called Silvester or 'of

the wood') went crazy in the woods and had a terrible vision of a battle-axe flying in the air.

28 Burrow and Turville-Petre, *Book of Middle English*, p. 241, from British Library, London, MS Harley 2253.

29 Processing around parish boundaries and/or 'beating the bounds' was an activity usually carried out at Rogationtide, just before Whitsun, and therefore close to the time when Robin Hood events were held. Attendance was made compulsory by the Church: Ronald Hutton, *The Stations of the Sun: A History of the Ritual Year in Britain* (Oxford, 1996), pp. 277–81; Eamon Duffy, *The Stripping of the Altars: Traditional Religion in England, 1400–1580* (New Haven, CT, and London, 1992), pp. 136–9.

30 Corinne Saunders, *The Forest of Medieval Romance: Avernus, Broceliande, Arden* (Woodbridge, 1993), pp. 132–62. There are more ecologically based readings in Gillian Rudd, *Greenery: Ecocritical Readings of Late Medieval English Literature* (Manchester and New York, 2007), and in Sarah Harlan-Haughey, *The Ecology of the English Outlaw in Medieval Literature: From Fen to Greenwood* (London and New York, 2016), pp. 143–77, in particular.

31 Lesley Coote, 'Journeys to the Edge: Self-identity, Salvation and Outlaw(ed) Space', in *Robin Hood in Greenwood Stood: Alterity and Context in the English Outlaw Tradition*, ed. Stephen Knight (Turnhout, 2011), pp. 47–66, discusses the idea of boundaries in Robin Hood stories in this context.

32 Ohlgren and Matheson, *Early Rymes*, pp. 143–4, ll. 1687–98, 1701–4.

33 Hathaway et al., *Fouke*, p. 22.

34 Ibid., p. 49.

35 Ibid., pp. 49–50.

36 Paris and Robert, *Miracles*, vol. V, p. 5, ll. 16–19.

37 Pollard, *Imagining Robin*, pp. 156–83.

38 Nancy Mason Bradbury and Scott Bradbury, eds, *The Dialogue of Solomon and Marcolf* (Kalamazoo, MI, 2012), p. 15. The best study, with much manuscript and textual information on the Latin versions, is Jan M. Ziolkowsi, *Solomon and Marcolf* (Cambridge, MA, 2008).

39 Bradbury and Bradbury, *Dialogue*, p. 5.

40 Marcolf tells a story: Solomon's mother cooked a vulture's heart in the oven on a piece of bread. She gave Solomon the heart to eat, from which he derived his wisdom, then threw the bread at Marcolf. Marcolf's 'alternative' wisdom derived from the infusion of the bread with the fluid from the vulture's heart. The story also neatly describes the 'trickle down' transmission of learning and culture, from the top to the bottom of society.

41 Bradbury and Bradbury, *Dialogue*, p. 43.

42 The letter not the spirit, as with *Till Eulenspiegel*.

43 There follows a comic (in)version of the well-known story of Solomon's judgement between the two women who both claim the same child as their own. Solomon orders that the child should be cut in half, and one half given to each woman, whereupon the real mother offers to give way to preserve the child's life. Marcolf goes out into the street and begins a rumour that the king will rescind his judgement, whereupon the mother rouses her neighbours, and the women go to complain against

the king. Solomon, despite his avowals of female worth, is driven to curse women. Bradbury and Bradbury, *Solomon and Marcolf*, pp. 53–61.

44 This is the theme of Chaucer's *Tale of Melibee*. See Chapter Two for Caxton's comments on *Reynard*.

SIX: ROBIN HOOD AND OTHER TRICKSTERS

1 See Chapter Three.

2 Thomas H. Ohlgren, 'Edwardus Redivivus in A Gest of Robyn Hode', *Journal of English and Germanic Philology*, XCIX (2000), pp. 1–29, addresses this problem.

3 Francis James Child, ed., *The English and Scottish Popular Ballads*, 2nd edn, 5 vols (New York, 1965), vol. v, p. 79, ll. 20–21.

4 Ibid., p. 80, ll. 48–9.

5 Mark Truesdale, *The King and Commoner Tradition* (London and New York, 2018), is a detailed study of this type of narrative; Mark Truesdale, 'Robin Hood and the King and Commoner Tradition: "Þe best archer of ilkon, / I durst mete hym with a stone"', in *Robin Hood and the Outlaw/ed Literary Canon*, ed. Alexander Kaufman and Lesley Coote (London and New York, 2018), pp. 69–88.

6 Albrecht Classen, 'Transgression and Laughter, the Scatological and Epistemological: New Insights into the Pranks of Till Eulenspiegel', *Medievalia et Humanistica*, XXXIII (2007), pp. 41–61.

7 Paul Oppenheimer, ed. and trans., *Till Eulenspiegel: His Adventures* (Oxford and New York, 1995), pp. 38–9, 42–3, 112–13. I have used Oppenheimer's excellent translation from Old High German.

8 This is the influence of 'rulership advice' literature.

9 The owl was also closely associated with the craft of printing, Athena being the goddess of crafts. She was, of course, the goddess of war as well.

10 Oppenheimer, *Till*, p. xxi.

11 Robert S. Sturges, ed. and trans., *Aucassin and Nicolette: A Facing-page Edition and Translation* (Ann Arbor, MI, 2015), is the most accessible edition. In *Aucassin*, the actual peasants are described in a similar, bestial, manner; see Paul Freedman, *Images of the Medieval Peasant* (Stanford, CA, 1999), p. 140.

12 Nancy Mason Bradbury and Scott Bradbury, eds, *The Dialogue of Solomon and Marcolf: A Dual-language Edition from Latin and Middle English Printed Editions* (Kalamazoo, MI, 2012), pp. 26–7; also available from TEAMS Middle English Texts, http://d.lib.rochester.edu, accessed 15 February 2019.

13 Helen Cooper, ed., *Sir Thomas Malory Le Morte Darthur: The Winchester Manuscript* (Oxford, 1998), pp. 52–3.

14 Kathryn Gravdal, *Vilain and Courtois: Transgressive Parody in French Literature of the Twelfth and Thirteenth Centuries* (Lincoln, NE, 1989), pp. 13–17.

15 E. J. Hathaway et al., eds, *Fouke le FitzWaryn*, Anglo-Norman Texts 26–8 (Oxford, 1975), p. 43.

16 Ibid., p. 44.

17 Thomas H. Ohlgren and Lister M. Matheson, eds, *Early Rymes of Robyn Hood: An Edition of the Texts, ca. 1425 to ca. 1600* (Tempe, AZ, 2013), pp. 66, 69–70, ll. 150–51, 250–53. Also Susan Crane, *The Performance of Self: Ritual, Clothing and Identity during the Hundred Years' War* (Philadelphia, PA, 2002), pp. 10–38.
18 Larry D. Benson and F. N. Robinson, eds, *The Riverside Chaucer* (Oxford, 1988), p. 120, 'The Wife of Bath's Prologue and Tale', ll. 1009–18.
19 A. J. Pollard, *Imagining Robin Hood: The Late-Medieval Stories in Historical Context* (London and New York, 2004), pp. 29–56.
20 Ohlgren and Matheson, *Early Rymes*, p. 106, ll. 433–6, 445–6.
21 Gravdal, *Vilain and Courtois*, pp. 56–80.
22 *The Knight who Could Make Cunts Talk* is a comic tale that also presents an impoverished knight: see Chapter Seven for more on this.
23 Eustace disguises himself at various times as a Cistercian monk, shepherd, pilgrim, peasant, charcoal burner, potter, leper, cripple, pastry seller, young woman and even a bird.
24 Denis Joseph Conlon, ed., *Li romans de Witasse le Moine* (Chapel Hill, NC, 1972), p. 45, ll. 224–31.
25 Ibid., p. 39, ll. 6–16.
26 There are many editions and translations of medieval Reynard stories. The most accessible in English is that of Douglas Owen, *The Romance of Reynard the Fox* (Oxford, 1994). For the Flemish story with parallel translation: André Bouwman et al., eds, *Of Reynaert the Fox: Text and Facing Translation of the Middle Dutch Beast Epic Van den Vos Reynaerde* (Amsterdam, 2009). For Reynard as an anti-hero: Joseline Bidard, 'Reynard the Fox as Anti-hero', in *Heroes and Heroines in Medieval English Literature: Presented to André Crépin on the Occasion of his Sixty-fifth Birthday,* ed. Leo Carruthers (Cambridge, 1994), pp. 119–23.
27 This episode also carries traces of Charlemagne's attempt to judge the quarrel between Roland and his evil-intentioned uncle, Ganelon, in the *Chanson de Roland.*
28 Bodleian Library, Oxford, MS Digby 86: this poem is on folios 138–40.
29 Kenneth Varty, *Reynard the Fox: A Study of the Fox in Medieval English Art* (Leicester, 1967), has many examples. Varty's viewpoint has been challenged by Norman Blake, who argues that foxes in English literature and art are not necessarily Reynard. However, Varty's examples are very convincing. Norman Blake, 'Reynard the Fox in England', in *Aspects of Medieval Animal Epic*, ed. E. E. Rombauts and A. A. Welkenhuysen (Louvain and The Hague, 1975), pp. 53–65. Also N. F. Blake, 'English Versions of Reynard the Fox in the Fifteenth and Sixteenth Centuries', *Studies in Philology*, LXII (1965), pp. 63–100. For an exposition of Reynard in the context of other beasts, see Jill Mann, *From Aesop to Reynard: Beast Literature in Medieval Britain* (Oxford and New York, 2009).
30 This does not mean that the human peasant class is depicted with any more sympathy by the makers of Reynard stories than they are by the composer of the contemporary romance of *Fouke FitzWaryn.*
31 See Chapter Eight; also Pollard, *Imagining Robin*, pp. 156–83.
32 Thomas Wright, ed. and trans., *The Political Songs of England: From the Reign of John to that of Edward II* (Hildesheim, 1968), pp. 231–6,

233–4. Trailbaston was instigated by Edward I in the first decade of the fourteenth century in order to combat disorder. Itinerant royal justices would hold courts in towns and cities, trying local felons. A *bastoun* was a strong club, often with metal bands and nails used to strengthen it and to enhance its quality as a weapon. Trailbaston commissions could be, as they are here, perceived as creating more outlaws and highway robbers.

33 Wright, *Political Songs*, p. 234. The word 'ploy', as used here, may be *plait*, a plea or lawsuit (the speaker is talking about a legal situation), or *ploie*, a strap or bond (the speaker continually refers to being in prison), or even *plaie*, a wound or injury (in the sense of harm). I have followed Wright and translated it as 'plea', which seems the more obvious given the legal subtext of the poem.

34 Willem Noomen and Nico van den Boogaard, eds, *Nouveau Recueil complet des fabliaux*, 10 vols (Assen, 1983–98), vol. x, pp. 146–7. The classic edition is by G. Reynaud de Lage, *Trubert: Fabliau du XIIIe siècle* (Paris and Geneva, 1974), although there is a more recent one by C. Donà, *Douin de Lavesne: Trubert* (Parma, 1994). I have used the Noomen text, as it is very clear and relatively available in many academic libraries.

35 Noomen and Boogaard, *Recueil*, vol. x, p. 188, ll. 7–9.

36 In her sole appearance in the *Chanson de Roland*, Aude falls down dead when she hears that Roland has been killed.

37 Noomen and Boogaard, *Recueil*, vol. x, pp. 191–2, ll. 151–7.

38 Ibid., p. 192, ll. 172–5.

39 Ibid., p. 193, ll. 209–14.

40 Ibid., p. 194, ll. 259–60.

41 Ibid., p. 197, ll. 387–90.

42 Ibid., p. 205, ll. 693–4.

43 A medieval audience would have recognized this as an '*Audigier*-type' moment, especially when the coward Trubert is carried forward on his charger, back to front, in ill-fitting armour.

44 Noomen and Boogaard, *Recueil*, vol. x, p. 252, ll. 2567–8.

45 Ibid., p. 253, l. 2596.

46 Ibid., p. 188, l. 13.

47 Ibid., p. 209, ll. 888–9.

48 *Robin Hood and the Potter*, ll. 282–4; Ohlgren and Matheson, *Early Rymes*, p. 37.

49 Noomen and Boogaard, *Recueil*, vol. x, p. 209, l. 834.

50 Enid Welsford, *The Fool: His Social and Literary History* (Gloucester, MA, 1966), pp. 115–25; Judith Diane McCrary, 'The Fool in Medieval French Drama', PhD thesis, University of Michigan (Ann Arbor), 1976, pp. 15–44.

51 Ohlgren, *Early Rymes*, p. 34, ll. 205–11.

52 Ibid., p. 35, ll. 218–24.

53 Ibid., pp. 9–10, ll. 95–100.

54 Non-noble (male) traitors were taken to the place of execution tied to hurdles, behind a horse, then hanged by the neck, taken down alive, slit open, their bowels and intestines removed and burned in front of their eyes, and then castrated, beheaded and cut into four pieces, for display in public places. The nobly born could be 'mercifully' beheaded,

although they might be subjected to ritualized humiliation first, as Edward I did with Sir Simon Fraser (his coat of arms was reversed and his shield broken over his head) and Edward II with Thomas of Lancaster, who had to ride backwards to his execution, his face to the horse's tail.

55 Thomas H. Ohlgren, 'The "Marchaunt" of Sherwood: Mercantile Ideology in *A Gest of Robyn Hode*', in *Robin Hood in Popular Culture*, ed. Thomas Hahn (Cambridge, 2000), pp. 175–90; also Jean-Charles Payen, *Trubert ou le triomphe de la marginalité* (Aix-en-Provence, 1978), and Daron Burrows, 'Trubert: Transgression, Revolution, Abjection', *Reinardus*, XIX (2006), pp. 37–52.

56 Crane, *Performance of Self*, gives detailed examples of the importance of appearances.

SEVEN: ROBIN HOOD AND THE COMIC TALE

1 On English-language versions, see John Hines, *The Fabliau in English* (London, 1993), and for English and translations of *fabliau* stories from seven different languages, there is Derek Brewer, *Medieval Comic Tales*, 3rd edn (Cambridge, 2008). There is considerable literature on French stories, the most accessible being Brian J. Levy, *The Comic Text: Patterns and Images in the Old French Fabliaux*, Faux Titre 186 (Amsterdam, 2000).

2 The story is translated into modern English in Brewer, *Comic Tales*, pp. 55–8.

3 There are several intertextual references in the Trubert story; the shabby appearance of Trubert's sister is similar to that of the lady wronged by Perceval in the *Conte du Graal*, Trubert's rusty old armour and his cowardly but successful attack on King Golias's champion is a reference to mock romance (as in *Audigier*), and there is blasphemous reference to the Annunciation and the Immaculate Conception of the Virgin Mary in the pregnancy of Rosette (whose name, 'little Rose', associates her with the Virgin in a similar way to the name of 'Marion' the shepherdess), in a comic inversion of biblical narrative.

4 Willem Noomen and Nico van den Boogaard, eds, *Nouveau Recueil complet des fabliaux,* 10 vols (Assen, 1983–98), vol. X, p. 250, ll. 2482–3.

5 Ibid., vol. IV, pp. 305–12, quote p. 311, ll. 93–6 .

6 Ibid., vol. II, pp. 153–90.

7 Bibliothèque Nationale, Paris, MS fr. 837.

8 Larry D. Benson and N. F. Robinson, eds, *The Riverside Chaucer*, 3rd edn (Oxford, 1988), p. 134, 'The Summoner's Tale', ll. 2144–8.

9 Noomen and Boogaard, *Recueil*, vol. VIII, pp. 209–14.

10 Andrew Cowell describes this as 'comic realism', and offers a detailed examination of what it means, in *At Play in the Tavern: Signs, Coins and Bodies in the Middle Ages* (Ann Arbor, MI, 1999), pp. 1–9.

11 *La Borgoise d'Orlians*: a wife is intending to deceive her husband with a priest. The husband's niece spies on them and reports their plans to him, and he determines to expose them. He pretends to go away on business, and then meets his wife under cover of darkness in the place where she has agreed to meet the priest. The wife is not deceived, but

lets him in and hides him in an upstairs room. She then goes back to meet her lover, and brings him back to her bed. After a while, she arranges a meal for the household servants, then asks them to rid her of a clerk who has been pestering her for sex. He is hiding in the small upstairs room. The servants get clubs and sticks, go upstairs and beat the husband black and blue, then throw him on to the dung heap. The *borgoise* feeds her lover and 'entertains' him all night, then goes to her husband, who has been fetched indoors by his servants. She gives him a bath and salves his wounds. He was beaten, she says, because the servants mistook him for a clerk who had been pestering her, as she had rejected his advances and was determined to remain loyal to her husband. Her husband believes her, and she carries on living happily with him while also entertaining her lover. Noomen and Boogaard, *Recueil*, vol. IV, pp. 305–12. In *La Sainteresse*, a bourgeois husband is proud of the fact that his wife is faithful and shows off around the town about it. His wife vows to make him a liar. One day a young chancer comes to the door dressed as a woman. On being admitted by the husband, s/he says that the wife has sent for her/him for medical treatment. The 'lady' doctor and the wife go upstairs, where they have (energetic) sex three times, before returning to the husband. He pays the 'lady' doctor well, and s/he then leaves: ibid., vol. IV, pp. 305–12.

12 See Mary Jane Stearns Schenck, *The Fabliaux: Tales of Wit and Deception*, Purdue University Monographs in Romance Languages 25 (Amsterdam and Philadelphia, 1987), p. 43, for more on settings.

13 Thomas H. Ohlgren and Lister M. Matheson, eds, *Early Rymes of Robyn Hood: An Edition of the Texts, ca. 1425 to ca. 1600* (Tempe, AZ, 2013), p. 15: *Robin Hood and the Monk*, ll. 282–5.

14 Ibid., p. 70, ll. 260–65.

15 In *Dame Sirith*, a clerk falls in love/lust with a beautiful but pious and faithful young wife. Distraught, he seeks the help of an old 'wise woman', Dame Sirith. In return for lots of cash and good clothing, she agrees to help. She rubs pepper into the eyes of her dog and visits Margery. She says that the dog is her daughter, who changed into a dog because she rejected the advances of a poor young clerk. The petrified Margery accepts the young lover, and Dame Sirith gets her money: Brewer, *Comic Tales*, pp. 47–51, has a version of the story. In *La Pucele qui voloit voler* (The Girl Who Wanted to Fly), a chaste but proud young girl refuses to marry, but is convinced that she can learn to fly. A lusty priest persuades her that he can teach her to do this. He tells her that his kisses will help her to grow a beak, and that sex will help her to grow a tail. After a while, she grows neither of these, but she does become pregnant: Noomen and Boogaard, *Recueil*, vol. VI, pp. 157–70.

16 Ibid., pp. 169–70. On *fabliau* morality, see also Edith Joyce Benkov, 'Les Fabliaux: Jugements Risibles', PhD thesis, University of California, Los Angeles, 1979.

17 Noomen and Boogaard, *Receuil*, vol. III, pp. 377–403.

18 For the boastful husband, see *La Sainteresse*. In *Le Chevalier qui fist sa fame confesse* (The Knight Who Gets his Wife to Confess), a knight has had a happy marriage to an honourable, faithful wife. As she lies dying,

he dresses as a priest and takes her confession. He discovers that she has been keeping her serial unfaithfulness hidden from him: ibid., vol. III, pp. 229–43.

19 Ibid., vol. III, pp. 3–44.

20 Benson and Robinson, *Riverside Chaucer*, p. 109, 'The Wife of Bath's Prologue and Tale', ll. 333–4.

21 Unlike Eustace the Monk, who imposes a truth test to see if a merchant is honest enough to take a message to the Count of Boulogne for him. He also gives the merchant a palfrey from the ten horses he has stolen from him, rather like Robin Hood and the Potter.

22 For example, *Le Pretre qui abevete* (The Priest Who Peeped): a lover-priest spies on his lover and her husband through a hole in the door as they eat. When he enters the house, the priest asks what they have been doing. The husband says they have been eating, to which the priest replies that he saw them making love. If the priest eats with the wife, her husband will see the same thing. The husband goes outside and peeps through the hole, while the priest makes love to his wife. This makes the husband extremely angry, but the priest says that they were only eating – and the husband is calmed: Noomen and Boogaard, *Receuil*, vol. VIII, pp. 301–9.

23 A monk dreams that he is in a market, where the goods for sale are women's genitalia. On reaching out for one, he puts his hand into a heap of thorns. Badly hurt, he repents his lewd thoughts: ibid., vol. x, pp. 265–75.

24 Ibid., vol. IV, pp. 93–106.

25 The priest is caught in flagrante by his mistress's husband, falls into the river and drowns, his erection intact. The fisherman pulls the detached penis from the river and shows it to his wife, who has claimed that she will love him whether he can satisfy her sexually or not. The wife is distraught, and makes ready to leave. He then tells her to feel inside his breeches, where his own 'tool' is still intact: ibid., vol. IV, pp. 109–29. Of course, 'what women want' is the subject of the Wife of Bath's tale in *The Canterbury Tales*, too.

26 For example, in *Le Testament de l'ane* (The Donkey's Will), a greedy priest is allowed to leave his donkey buried in consecrated ground, but only when he gives twenty livres to the bishop, claiming that the ass has left it to the Church. The moral is 'don't be a miser': ibid., vol. IX, pp. 239–50. In *Brunain, La Vache du prestre* (Brunain, the Priest's Cow), a greedy priest tells a peasant that God will bless those who give to the Church by giving them even more than they have given. The peasant gives the priest his only cow. Later, the cow wanders back home, bringing the priest's cow with it. The peasant blesses God, who really has doubled the gift. The priest has to 'put up and shut up': ibid., vol. V, pp. 41–8.

27 Ibid., vol. I, pp. 3–28, quotes on pp. 27–8.

28 Brewer gives a Latin version in translation: Brewer, *Comic Tales*, pp. 147–8. A French version, in which the husband sells the child to slavers, is *L'Enfant qui fu remis au soleil* (The Child Who Was Put Back Out in the Sun): Noomen and Boogaard, *Recueil*, vol. V, pp. 211–21.

29 Ohlgren and Matheson, *Early Rymes*, p. 9, l. 34.

30 The boy in Chaucer's tale is murdered by Jews, but the Virgin keeps him alive for long enough to tell his tale and receive extreme unction so that he can attain Paradise: Benson and Robinson, *Riverside Chaucer*, pp. 209–12.
31 Noomen and Boogaard, *Recueil*, vol. III, pp. 47–173.
32 Ibid., pp. 85, 87.
33 Ibid., p. 95.
34 Ibid., p. 129.
35 Thorlac Turville-Petre, *England the Nation: Language, Literature and National Identity, 1290–1340* (Oxford, 1996), pp. 199–203.
36 On the basis that Robin gives her a ring (a lover's gift, as Queen Fière gives to Reynard) and can rely on her complicity. We actually see only her good humour and her liking for free gifts in the still extant story, though.
37 John Southworth, *The English Medieval Minstrel* (Woodbridge, 1989), pp. 157–8.
38 The Beverley 'king' is depicted on the 'minstrel' pillar in St Mary's Church in Beverley.
39 E. J. Hathaway et al., eds, *Fouke le FitzWaryn*, Anglo-Norman Texts 26–8 (Oxford, 1975), p. 32.
40 Noomen and Boogaard, *Recueil*, vol. II, pp. 79–105.
41 Ibid., vol. I, pp. 129–59.
42 William Paden, ed. and trans., *The Medieval Pastourelle*, 2 vols (New York and London, 1987), vol. I, pp. 202–3 (Colin Muset, 1230–1270).
43 Rossell Hope Robbins, ed., *Secular Lyrics of the XIV and XV Centuries*, 2nd edn (Oxford, 1955), pp. 15–16; poem from British Library, MS Sloane 2593, fol. 11v.
44 The minstrel could also act as a fool. Southworth notes a Roger and a John le Follus (the fool), who were also huntsmen and foresters in the reigns of Henry II, of John and of Henry III (from *c.* 1180 into the early 1200s). John le Follus had charge of a large pack of hounds for King John in 1210. Roger was rewarded with a house and land; John received 21*d.* a day from Henry III in 1242, but was later given land. One of his jobs was to travel around, providing venison for the king. Minstrels also taught and entertained royal children as well as adults, and performed for ecclesiastical lords as well as secular ones. Minstrels travelled singly or in pairs: Southworth, *The English Medieval Minstrel*, pp. 55–87, 142–52.

EIGHT: ROBIN HOOD AND THE MEDIEVAL PAST

1 Alexandra F. Johnston and Sally-Beth MacLean, 'Reformation and Resistance in Thames/Severn Parishes: The Dramatic Voice', in *The Parish in English Life*, ed. Katherine L. French, Gary C. Gibbs and Beat A. Kümin (Manchester and New York, 1997), pp. 178–202.
2 For Machyn and his association with performance in London, see John Marshall, 'Revisiting and Revising Robin Hood in Sixteenth-century London', in *Robin Hood in Outlaw/ed Spaces: Media, Performance, and Other New Directions*, ed. Lesley Coote and Valerie B. Johnson (London and New York, 2017), pp. 111–31.

3 Mary Erler, *Records of Early English Drama: Ecclesiastical London* (Toronto, Buffalo and London, 2008), p. xxxi.
4 Thomas H. Ohlgren, *Robin Hood: The Early Poems, 1465–1560: Texts, Contexts and Ideology* (Newark, NJ, 2007), p. 18.
5 Ibid., pp. 19–20.
6 Ibid., p. 50, quotes from Richard Pynson's 1493 edition.
7 This and other fifteenth-century examples in similar vein, are cited by Alan J. Fletcher, *Preaching, Politics and Poetry in Late Medieval England* (Dublin, 1998), pp. 145, 166: see also Ohlgren, *The Early Poems*, pp. 50–51, who contextualizes them further.
8 Dora Mortimer Grisdale, ed., *Three Middle English Sermons from the Worcester Chapter Manuscript F 10* (Leeds, 1939), p. 8.
9 Passus v.ll.395–7. George Kane and E. Talbot Donaldson, eds, *Will's Visions of Piers Plowman, Do-well, Do-better and Do-best* (London, 1975), p. 331; A.V.C. Schmidt, ed., *William Langland: The Vision of Piers Plowman, a Complete Edition of the B-text* (London, 1978), p. 56.
10 Wendy Scase, *Piers Plowman and the New Anticlericalism* (Cambridge, 1989), p. 123.
11 Erler, *Records*, p. xxxi, notes Sir Richard Morrison's suggestion that Henry VIII should use anti-papal versions to replace the 'lewd and ribald' Robin Hood plays found everywhere; Peter Happé, 'Protestant Adaptation of the Saint Play', in *The Saint Play in Medieval Europe*, ed. Clifford Davidson (Kalamazoo, MI, 1986), pp. 205–40, gives a general overview, including Bale.
12 Rosalind Couklin Hays and C. E. McGee, eds, *Records of Early English Drama: Dorset and Cornwall* (Toronto, Buffalo and London, 1999), pp. 506–8, 516–17. Later, other festivals such as Elizabeth I's accession date (17 November) were substituted.
13 James Stokes, ed., *Records of Early English Drama: Somerset*, 2 vols (Toronto, Buffalo and London, 1996), vol. I, pp. 52–5, 57.
14 Stokes, ed., *Early English Drama: Somerset*, vol. I, p. 321.
15 See Chapter Three for these.
16 Alexander L. Kaufman, *The Historical Literature of the Jack Cade Rebellion* (Farnham, 2009), pp. 120–21.
17 Richard B. Dobson and John Taylor, eds, *Rymes of Robyn Hood: An Introduction to the English Outlaw* (Stroud, 1977), pp. 3–4; James Holt, *Robin Hood*, revd edn (London, 1989), pp. 149–52.
18 Kaufman, *Jack Cade*, p. 178.
19 Hays and McGee, *Records*, pp. 468–9.
20 Holt, *Robin Hood*, pp. 148–9.
21 John M. Wasson, ed., *Records of Early English Drama: Devon* (Toronto, Buffalo and London, 1986), p. 119. 'Robyn whode & lytell Iohn' appear again, in the churchwardens' accounts of St John's Bow in 1553–4; ibid., p. 145.
22 James M, Gibson, ed., *Records of Early English Drama: Kent*, 3 vols (Toronto, Buffalo and London, 2002), vol. II, pp. 426–7.
23 Ronald Hutton, *The Rise and Fall of Merry England: The Ritual Year, 1400–1700* (Oxford and New York, 1994), pp. 140–41.

24 R. W. Ingram, ed., *Records of Early English Drama: Coventry* (Manchester, Toronto, Buffalo and London, 1981), p. 273.

25 I am here following, and adapting, arguments put forward by Mary Ellen Lamb in *The Popular Culture of Shakespeare, Spenser and Jonson* (London and New York, 2006), pp. 1–22.

26 This does not mean that ballads derived from oral traditions, although they might pretend to do so.

27 Leslie Shepard, *The Broadside Ballad: A Study in Origins and Meaning* (London, 1962), pp. 23–8.

28 For the period 1576–1640 Adam Fox estimates publication of around 300,000 units, at a rate of over five hundred titles a year by 1640. Adam Fox, *Oral and Literate Culture in England, 1500–1700* (Oxford, 2000), p. 14.

29 Fox speaks of 'a prevailing, male-dominated, culture which typically characterized women as creatures of the spoken word': ibid., p. 177.

30 For Robin Hood as a warning about turning to crime, see Stephen Basdeo, 'Robin Hood the Brute: Representations of the Outlaw in Eighteenth-century Criminal Biography', *Law, Crime and History*, VI (2016), pp. 54–70.

31 Francis James Child, ed., *The English and Scottish Popular Ballads*, 5 vols (Boston, 1882–98), vol. III, pp. 133–6, 120–28, 218–19.

32 The Pinder of Wakefield is also the subject of the anonymous play *George a Greene*, first published in 1599 but performed a decade earlier than the date of publication. Edwin Davenport, 'The Representation of Robin Hood in Elizabethan Drama: George a Greene and Edward I', in *Playing Robin Hood: The Legend as Performance in Five Centuries*, ed. Lois Potter (Newark, NJ, 1998), pp. 45–62. There were also two prose biographies, of 1632 and 1706 respectively.

33 Child, *Ballads*, vol. III, pp. 214–17, 196–205. See also *The Jolly Pinder of Wakefield*, ibid., pp. 129–32.

34 *Robin Hood's Death*: ibid., pp. 102–7. In both cases he is bled to death by the prioress of Kirklees; in one version he is buried beside the road, and in the other version he (more famously) shoots an arrow out of the window to mark the place where his body shall lie. This contrasts with the fifteenth-century *Robin and Gandeleyn*, where he is simply shot in the woods and left to lie there.

35 Ibid., pp. 147–50, 154–5, 144–7.

36 Ibid., pp. 140–43.

37 John C. Meagher and Arthur Brown, eds, *The Downfall of Robert Earl of Huntingdon*, Malone Society Reprints (Oxford, 1965). In Munday's companion play, *The Death of Robert Earl of Huntingdon*, Robin dies early in the play, which is really about his chaste young widow: John C. Meagher and Arthur Brown, eds, *The Death of Robert Earl of Huntingdon*, Malone Society Reprints (Oxford, 1965). Both plays are edited in a single volume by John C. Meagher in *The Huntingdon Plays: A Critical Edition of The Downfall and The Death of Robert Earl of Huntingdon* (New York, 1980). See also Jeffrey L. Singman, 'Munday's Unruly Earl', in *Playing Robin Hood*, ed. Potter, pp. 63–76.

38 Lois Potter reveals an additional debt to Rostand's *Cyrano de Bergerac*: Lois Potter, 'Robin Hood and the Fairies: Alfred Noyes' Sherwood', in

Robin Hood: Medieval and Post-medieval, ed. Helen Phillips (Dublin, 2005), pp. 167–80.

39 Act v, Scene 1; Alfred Noyes, *Robin Hood: A Play in Five Acts* (Edinburgh and London, 1926), p. 118. The first scene of Noyes's play was adapted by John Irvin for the opening scene of his 1991 film.

40 Natalie Kononenko, 'Clothes Unmake the Social Bandit: Sten'ka Razin and the Golyt'ba', in *Playing Robin Hood*, ed. Potter, pp. 111–35 (Russia); Yoshiko Uéno, 'Robin Hood in Japan', ibid., pp. 136–58; and 'Murayama's Robin Hood: The Most Radical Variant in Japan', in *Robin Hood in Popular Culture: Violence, Transgression and Justice*, ed. Thomas Hahn (Cambridge, 2000), pp. 265–72. Anna Czarnowus, 'The Legend of Janosik and the Polish Novel about Robin Hood as Continuations of the Medieval Outlaw Tradition', in *Robin Hood and the Outlaw/ed Literary Canon*, ed. Lesley Coote and Alexander L. Kaufman (London and New York, 2018), pp. 167–84. For Robin Hood in Germany and Scandinavia, see Kevin Carpenter, *Robin Hood: Die Vielen Gesichter des Edlen Raubers / The Many Faces of that Celebrated English Outlaw* (Oldenburg, 1995).

41 *Robin and Marian* (dir. Richard Lester, 1976). Angus Donald's *Outlaw* (London, 2009) is the first novel in a series. Stephen R. Lawhead has produced a trilogy, setting Robin against a mystical, 'Celtic' background in *Hood*, *Scarlet* and *Tuck* (London, 2006, 2007, 2008): Adam Thorpe, *Hodd* (London, 2010).

42 This is mirrored in Ridley Scott's 2010 film, where Robin and his friends have been similarly condemned, leading ultimately to Robin's masquerade as a dead man.

43 For more information on the late eighteenth-century stage Robin Hoods, see Linda V. Troost, 'Robin Hood Musicals in Eighteenth-century London', in *Robin Hood in Popular Culture*, ed. Hahn, pp. 251–64.

44 Terry never got to play the part, as her actor/impresario husband (Henry Irving) withdrew from the project. The play was first produced on stage in New York, not London, with Ada Rehan in the title role. Lois Potter, 'The Apotheosis of Maid Marian', in *Playing Robin Hood*, ed. Potter, pp. 182–204.

45 Many of Hobsbawm's social bandits hail from the Americas; Eric Hobsbawm, *Bandits*, 2nd edn (London, 2000); also Max Harris, 'Sweet Moll and Malinche: Maid Marian Goes to Mexico', in *Playing Robin Hood*, ed. Potter, pp. 101–10.

46 Joseph Ritson, ed., *Robin Hood: A Collection of all the ancient poems, songs, and ballads now extant relative to that celebrated English outlaw, to which are prefixed historical anecdotes of his life*, 2nd edn, 2 vols (London and York, 1832), p. viii.

47 For a telling comparison between the two, see Alan T. Gaylord, '". . . something of the air of a celebration": Scott, Peacock, and Maid Marian', in *Telling Tales and Crafting Books: Essays in Honor of Thomas H. Ohlgren,* ed. Alexander L. Kaufman, Shaun F. D. Hughes and Dorsey Armstrong (Kalamazoo, MI, 2016), pp. 203–14.

48 Chapter Twenty; taken from Sir Walter Scott, *Ivanhoe* (London, 1964), p. 174.

49 Lorraine Kochanske Stock, 'Recovering Reginald de Koven's and Harry Bache Smith's "Lost" Operetta Maid Marian', in *Images of Robin Hood: Medieval to Modern*, ed. Lois Potter and Joshua Calhoun (Newark, NJ, 2008), pp. 256–65.

50 Howard Pyle, *The Merry Adventures of Robin Hood* (New York, 1883); on Pyle's illustrations and their immediate influence: Jill May, 'Robin Hood's Home Away from Home: Howard Pyle and his Art Students', in *Images of Robin Hood*, ed. Potter and Calhoun, pp. 138–87.

51 Ian Wojcik-Andrews, 'Children's Literature Canon, Robin Hood, Children's Literature Criticism', in *Robin Hood and the Outlaw/ed Canon*, ed. Coote and Kaufman, pp. 205–20. See also Michael R. Evans, '"A Song of Freedom": Geoffrey Trease's Bows Against the Barons', in *Images of Robin Hood*, ed. Potter and Calhoun, pp. 188–96.

52 Marcia Williams, *The Adventures of Robin Hood*, 2nd edn (London, 2007). In online fanzine and gaming scenarios, audiences are creating their own narratives. See Thomas Rowland, '"And Now Begins Our Game": Revitalizing the Ludic Robin Hood' and Kristin Noone, 'Highwaymen, Robbers, and Rogues in the Twentieth Century: A New Outlaw Fantasy', both in *Robin Hood in Outlaw/ed Spaces: Media, Performance, and Other New Directions*, ed. Lesley Coote and Valerie B. Johnson (London and New York, 2017), pp. 175–88 and 88–98 respectively. On modern romance novels, see Valerie B. Johnson, 'What a Canon Wants: Robin Hood, Romance Novels, and Carrie Lofty's *What a Scoundrel Wants*', in *Robin Hood in Outlaw/ed Spaces*, ed. Coote and Johnson, pp. 184–204.

53 For the Armitage family, see David Hepworth, 'A Grave Tale', in *Medieval and Post-medieval*, ed. Phillips, pp. 91–112. More detail on Harrogate and Knaresborough as 'health tourism' centres in the seventeenth and eighteenth centuries is given in Tim Thornton, *Prophecy, Politics and the People in Early Modern England* (Woodbridge, 2006), pp. 163–78.

54 Child, *Ballads*, vol. III, p. 47. He also had a 'cave', a 'cross' and a 'stoop' in the area.

55 Helen Phillips, 'Forest, and Town, and Road: The Significance of Places and Names in Some Robin Hood Texts', in *Robin Hood in Popular Culture*, ed. Hahn, pp. 197–214.

56 Stephen Knight, 'Quite Another Man: The Restoration Robin Hood', in *Playing Robin Hood*, ed. Potter, pp. 167–81.

Select Bibliography

Major works cited: for minor citations see References.

PRIMARY SOURCES: MANUSCRIPTS

Cambridge, Trinity College, MS R.2.64
Cambridge, University Library, MS Ee.4.35
Cambridge, University Library, MS Ff.5.48
London, British Library, Additional MS 42130
London, British Library, MS Cotton Nero Dii
London, British Library, MS Sloane 2593
Paris, Bibliothèque Nationale, MS fr. 12483

PRIMARY SOURCES: EDITIONS

Benson Larry D., and F. N. Robinson, eds, *The Riverside Chaucer*, 3rd edn (Oxford, 1988)

Blake, Norman F., ed., *The History of Reynard the Fox* (Oxford, 1970)

Bradbury, Nancy Mason, and Scott Bradbury, eds, *The Dialogue of Solomon and Marcolf: A Dual-language Edition from Latin and Middle English Printed Editions* (Kalamazoo, MI, 2012)

Burgess, Glyn S., ed. and trans., *Two Medieval Outlaws: Eustace the Monk and Fouke Fitz Waryn* (Woodbridge, 1997)

Child, Francis James, ed., *The English and Scottish Popular Ballads*, 2nd edn, 5 vols (New York, 1965)

Conlon, Denis Joseph, ed., *Li Romans de Witasse le Moine* (Chapel Hill, NC, 1972)

Cooper, Helen, ed., *Sir Thomas Malory Le Morte Darthur: The Winchester Manuscript* (Oxford, 1998)

Davis, Norman, ed., *Paston Letters and Papers of the Fifteenth Century*, 2 vols (Oxford, 1971)

Dobson, Richard B., and John Taylor, eds, *Rymes of Robyn Hood: An Introduction to the English Outlaw* (Stroud, 1977)

Donà, C., ed., *Douin de Lavesne: Trubert* (Parma, 1994)

Downing, Janay Young, ed., 'A Critical Edition of Cambridge University MS Ff.5.48', PhD thesis, University of Washington, 1969

Dufournet, Jean, ed., *Le Jeu de Robin et de Marion* (Paris, 1989)
Erler, Mary C., ed., *Records of Early English Drama: Ecclesiastical London* (Toronto, Buffalo and London, 2008)
Fourrier, Anthime, ed., *Jean Froissart, 'dits' et 'débats'* (Geneva, 1979)
Freebairn, R., ed., *John Major: Historia Majoris Britanniae* (Edinburgh, 1740)
Fukumoto, Naoyuki, Noboru Harano and Satoru Suzuki, eds, *Le Roman de Renart, édité d'après les manuscrits C et M*, 2 vols (Paris and Tokyo, 1983)
Galloway, David, ed., *Records of Early English Drama: Norwich, 1540–1642* (Toronto and London, 1984)
George, David, ed., *Records of Early English Drama: Lancashire* (Toronto, Buffalo and London, 1991)
Gibson, James M., ed., *Records of Early English Drama: Kent*, 3 vols (Toronto, Buffalo and London, 2002)
Green, Richard Leighton, *The Early English Carols*, 2nd edn (Oxford, 1977)
Gros, Gérard, ed., Judith M. Davis and F.R.P. Akehurst, trans., *Our Lady's Lawsuits in L'Advocacie de Nostre Dame and La Chapelerie Nostre Dame de Baiex* (Tempe, AZ, 2011)
Hamilton, Rita, and Janet Perry, eds and trans., *The Poem of the Cid: A Bilingual Edition with Parallel Text*, 2nd edn (London, 1984)
Hathaway, E. J., et al., eds, *Fouke le FitzWaryn*, Anglo-Norman Texts 26–8 (Oxford, 1975)
Hays, Rosalind Couklin, and C. E. McGee, eds, *Records of Early English Drama: Dorset and Cornwall* (Toronto, Buffalo and London, 1999)
Heyworth P. L., *Jack Upland, Friar Daw's Reply and Upland's Rejoinder* (Oxford, 1968)
Ingram, R. W., ed., *Records of Early English Drama: Coventry* (Manchester, Toronto, Buffalo and London, 1981)
Joynes, Andrew, ed. and trans., *Medieval Ghost Stories: An Anthology of Miracles, Marvels and Prodigies* (Woodbridge, 2001)
Jubinal, Achille, *Nouveau receuil de contes, dits, fabliaux et autres pieces inédits des XIIIe, XIVe et XVe siècles*, 2 vols (Geneva, 1975)
Kane, George, and E. Talbot Donaldson, eds, *Will's Visions of Piers Plowman, Do-well, Do-better and Do-best* (London, 1975)
Klausner, David N., ed., *Records of Early English Drama: Herefordshire and Worcestershire* (Toronto, Buffalo and London, 1990)
Kunstmann, Pierre, ed., *Miracles de Nostre Dame: Tirés du Rosarius* (Ottawa and Paris, 1991)
Lage, G. Reynaud de, ed., *Trubert: Fabliau du XIIIe siècle* (Paris and Geneva, 1974)
Löseth, E., ed., *Robert le Diable: Roman d'aventures*, Société des Anciens Textes Français (Paris, 1903)
Louis, Cameron, ed., *Records of Early English Drama: Sussex* (Turnhout and Toronto, 2000)
Maddox, Donald, and Sara Sturm-Maddox, eds, *Parisian Confraternity Drama of the Fourteenth Century: The Miracles de Nostre Dame par personnages* (Turnhout, 2008)
Mills, Maldwyn, ed., 'Sir Gowther', in *Six Middle English Romances* (London, 1973), pp. 143–68

Montaiglon, Anatole de, and Gaston Raynaud, eds, *Recueil generale et complet des fabliaux des XIIIe et XIVe siècles imprimés et inédits: Publiés avec notes et variants d'après les manuscrits*, 6 vols (Paris, 1872–90)
Morey, James H., ed., *Prik of Conscience* (Kalamazoo, MI, 2012)
Murray, J.A.H., ed., *The Romance and Prophecies of Thomas of Erceldoune*, Early English Text Society Original Series 61 (London, 1875)
Noomen, Willem, and Nico van den Boogaard, eds, *Nouveau Recueil complet des fabliaux*, 10 vols (Assen, 1983–98)
Noyes, Alfred, *Robin Hood: A Play in Five Acts* (Edinburgh and London, 1926)
Ohlgren, Thomas H., ed., *Medieval Outlaws: Ten Tales in Modern English* (Stroud, 1998)
Ohlgren, Thomas H., and Lister M. Matheson, eds, *Early Rymes of Robyn Hood: An Edition of the Texts, ca. 1425 to ca. 1600* (Tempe, AZ, 2013)
Owen, Douglas, *The Romance of Reynard the Fox* (Oxford, 1994)
Paden, William, ed. and trans., *The Medieval Pastourelle*, 2 vols (New York and London, 1987)
Pàlsson, Hermann, and Paul Edwards, ed. and trans., *Egil's Saga* (Harmondsworth, 1976)
Pàlsson, Hermann, and Magnus Magnusson, eds and trans., *King Harald's Saga: Hardradi of Norway* (Harmondsworth, 1966)
Paris, Gaston, and Ulysse Robert, eds, *Miracles de Nostre Dame par personnages*, 7 vols (Paris, 1876–83)
Pollard, A. W., and G. R. Redgrave, eds, *A Short Title Catalogue of Books Printed in England, Scotland and Ireland and of English Books Printed Abroad, 1475–1640* (London, 1950)
Proudfoot, G. R., ed., *Records of Plays and Players in Lincolnshire, 1300–1585*, Malone Society Collections VIII (Oxford, 1974)
Ritson, Joseph, ed., *Robin Hood: A Collection of all the ancient poems, songs, and ballads now extant relative to that celebrated English outlaw, to which are prefixed historical anecdotes of his life* [1795], 2nd edn, 2 vols (London and York, 1832)
Robbins, Rossell Hope, ed., *Secular Lyrics of the XIV and XV Centuries*, 2nd edn (Oxford, 1955)
Schmidt, A.V.C., ed., *William Langland: The Vision of Piers Plowman, a Complete Edition of the B-Text* (London, 1978)
Schwam-Baird, Shira I., and Milton G. Scheuermann, eds and trans., *Le Jeu de Robin et de Marion* (New York, 1994)
Somerset, Alan J., ed., *Records of Early English Drama: Shropshire*, 2 vols (Toronto, Buffalo and London, 1994)
Stevenson, J., ed., *Ralph of Coggeshall: Chronicon Anglicanum*, Rolls Series 66 (London, 1875)
Stokes, James, ed., *Records of Early English Drama: Somerset*, 2 vols (Toronto, Buffalo and London, 1996)
Taylor, Simon, and D.E.R. Watt, eds, *Scotichronicon by Walter Bower in Latin and English*, 8 vols (St Andrews, 1987–94)
Thoms, William J., ed., *Robert the Deyull, Emprynted in Flete-strete at the sygne of the sonne by Wynkyn de Worde* (Edinburgh, 1904); http://eebo.chadwyck.com

Treharne, Elaine, ed., *Old and Middle English, c. 890–c. 1450: An Anthology*, 3rd edn (Oxford, 2010)
Varty, Kenneth, ed., *Le Jeu de Robin et de Marion, précédé du Jeu du pelerin* (London, 1960)
Wasson, John M., ed., *Records of Plays and Players in Norfolk and Suffolk, 1330–1642*, Malone Society Collections XI (London, 1981)
—, *Records of Early English Drama: Devon* (Toronto, Buffalo and London, 1986)
Wright, Thomas, ed. and trans., *The Political Songs of England*, 5 vols (Hildesheim, 1968)

SECONDARY SOURCES: ESSAY COLLECTIONS (FOR INDIVIDUAL ESSAYS SEE REFERENCES)

Carpenter, Kevin, ed., *Robin Hood: Die Vielen Gesichter des Edlen Raubers / The Many Faces of that Celebrated English Outlaw* (Oldenburg, 1995)
Coote, Lesley, and Valerie B. Johnson, eds, *Robin Hood in Outlaw/ed Spaces: Media, Performance and Other New Directions* (London, 2017)
Fein, Susanna, and Michael Johnston, eds, *Robert Thornton and his Books: Essays on the Lincoln and London Thornton Manuscripts* (York, 2014)
Hahn, Thomas, ed., *Robin Hood in Popular Culture: Violence, Transgression and Justice* (Cambridge, 2000)
Kaufman, Alexander L., ed., *British Outlaws of Literature and History: Essays on Medieval and Early Modern Figures from Robin Hood to Twm Shon Catty* (Jefferson, NC, 2011)
Kaufman, Alexander L., and Lesley Coote, eds, *Robin Hood and the Outlaw/ed Literary Canon* (London and New York, 2018)
Kaufman, Alexander L., Shaun F. D. Hughes and Dorsey Armstrong, eds, *Telling Tales and Crafting Books: Essays in Honor of Thomas H. Ohlgren* (Kalamazoo, MI, 2016)
Knight, Stephen, ed., *Robin Hood in Greenwood Stood: Alterity and Context in the English Outlaw Tradition* (Turnhout, 2011)
Phillips, Helen, ed., *Robin Hood: Medieval and Post-medieval* (Dublin, 2005)
Potter, Lois, ed., *Playing Robin Hood: The Legend as Performance in Five Centuries* (Newark, NJ, 1998)
Potter, Lois, and Joshua Calhoun, eds, *Images of Robin Hood: Medieval to Modern* (Newark, NJ, 2008)

SECONDARY SOURCES: CRITICAL WORKS

Anderson, M. D., *Drama and Imagery in English Medieval Churches* (Cambridge, 1963)
Badham, Sally, *Seeking Salvation: Commemorating the Dead in the Late-medieval English Parish* (Donington, 2015)
Bakhtin, Mikhael, *Rabelais and his World*, trans. Hélène Iswolsky (Bloomington, IN, 1984)
Barker, Juliet, *The Tournament in England, 1100–1400* (Woodbridge, 1986)
Barron, Caroline, 'The Parish Fraternities of Medieval London', in *The Church in Pre-Reformation Society: Essays in Honour of F.R.H. du Boulay*,

ed. Caroline Barron and Christopher Harper-Bill (Woodbridge, 1985), pp. 13–37

Benkov, Edith Joyce, 'Les Fabliaux: Jugements Risibles', PhD thesis, University of California, Los Angeles, 1979

Bennett, Richard J., *Community, Class and Cohesion: Cheshire and Lancashire Society in the Age of Sir Gawain and the Green Knight* (Cambridge, 1983)

Bidard, Joseline, 'Reynard the Fox as Anti-hero', in *Heroes and Heroines in Medieval English Literature: Presented to André Crépin on the Occasion of his Sixty-fifth Birthday*, ed. Leo Carruthers (Cambridge, 1994), pp. 119–23

Billington, Sandra, *Mock Kings in Medieval Society and Renaissance Drama* (Oxford, 1991)

—, *Midsummer: A Cultural Sub-text from Chrétien de Troyes to Jean Michel* (Turnhout, 2000)

Blake, Norman F., 'English Versions of Reynard the Fox in the Fifteenth and Sixteenth Centuries', *Studies in Philology*, LXII (1965), pp. 63–100

—, 'Reynard the Fox in England', in *Aspects of Medieval Animal Epic*, ed. E. E. Rombauts and A. A. Welkenhuysen (Louvain and The Hague, 1975), pp. 53–65

Brownlee, Kevin, 'Transformations of the Couple: Genre and Language in the Jeu de Robin et de Marion', *French Forum*, XIV, supplement 1 (December 1989), pp. 419–43

Bruckner, Matilda Tomaryn, 'The Shape of Romance in Medieval France', in *The Cambridge Companion to Medieval Romance*, ed. Roberta L. Krueger (Cambridge, 2000)

Burgess, Clive, 'Time and Place: The Late Medieval English Parish in Perspective', in *The Parish in Late Medieval England*, ed. Clive Burgess and Eamon Duffy (Donington, 2006), pp. 1–28

Burrows, Daron, 'Trubert: Transgression, Revolution, Abjection', *Reinardus*, XIX (2006), pp. 37–52

Camille, Michael, *Image on the Edge: The Margins of Medieval Art* (London, 1992)

Carruthers, Mary, *The Book of Memory: A Study of Memory in Medieval Culture*, 2nd edn (Cambridge, 2008)

Christiansen, C. Paul, 'The Rise of London's Book Trade', in *Cambridge History of the Book, 1400–1557*, ed. Lotte Hillinga and Joseph B. Trapp (Cambridge, 1999), pp. 128–47

Clark, Robert L. A., 'Gautier's Wordplay as Devotional Ecstasy', in *Gautier de Coinci: Miracles, Music and Manuscripts*, ed. Kathy M. Krause and Alison Stones (Turnhout, 2006), pp. 113–26

Classen, Albrecht, 'Transgression and Laughter, the Scatological and Epistemological: New Insights into the Pranks of Till Eulenspiegel', *Medievalia et Humanistica*, XXXIII (2007), pp. 41–61

Cooper, Helen, *The Pastoral: Medieval into Renaissance* (Ipswich and Totowa, NJ, 1977)

Cowell, Andrew, *At Play in the Tavern: Signs, Coins and Bodies in the Middle Ages* (Ann Arbor, MI, 1999)

Crane, Susan, *The Performance of Self: Ritual, Clothing and Identity during the Hundred Years' War* (Philadelphia, PA, 2002)

Cruse, Mark, Gabriella Parussa and Isabelle Ragnard, 'The Aix "Jeu de Robin et Marion": Image, Text, Music', *Studies in Iconography*, XXV (2004), pp. 1–46

Davidson, Clifford, 'The Middle English Saint Play', in *The Saint Play in Medieval Europe*, ed. Clifford Davidson (Kalamazoo, MI, 1986), pp. 31–122

Davis, Judith M., 'Giving the Devil his Due: Justice and Equity in *L'Advocacie Nostre Dame*', in *Courtly Arts and the Art of Courtliness: Selected Papers from the Eleventh Triennial Congress of the International Courtly Literature Society, University of Wisconsin, Madison, 29 July–4 August 2004* (Cambridge, 2006), pp. 373–84

Duffy, Eamon, *The Stripping of the Altars: Traditional Religion in England, 1400–1580* (New Haven, CT, and London, 1992)

—, *Marking the Hours: English People and their Prayers, 1240–1570* (New Haven, CT, and London, 2006)

Emden, Alfred B., *A Biographical Register of the University of Cambridge to 1500* (Cambridge, 1963)

Evans, Mary Jane, 'Amis et Amille and Robert le Dyable: A Contextual Appreciation of Two of the Miracles de Nostre Dame par personnages', PhD thesis, Duke University, 1981

Farnhill, K., *Guilds and the Parish Community in Late Medieval East Anglia, c. 1470–1550* (York, 2001)

Flood, Victoria, *Prophecy, Politics and Place in Medieval England* (Cambridge, 2016)

Ford, Margaret Lane, 'The Private Ownership of Printed Books', in *Cambridge History of the Book, 1400–1557*, ed. Lotte Hillinga and Joseph B. Trapp (Cambridge, 1999), pp. 205–28

Foster, Frances Allen, *A Study of the Middle-English Poem known as the Northern Passion and its Relation to the Cycle Plays* (London, 1914)

Fox, Adam, *Oral and Literate Culture in England, 1500–1700* (Oxford, 2000)

Freedman, Paul, *Images of the Medieval Peasant* (Stanford, CA, 1999)

French, Katherine, 'Parochial Fund-raising in Late Medieval Somerset', in *The Parish in English Life*, ed. Katherine L. French, Gary C. Gibbs and Beat A. Kümin (Manchester and New York, 1997), pp. 115–32

Gaucher, Élisabeth, *Robert le Diable: Histoire d'une legende* (Paris, 2003)

Gaunt, Simon, 'Romance and other Genres', in *The Cambridge Companion to Medieval Romance*, ed. Roberta L. Krueger (Cambridge, 2000)

Gravdal, Kathryn, *Vilain and Courtois: Transgressive Parody in French Literature of the Twelfth and Thirteenth Centuries* (Lincoln, NE, 1989)

Happé, Peter, *English Drama before Shakespeare* (London and New York, 1999)

Harlan-Haughey, Sarah, *The Ecology of the English Outlaw in Medieval Literature: From Fen to Greenwood* (London and New York, 2016)

Harris, B. E., *The Victoria County History of Cheshire*, vol. II (Oxford, 1979)

Higham, N. J., *A Frontier Landscape: The North West in the Middle Ages* (Macclesfield, 2004)

Hines, John, *The Fabliau in English* (London, 1993)

Hirsch, Rudolf, *Printing, Selling and Reading, 1450–1550* (Wiesbaden, 1974)

Hobsbawm, Eric, *Bandits* (London, 1969)

Holt, James, *Robin Hood*, revd edn (London, 1989)
Howe, Emily, et al., *Wall Paintings of Eton* (London, 2011)
Humphrey, Chris, *The Politics of Carnival: Festive Misrule in Medieval England* (Manchester, 2001)
Hutton, Ronald, *The Rise and Fall of Merry England: The Ritual Year, 1400–1700* (Oxford and New York, 1994)
—, *The Stations of the Sun: A History of the Ritual Year in Britain* (Oxford, 1996)
Johnston, Alexandra F., and Sally-Beth MacLean, 'Reformation and Resistance in Thames/Severn Parishes: The Dramatic Voice', in *The Parish in English Life*, ed. Katherine L. French, Gary C. Gibbs and Beat A. Kümin (Manchester and New York, 1997), pp. 178–202
Jones, Mike Rodman, *Radical Pastoral, 1381–1594: Appropriation and the Writing of Religious Controversy* (Farnham, 2011)
Kaufman, Alexander L., *The Historical Literature of the Jack Cade Rebellion* (Farnham, 2009)
Keen, Maurice, *The Outlaws of Medieval Legend* (London, 1961)
Kendall, Elliot, *Lordship and Literature: John Gower and the Politics of the Great Household* (Oxford and New York, 2008)
Knight, Stephen, *Robin Hood: A Complete Study of the English Outlaw* (Oxford, 1994)
—, *Robin Hood: A Mythic Biography* (Ithaca, NY, and London, 2003)
—, *Reading Robin Hood: Content, Form and Reception in the Outlaw Myth* (Manchester, 2015)
Koopmans, Jelle, *Le Théâtre des exclus au moyen âge: Hérétiques, sorcières et marginaux* (Paris, 1997)
Lamb, Mary Ellen, *The Popular Culture of Shakespeare, Spenser and Jonson* (London and New York, 2006)
Levy, Brian J., *The Comic Text: Patterns and Images in the Old French Fabliaux*, Faux Titre 186 (Amsterdam, 2000)
Little, Katherine C., *Confession and Resistance: Defining the Self in Late Medieval England* (Notre Dame, IN, 2006)
Lundeen, Stephanie Thompson, 'Dressing Down: Aristocratic Identity in *Le Jeu de Robin et Marion*', *Essays in Medieval Studies*, XXII (2005), pp. 67–74
McCrary, Judith Diane, 'The Fool in Medieval French Drama', PhD thesis, Columbia, University of Missouri, 1976
Mann, Jill, *From Aesop to Reynard: Beast Literature in Medieval Britain* (Oxford and New York, 2009)
Marshall, John, '. . . goon in-to Bernysdale: The Trail of the Paston Robin Hood Play', *Leeds Studies in English*, n.s. XXXII (2001), pp. 345–68
—, 'Gathering in the Name of the Outlaw: REED and Robin Hood', in *REED in Review: Essays in Celebration of the First Twenty-five Years*, ed. Audrey Douglas and Sally-Beth MacLean (Toronto, Buffalo and London, 2006), pp. 65–80
—, 'Picturing Robin Hood in Early Print and Performance: 1500–1590', in *Images of Robin Hood: Medieval to Modern*, ed. Lois Potter and Joshua Calhoun (Newark, NJ, 2008), pp. 60–81
Meale Carol L., and Julia Boffey, 'Gentlewomen's Reading', in *The*

Cambridge History of the Book in Britain, 1400–1557, ed. Lotte Hellinga and Joseph B. Trapp (Cambridge, 1999), pp. 526–40
Mish, Charles C., 'Reynard the Fox in the Seventeenth Century', *Huntington Library Quarterly*, XVII (1954), pp. 327–44
Murphy, Diane, *Medieval Mystery Plays as Popular Culture: Performing the Lives of Saints* (Lewiston, Queenston and Lampeter, 2006)
Nelson, Ingrid, *Lyric Tactics: Poetry, Genre and Practice in Later Medieval England* (Philadelphia, PA, 2016)
Nuttall, Jenni, *The Creation of Lancastrian Kingship: Literature, Language and Politics in Late Medieval England* (Cambridge and New York, 2007)
Ohlgren, Thomas H., 'Edwardus Redivivus in "A Gest of Robyn Hode"', *Journal of English and Germanic Philology*, XCIX/1 (2000), pp. 1–29
—, 'The "Marchaunt" of Sherwood: Mercantile Ideology in *A Gest of Robyn Hode*', in *Robin Hood in Popular Culture*, ed. Thomas Hahn (Cambridge, 2000), pp. 175–90
—, *Robin Hood: The Early Poems, 1465–1560: Texts, Contexts and Ideology* (Newark, NJ, 2007)
Payen, Jean-Charles, *Trubert ou le triomphe de la marginalité* (Aix-en-Provence, 1978)
Pollard, A. J., *Imagining Robin Hood: The Late-medieval Stories in Historical Context* (London and New York, 2004)
Rosewell, Roger, *The Eton College Chapel Wall Paintings: England's Forgotten Masterpieces* (Woodbridge, 2014)
Rubin, Miri, *Mother of God: A History of the Virgin Mary* (London and New York, 2009)
Rudd, Gillian, *Greenery: Ecocritical Readings of Late Medieval English Literature* (Manchester and New York, 2007)
Runnalls, Graham, 'Medieval Trade Guilds and the *Miracles de Nostre Dame par personnages*', in *Parisian Confraternity Drama of the Fourteenth Century: The Miracles de Nostre Dame par personnages*, ed. Donald Maddox and Sara Sturm-Maddox (Turnhout, 2008), pp. 29–66
Sajavaara, Kari, 'The Sixteenth-century Editions of Robert the Devil', *Neuphilologische Mitteilungen*, LXXX (1979), pp. 335–47
Sartore, Melissa, *Outlawry, Governance and Law in Medieval England* (New York, 2013)
Saunders, Corinne, *The Forest of Medieval Romance: Avernus, Broceliande, Arden* (Woodbridge, 1993)
Schenck, Mary Jane Stearns, *The Fabliaux: Tales of Wit and Deception*, Purdue University Monographs in Romance Languages 25 (Amsterdam and Philadelphia, 1987)
Shepard, Leslie, *The Broadside Ballad: A Study in Origins and Meaning* (London, 1962)
Smith, Geri L., *The Medieval French Pastourelle Tradition* (Gainesville, FL, 2009)
Southworth, John, *The English Medieval Minstrel* (Woodbridge, 1989)
Truesdale, Mark, *The King and Commoner Tradition* (London and New York, 2018)
Turville-Petre, Thorlac, *England the Nation: Language, Literature and National Identity, 1290–1340* (Oxford, 1996)

Varty, Kenneth, *Reynard the Fox: A Study of the Fox in Medieval English Art* (Leicester, 1967)
—, 'Le Mariage, la courtoisie et l'ironie comique dans *le Jeu de Robin et de Marion*', *Marche Romaine*, XXX (1980), pp. 287–92
—, *Renard, Renart, Reinaert and Other Foxes in Medieval England: The Iconographic Evidence* (Amsterdam, 1999)
Waller, Gary, *The Virgin Mary in Late Medieval and Early Modern English Literature and Popular Culture* (Cambridge and New York, 2011)
Welsford, Enid, *The Fool: His Social and Literary History* (Gloucester, MA, 1966)
White, Paul Whitfield, 'Holy Robin Hood! Carnival, Parish Guilds and the Outlaw Tradition', in *Tudor Drama Before Shakespeare, 1485–1590: New Directions for Research, Criticism and Pedagogy*, ed. Lloyd Edward Kermode, Jason Scott-Warren and Martine van Elk (New York, 2004), pp. 67–89
Wiles, David, *The Early Plays of Robin Hood* (Woodbridge, 1981)
Winchester, Angus J. L., 'Baronial and Manorial Parks in Medieval Cumbria', in *The Medieval Park: New Perspectives*, ed. Robert Liddiard (Macclesfield, 2007)
Wiseman, T. P., *The Myths of Rome* (Liverpool, 2004)
Zink, Michel, *La Pastourelle: Poésie et folklore au moyen âge* (Paris, 1972)

FILMS AND TELEVISION

The Adventures of Robin Hood (dir. Michael Curtiz/William Keighley, 1938)
Maid Marian and her Merry Men (dir. Tony Robinson, 1989–94)
Robin and Marian (dir. Richard Lester, 1976)
Robin Hood (dir. Allan Dwan, 1922)
Robin Hood (dir. Wolfgang Reitherman, 1973)
Robin Hood (dir. John Irvin, 1991)
Robin Hood (dir. Dominic Minghella/Foz Allan, 2006–9)
Robin Hood (dir. Ridley Scott, 2010)
Robin Hood (dir. Otto Bathurst, 2018)
Robin Hood: Men in Tights (dir. Mel Brooks, 1993)
Robin Hood, Prince of Thieves (dir. Kevin Reynolds, 1991)
Robin of Sherwood (dir. Richard Carpenter, 1984–6)

Acknowledgements

Many people have contributed to this book, from the staff of the libraries, repositories and other sites I have visited and whose books and images appear in these pages, to the students and colleagues who have studied and discussed 'the outlaw' with me over the years. Particular thanks are due to colleagues in the International Association for Robin Hood Studies, who have responded to my queries and presentations, especially Professor Alexander Kaufman of Ball State University, whose encouragement and enthusiasm has been without price. My colleague at the University of Hull, Professor Veronica O'Mara, provided invaluable comments and suggestions concerning the books and manuscripts, and the entire concept of the volume owes its origin to my late colleague and friend Dr Brian Levy, Reader in Old French at this university, with whom I studied, taught and wrote about outlaws for so long, and who introduced me to the joy of medieval French scatology.

I also need to extend extensive and heartfelt thanks to Michael Leaman and his team at Reaktion Books, most notably to my patient, sharp-eyed and indefatigable editor Martha Jay, and to Alexandru Ciobanu, who dealt skilfully and insightfully with the illustrations. Both were much more than helpful, and this is, inevitably, as much their volume as mine.

As ever, nothing would have been possible without the endless patience and encouragement of my husband David, who provided a spirit of calm amid the chaos and turbulence of working and writing. With barely perceptible effort, he manages to keep me going when things get rough.

Photo Acknowledgements

The author and publishers wish to express their thanks to the below sources of illustrative material and/or permission to reproduce it:

© Chapter of York, reproduced by kind permission: p. 96; reproduced by kind permission of Cley Parish Church Council: pp. 170, 171; photos Lesley Coote: pp. 21, 40, 194, 196, 197; Library of Congress, Prints and Photographs Division, Washington, DC: p. 58; reproduced by permission of the National Library of Scotland, Edinburgh: p. 6; from Howard Pyle, *The Merry Adventures of Robin Hood of Great Renown in Nottinghamshire* (New York, 1883), photo courtesy University of California Libraries: p. 188 (bottom); from Joseph Ritson, *Robin Hood: A Collection of All the Ancient Poems, Songs, and Ballads*, vol. II (London, 1832), photos courtesy University of Pittsburgh Library: pp. 183, 188 (top); reproduced by kind permission of the Syndics of Cambridge University Library, SEL.5.18: p. 62; © www.misericords.co.uk 2019, photos courtesy Dominic Strange: pp. 117, 144.

Immanuel Giel, the copyright holder of image on p. 30, has published it online under conditions imposed by a Creative Commons Attribution-ShareAlike 4.0 International License.

Readers are free to:
share – copy and redistribute the material in any medium or format.
adapt – remix, transform, and build upon the material for any purpose, even commercially.

Under the following terms:
attribution – You must give appropriate credit, provide a link to the license, and indicate if changes were made. You may do so in any reasonable manner, but not in any way that suggests the licensor endorses you or your use.
share alike – If you remix, transform, or build upon the material, you must distribute your contributions under the same license as the original.

Index

Page numbers in *italics* indicate illustrations.